# THE COMMUNITY JUNIOR COLLEGE

# THE COMMUNITY JUNIOR COLLEGE

## THIRD EDITION

JAMES W. THORNTON, JR.
University of Hawaii
Honolulu Community College

JOHN WILEY & SONS, INC.
New York    London    Sydney    Toronto

# PREFACE

The preface to the first edition of *The Community Junior College* in 1960 made a prediction about the growth of the institution by 1970:

> The January 1960 issue of the *Junior College Directory* names 677 junior colleges of all types with enrollments totaling 905,062. The total full-time equivalent for instructors was 24,022. It is entirely possible that another decade will see as many as 800 colleges, with 2,000,000 students and at least 40,000 full-time equivalent instructors.

That prediction has turned out to be approximately correct in only one of its figures, the total number of students. The 1971 *Directory* of the American Association of Junior Colleges reports 1091 colleges, with the October, 1970 total enrollment of 2,499,837, and total faculty of 109,345. The figures for the two years are not entirely comparable, since the basis for reporting was changed during the decade; but the conclusion is inescapable that the rate of establishment of new colleges and the addition of new full-time and part-time faculty members outstripped even an optimistic prediction.

Numerical growth was not the only major change in community junior colleges during the decade. More than 100 senior institutions introduced programs for the preparation of teachers and administrators for these colleges. Several states engaged in energetic efforts to develop systems of community colleges that would provide a campus within commuting distance of almost every high school graduate in the state. Multi-campus districts became common, and the architecture of newly established community colleges attracted national attention and won several architectural prizes. It is not too much to say that during the sixties the community junior college finally attained full status as a member of the higher education establishment in the United States. In addition, eight nations began the development of institutions similar to the community junior college, drawing on the experience of American educators for guidance in their efforts.

The literature of the community colleges also increased in volume and in diversity of focus, in response to the growing need for materials for the layman, the graduate student of higher education, the intern teacher in training programs, and the prospective administrator. Problems of title for the institutions arose. The early appelation "junior college" disappeared almost entirely from the names of publicly supported colleges, and was supplanted by "community college." In an attempt to be inclusive in their nomenclature, several authors accepted the term "two-year college."

Increased numbers of instructors with better preparation for their work in community colleges led to the establishment of influential faculty associations, in some states with the sanction of legislative enactments defining their obligations and rights. Students also began to form associations for the discussion of statewide problems of status and improvement for their college systems.

All of these developments led to the decision to refine and expand the text of *The Community Junior College* in this third edition. Major sections of the second edition have been omitted, since the nationwide establishment of community colleges has made some of the discussion less essential than it was in 1966. Completely new materials have been introduced in every chapter in order to recognize new trends in curriculum and in administration. The basic aim of the book remains the same: to provide graduate students who intend to teach in community colleges with a useful and practical introduction to the principles and practices of the most vital and rapidly expanding segment of all American education.

It is a privilege to be able to recognize certain direct personal obligations incurred in the preparation of this third edition. The faculty, administration, and clerical staff of Honolulu Community College have helped in ways they often did not realize. In conversations and in their daily work they have clarified emerging trends and exemplified contemporary concerns of community college workers. After more than a decade of freedom from the daily stresses of administration, I found it must refreshing to be welcomed by such a diversified, dedicated, and cooperative band of colleagues, both in the college offices and classrooms. Special gratitude is due Mr. Noel Grogan, who agreed both to do library research and to present an "under thirty" critique of the work in progress. His suggestions have been influential in sharpening my awareness and in introducing new emphases throughout the work. Once again, Cyrilla Thornton contributed loyally by constant encouragement and by protecting me from distraction during the rare hours and half-days I was able to find for concentration on the revision.

During the seventies, tens of thousands of new teachers will join community college faculties. I offer them this book as an introduction to a fascinating, realistic, engrossing, innovative, creative, and richly rewarding career in an arena where the action is.

Honolulu, Oahu, Hawaii                    James W. Thornton, Jr.

# CONTENTS

x    Contents

# THE COMMUNITY
# JUNIOR COLLEGE

# I

---

# BACKGROUNDS OF THE COMMUNITY JUNIOR COLLEGE

# 1 | Issues in Higher Education

The community junior colleges are one segment of some 2550 American institutions that offer education beyond the high school. Many uncoordinated influences have led to the establishment of different but sometimes competing kinds of opportunity for higher education. Americans' appetite for learning has been such that students and financial support have been forthcoming for universities private and public, professional schools, liberal arts colleges, institutes of technology, land-grant colleges of agriculture and mechanical arts, theological seminaries, teachers' colleges, normal schools, vocational institutes, and junior colleges. Institutions which were originally established to achieve one purpose have expanded to include other purposes, until accurate classification of American colleges and universities is almost impossible.

During the last quarter of the twentieth century, American higher education will face

3

shifting trends in enrollments and increased urgency of its recognized tasks. New kinds of education are required by a much greater proportion of the population, young and old, than ever before. As the diversity of the student body and the scope of available education increase, costs will also rise. Acquaintance with some of the issues which confront all of higher education is basic to understanding the nature and function of the community junior college. Several of these issues are discussed briefly in Chapter 1.

## A. Definition of Purposes

There has never been an unambiguous and fully accepted statement of the purposes of American higher education. Because of the complexity of its organization, there probably never will be. One school of thought emphasizes the concept that man is distinguished from the rest of the animal kingdom by his rationality, and that cultivation of this reasoning power is the sole purpose of higher education. If a man can reason, the solution of problems of any nature is possible. Since the cultivation of sophisticated powers of reason demands concentrated thought and a great deal of reading and learned conversation, any other educational practice than reasoning is a distraction. Regardless of social need for the training of practitioners in medicine, law, cosmetology, or auto mechanics, in this view, such training should not be allowed to contaminate the cultivation of reason. This restrictive view has been ably presented, but has not been adopted by most American colleges.

A more usual approach to higher education has seen it as an instrument for human betterment. The college is not seen as an institution apart from and in a sense above society, admitting only a select few to its portals. Instead, emphasis has been placed on the changes in behavior that education is intended to bring about in students drawn from all segments of society.

Even during the nineteenth century, this position was foreshadowed by Newman in his *Idea of the University*. In an eloquent passage, he describes the personal and social graces to be developed in man as a result of his university education. His ideal graduate is a man of action in harmony with his environment and with his society, not simply a scholar who concentrates on the life of the mind.

Alfred North Whitehead also insisted on dual purposes of education: culture and expert knowledge. He defined culture as "activity of thought and receptiveness to beauty and humane feeling." Expert knowledge included both specialization and the ability to apply the expertise to practical ends. A merely well-informed man, he suggests, "is the most useless bore on God's earth." Knowledge unrelated to its application is "inert."

Neither Whitehead nor Newman rejected classical education—both were outstanding examples of its best potential. But both also recognized the dehumanizing effect of the emphasis on abstract knowledge and on pure research, if these were pursued as ends in themselves. They insisted, a half-century apart, that a fundamental purpose of higher education was the improvement of the quality of human life.

A more explicit emphasis on the social role of education is found just after World War II and during the period of most intense reaction to the first use of atomic bombs. The President's Commission on Higher Education (1947) stated that universities could no longer be merely instruments for producing an intellectual elite. Instead, the Commission believed that universal education is indispensable to the full and living realization of the democratic ideal.

During the sixties, this trend of thought became more explicit, and was elaborated not only by the scholars who study higher education but even more forcibly and vocally by students themselves. The demand for participation in development of the curriculum and for relevance in instruction are outgrowths of the philosophy that higher education is a part of life, an agent of society, and not an autonomous creation above and apart from the problems of daily living. Nevitt Sanford goes so far as to declare that individual development is the first and most important goal of higher education. This is not to deny the importance of other purposes such as creating and preserving culture and preparing specialists in technical skills or professions; it is simply to say that unless the college accepts the responsibility to teach so that students develop all of their capacities, other efforts of the colleges will be only partially successful.

It is clear that no single statement will suffice. The totality of American colleges and universities, and each of them individually, must accept a hierarchy of purposes. Emphasis will vary from campus to campus; but concentration solely on the intellect is no longer acceptable. A university medical officer tells of calling a mathematician to ask his consideration in helping a student with severe personal problems. The response was, "I'm here to teach math, not to baby-sit!" The attitude behind the remark exemplifies the extreme of separation of the intellect from the human being. College purposes during the rest of this century, at least, must recognize that the supporting society has an interest in the outcomes and that the students deserve a voice in the development and the implementation of the operative purposes of their college. The day of the ivory tower has passed; the college in the marketplace will continue to emphasize research and inherited wisdom. It will give primary emphasis, though, to the selection of instructional materials that contribute directly and effectively to the individual development of the humane qualities of their students.


## B. Increasing Enrollments

Every decade in the twentieth century has seen a sharp increase in degree-credit enrollments. The decade of the sixties saw enrollments more than double, from 3.5 million in fall 1960 to 7.2 million in fall 1970. Table I shows Office of Education predictions for fall 1977; growth is expected to continue, though not so rapidly as in previous periods. For comparison, data for three years are presented at seven-year intervals.

The relationships of the several factors in Table I permit several deductions. Since the increase in live births between the years when new students of 1963 and 1977 were born (i.e., 1945 and 1959) was from about 2.5 million to 3.7 million, or about 148% of the earlier year, the excess in enrollments (215% over the period covered Table I) probably results from:

1. A higher proportion of the age group enrolling,
2. a greater proportion of older persons enrolling,
3. students persisting in college longer,
4. larger numbers of graduate students.

TABLE I

Actual and Estimated Degree-Credit Enrollments, Numbers of Bachelor's Degrees, and Numbers of Faculty, Fall 1963, 1970, and 1977[a]

|  | Fall 1963 | Fall 1970 | Fall 1977 |
|---|---|---|---|
| Degree-Credit Enrollments | 4,495,000 | 7,181,000 | 9,684,000 |
| Bachelor's Degrees | 498,654 | 760,000 | 980,000 |
| Numbers of Faculty (Full and Part-time) | 355,542 | 524,000 | 665,000 |

[a]Source: Projections of Educational Statistics to 1977-78 (1968 edition) Washington, D.C.: U.S. Government Printing Office, 1968.

Even with the increase in enrollments, it is anticipated that the ratio between bachelor's degree graduates and total enrollment will decrease from 11% of the total enrollment in 1963 to an estimated 10.1% in 1977. This change indicates a longer period of study before the bachelor's degree, as well as a drop-out rate between enrollment and graduation of almost 60%. (In a period of zero population growth, if the same numbers enrolled every year and all remained to graduate, degrees should be 25% of undergraduate enrollment. A degree rate of only 10% indicates, among other factors, a high drop-out rate.)

Since 1961, the annual number of live births has been declining, and by 1979 (when these children reach college age), it is likely that first-time college enrollments will begin to stabilize or even drop off a little for at least a decade. Entering enrollments in elementary school are already declining. Total degree-credit enrollments, however, may continue to rise as a consequence of lower drop-out rates, more enrollments of older students, and a trend toward educational enrichment through longer periods of undergraduate study.

Another probable consequence of the projected growth in enrollments is an increase in the number of students per faculty member in higher education. Table I indicates a progression from 12.6:1 in 1963 to 13.9:1 in 1970, and an estimated 14.6:1 in 1977. Such an increase might indicate greater economy in utilization of instructor time as related to mediated instruction. On the other hand, it may result in an increase in large classes at the undergraduate level, with an accompanying deterioration in quality of instruction.

The very rapid growth in enrollments over recent years and the projection for the future is both a cause and a consequence of the increase in numbers of community junior colleges. If the youth of the nation had not demanded education, new colleges would not have been needed; if new colleges were not provided, existing colleges would have been unable to accommodate the growth that has occurred.

## C. Support of Higher Education

The evidence that enrollments in higher education will continue to increase, at least over the next two decades, leads to concern about sources of support for the total system of colleges and universities. Expressed as a percentage of gross national product, increases in costs have been slightly more rapid than increases in enrollment. Compared with the predicted doubling of enrollments shown in Table I over a 14-year period, the total current and capital share of GNP for higher education has more than doubled in a past period of 18 years. In 1950, these costs were 0.8 of 1% of GNP; in 1968, they were 1.9%. If the continuing expansion of the tasks and the enrollment of higher education is to be supported adequately, it is likely that increases equal to an additional 1% of GNP will be needed over the next decade.

This prediction is based on several justifications. There is little doubt that enrollments will continue to grow. Moreover, faculty salaries and numbers of faculty will also increase, both because of inflation and because of the attraction of competing occupations. Capital costs of colleges may be expected to increase as well, as more sophisticated instructional and research equipment is introduced as a partial response to increased enrollments. Not the least of the added costs will be those attributable to the open-door purposes of higher education. Education is accepted as one of the fundamental solutions to problems of ghetto living and unemployability. Reeducation, or developmental education, requires more personal contact between instructor and pupil than the education of students who have been academically successful since kindergarten. It is more expensive, and it is the unavoidable educational goal of the seventies.

Counter forces to these educational needs and their concomitant costs are also becoming more and more evident. State and local taxes have risen to the point that taxpayers' revolts against the expenses of education are common. The unrest and violence of students are capitalized by punitive legislators to justify cutting educational appropriations. In search of scapegoats for the massive problems of American life, bewildered adults are quick to blame the fiscally vulnerable colleges and universities for all the ills of society. In addition, the vogue of accountability in economic appraisal of higher education makes justification of increased costs more difficult.

These forces portend major changes in the support and in the control of higher education. Already student tuition and the federal share of costs have risen, as the shares of endowment, gifts, and state and local costs have diminished. Yet neither of these increases is a totally wholesome trend. Federal support has been expressed in categorical grants or contracts intended to achieve specific federal purposes. Often these funds have diverted the attention of administrators and faculty from their primary educational tasks; often they have caused funds from nonfederal sources to be diverted from their intended use so that institutions might qualify for the grant. Appropriation of Federal funds for the general support of higher education may be a necessary solution to the cost squeeze of the future. Categorical grants are more difficult to justify.

Increases in student fees may be similarly counter-productive. If national policy requires that more persons be educated to higher levels than ever before, then fewer barriers should be erected to keep students from education. Even tuition loans or deferred tuition are not acceptable solutions to the total need for an open-door policy. Rather, every effort should be expended to encourage able but impoverished students to achieve a college education.

In relation to the total problem of costs, the community junior college is a part of the answer. As a nonresidential two-year college situated near the students it serves, it can save money for the student and his family as well as for the taxpayer. Its emphasis on instruction rather than on the total pattern of university purposes makes it the appropriate agency to prepare and to certify students for advanced study, or to prepare and to certify them for immediate employment.

## D. Continuing Education

The increase in the number of degree-credit students is only the more obvious aspect of growth. In another expression of its faith in schooling, the American public has become a nation of students. No man can safely proclaim that his education is completed. Maturing school dropouts return to the community college in search of a functional literacy, to learn new skills, or to satisfy newly realized interest in general education. Skilled workers find their skills eroded by new technology and return to community colleges for retraining or for preparation for promotion. The enrichment of leisure is another inducement for lifelong learning, emphasized by shortened work weeks and early retirement.

A part of the need for continuing education is indicated by the levels of education of the population. Early returns of the 1970 census indicated that almost 29% of adults over 25 years of age had less than an eighth grade education; 5.8% had completed less than four years of school. It is true that 18.5% of adults had graduated from college—but the nation still had a higher percentage of inadequately educated citizens than it did of college graduates. Most of the skills of citizenship, such as political science, economics, and sociology, are not taught in elementary school or even in many secondary schools.

A highly technological society has critical problems of international commerce, domestic politics, conservation, health, production, distribution, and utilization of human talent, to name only a few of the problems. Allowing millions of citizens to lack both economic productivity and civic responsibility is extremely costly to society, both in welfare expenditures and in crime rates. Education is the price of survival of civilization; it should be a first priority on the national agenda.

It may be argued that the need is not truly a need for further opportunity for college study. Still, the colleges and community colleges are ideally equipped to develop appropriate curriculums for the educational needs of adults. They are deterred by their traditional patterns of schedule, admissions procedures, and course development; their facilities could be used more effectively if they were in operation every month of the year and more hours of the day than at present. With a conviction of the importance of continuing education, colleges will find the techniques to make it available.

The community junior college, situated in the heart of its community, is able to contribute importantly to continuing part-time education. It has already demonstrated that it can serve large numbers of part-time students. It has the potential and the mission of expanding its efforts to meet the effective demands of its several clienteles.

## E. Encouraging the Able Student

The college student body is a highly selected group; according to a study reported by Richard Pearson, almost 80% of college entrants scored in the upper half of a college aptitude test administered to high school graduates. The degree of selectivity is increased by the fact that approximately 25% of American youth drop out of high school and so are not included in the aptitude test distributions. This fact means that more than 80% of college entrants come from the upper half of academic aptitude distribution, if the base figure includes all American youth. It is reasonable to argue that this is as should be; most students should have demonstrated their ability to profit from college offerings. On the other hand, analyses of those who enter college tend to obscure an important set of data about those who do not enter college.

Aptitude test scores of students who did not enter college were examined in the same study. Forty percent of those high school graduates who did not go to college scored in the upper half of the aptitude distribution. It is difficult to argue that every able young person should go to college; but at least a sizable part of the able 40% of nonattenders should be able to benefit themselves and their society if they improved their understanding and knowledge through further education. Their early termination of schooling seems to indicate that precious human resources are not reaching their fullest development. There is a serious social challenge of stimulating able high-school graduates to desire further education, and of removing the barriers that now prevent them from pursuing it.

Many able nonattenders have abilities which are not traditionally valued by colleges; either they are not attracted to higher education or they leave it because nothing in the curriculum seems to have value or meaning to them. On the other hand, some of the broad social groups that now do not aspire to higher education after high school graduation at one time in history did not learn to read or write. Within the present century, parents in the same strata of society withdrew their children from school at 10 or 12 or 14 years of age. The fact that as many as 75% of 18-year-olds graduate from high school is a major step forward in social progress, but it should not obscure the companion fact that there are still important unmet educational needs.

A major area of unmet need is the identification, recruitment, and realistic preparation for higher study of able students from disadvantaged minorities. There has been a great deal of effort in the past decade directed to special programs for educationally deprived young people; some have been remarkably successful, while others have been handicapped by strife and mutual mistrust. The problem remains. Able young people from inner city slums and from poverty-stricken rural areas can use education as an avenue of escape from the dungeons of ignorance; but they are unable to succeed unaided. The aid they need is both financial and educational. Community junior colleges seem to be the appropriate existing agency to provide this kind of assistance. The solution is to provide early identification and guidance of talented young people whose prospects of choosing to go to college are not high. Local opportunities for higher education at minimum cost to the student must be developed along with curriculums clearly relevant to the demands of modern times. If these steps can be combined with opportunities for work, for grants, or for loans for student support, many students will be encouraged to complete two or four or even more years of college. The optimum plan has not yet been elaborated; but there is little doubt that the value to the nation of such an outcome would far exceed its cost.

## F. Rebellion on Campus

At least in the public view, the salient feature of higher education in the sixties was rebellion on campus. Student unrest has been a recurrent aspect of university life throughout the history of higher education. Medieval Bologna and Paris coped with violence and destruction, as did the small rural colleges of early America. The new aspects of recent disruptions include their worldwide occurrence, and the numbers of institutions that have been involved. Certainly one explanation for the popularity of revolt is the fact that students everywhere learn rapidly of the protests in any part of the world and are encouraged to vent their own very real dissatisfactions in like manner. But this is not at all intended to place the blame for unrest solely on communication; it would be much closer to the truth to suggest that a lack of communication is the main culprit.

Seemingly everyone with a pen has attempted to explain the causes of campus unrest, whether condemning the students or defending the necessity of their protests. Diagnosis from one camp or the other has been accepted as sufficient, without proceeding to prescription of adequate cures. Perhaps another summary of causes is unnecessary, but for the record a very brief statement is attempted.

Some of the causes of student protest inhere in conditions of the larger society off campus. Affluence certainly is a part of the problem, largely because it is so unusual in the history of mankind. The totality of conditions that may be subsumed under the heading of affluence have made it unnecessary, indeed impossible, for most young people to have responsible full-time jobs during their adolescent years. Their search for diversion has tended to alienate them from their far too busy elders; and because they miss the companionship and counsel of the more mature, they condemn as materialistic and inhuman the activities that engage their parents.

In the attempt to justify their rejection of these activities, they analyze the value systems of the establishment. They are quick to notice the chasm between the values that society promulgates in schools and from the pulpits and the behavior of adults. Their recognition of hypocrisy leads them to reject the ethos of the past; but they have no skill as yet to develop a substitute set of standards. The resulting *anomie* or normlessness robs them of a consistent and creative sense of direction; the activity of the moment is self-justifying.

Perhaps the most distressing social pressure on the young has been the anxiety that results from international policy. The draft seems to threaten them with forced participation in some of the most repulsive activities of the political and military establishment. Their inability to change the laws or to bring peace on any terms begets a level of frustration that they seek to discharge by the same sort of violence they condemn. It remains to be seen whether the enfranchisement of 18-year olds will bring about a lessening of disorderly protest.

In the university, the same frustrations have led to similar violent protest. A community of scholars is notoriously unable to reach agreement and action precipitously, whereas the young are by nature impatient and intransigent in their desire to see immediate corrections. Under the conditions of modern university life—the traditionalism of the entire academic process contrasted with the newly evident exasperation of sizable elements of the student-body—conflict is inevitable.

It does seem that the community colleges of American have been comparatively free of violence. This happy eventuality seems to derive from several factors. The nature of the students is one aspect of their unwillingness to join in disruption. They are more goal oriented in general than the university liberal arts student; they live in their own communities instead of in ghetto-like dormitories; many must work for their living expenses; and they are unlikely to spend the leisure hours they have in rap sessions on campus. Even the newly developing inner-city community colleges seem to have been more free of disruption than their nearby universities, perhaps because their teachers and administrators are more accessible and more responsive.

Instructors in the community colleges are more explicitly and whole-heartedly concerned with teaching than are the research oriented members of university faculties. In most communities, the local governing board is both closer to the voices of the students and their parents and more immediately responsive. There is not the gap in communication that may exist when a statewide board makes the policies for a number of institutions, relying for its information on layers of functionaries who are less and less in touch with students as their responsibility and authority increase.

So much for a summary analysis of a phenomenon about which books have been written, each exploring one or another aspect of the complex. Any attempt at prescription must be equally summary; but, to this author, it seems evident that the new task of the administrator is to keep in touch with the concerns of his faculty and his students, so that he may be able to foresee sources of trouble and correct them. Students must not be forced to conclude that there is no way of getting the attention of the establishment except through destruction. The eristic approach seeks to smash problems and those who present them; the heuristic approach seeks to solve problems reasonably and creatively. There is need for more of the latter in college administration.

## G. Instructional Innovation

A wholesome outgrowth of campus unrest has been a growing interest in achieving relevance by new approaches to instruction and curriculum.

The approach in several colleges has been to emphasize greater involvement of students in the planning and presentation of their courses. Thus, there have been several "free universities," organized by volunteer faculty of all degrees of academic prestige or lack of it, using for campus any available space near a recognized institution, and offering any course at the suggestion of anyone who wanted to teach it or of students who wanted to enroll in it. A times, the work of free universities is recognized by the nearby accredited institution; in other examples, a sort of armed truce exists between the two, and no credit is desired or granted.

A more formal innovative effort consists of satellite campuses for undergraduate studies in the humanities. These colleges are established as offshoots of their parent institution, drawing on the more venturesome and imaginative of the faculty for their administration and instruction. A comparatively unstructured curriculum is emphasized, stressing independent study, small group discussion, and comparatively little formal lecture. Examinations are often oral, and grading is reported in evaluative statements of instructors rather than simply in letters or pass-fail symbols. In essence, the satellite campus seeks to achieve the classical goals of education by using the classical materials of education, but also to add meaning and intensity to the student experience by emphasizing direct participation of the student both in planning and in investigation of the topics studied.

Interdisciplinary approaches to curriculum seek to break down the logical barriers between academic subjects, placing emphasis on the application of knowledge from any field to the understanding of real-life phenomena. The rationale of this effort is that few problems of mankind are purely economic or biological or political; most problems have aspects appropriate to many academic disciplines. The emphasis on interrelation arises from the developmental objective of education. Emphasis mainly on the discipline results in the profound exploration of a defined and limited area of knowledge. This abstraction, however, tends to draw attention away from the implications of the discipline for human life. The inter-disciplinary approach stresses the human aspects of knowledge, and so requires a greater degree of interpretation of related research, even though the amount of factual learning may be diminished.

Paralleling and supporting the pressure for innovation in curriculum is a trend toward innovation in method of instruction. The tendency toward more frequent use of independent study and seminars in undergraduate instruction has been mentioned. This trend brings a subtle change in the relationship between professor and student and results in changing concepts of grades. When the professor is seen as the authority who judges the quality of the recitation of the student, a precise grade is possible; the student either repeats what he has learned or demonstrates that he has not learned. When the development of the student's powers is the goal, however, the relation changes. The professor is no longer the judge of the student's repetitive efforts, but a counselor, guide, and friend. The outcome is not so much mastery of the text as changes in understanding and attitudes; these changes are not so susceptible to quantitative rating as the other kind. In response to these changes, new grading schemes have been developed. The pass-fail option simply allows the professor to attest either that the student worked on the materials of the course for a specified period of time, or that he gave insufficient evidence that he had made an effort to become involved with the problems. Late withdrawal from courses without penalty allows the student in effect to grade the course for himself: he may decide that he has done well enough to trust the instructor's evaluation and so take the final examination and the resulting symbol on his transcript. On the other hand, he may decide that he has not derived much benefit from the course, and so he simply withdraws near the end of the semester, leaving no evidence on the transcript that either he or the instructor "failed."

Another trend toward placing more responsibility for his education on the student is modular scheduling. This involves planning courses so that comparatively independent brief segments can be presented and evaluated, and scheduling them so that students may start at any time of the year. The practice makes problems for the registrar, but it does allow a student who decides to attend college at any time of the year (e.g., a returning veteran) to enter without having to wait several months. It also permits a student who decides in mid-term to drop a course to start another one. Employed persons who need only one segment of a course, also, might find it possible to use vacation time or released hours to attend without having to sign up for the entire semester or school year. This trend also is a sign of the change in emphasis of colleges, from ivory tower concern with the discipline only to concentration on the behavioral outcomes of instruction in the lives of students.

## H. The Diversity of Institutions

A good many American institutions of higher education began during the nineteenth century with precise and specialized educational purposes, as colleges of medicine or technological institutes or normal schools. At that time, it was possible to classify institutions by their major educational purposes. The growth in enrollments during the twentieth century, however, has blurred distinctions among types of institutions as all move toward comprehensive offerings. Normal schools are now universities in fact as well as in name; institutes of technology boast of the quality of their offering in humanities. The major basis for classification has become the length of study appropriate at each institution. In 1969-70, the American educational establishment included 2551 colleges, institutes, and universities. Among them were:

903  colleges offering two but less than four years beyond high school,
754  colleges offering four-or five-year baccalaureate degrees,
 81  institutions offering the first professional degree,
425  institutions offering the master's degree,
 92  institutions offering study beyond the master's but less than doctorate,
296  offering doctorate degrees.

It seems that there is a sufficient variety of institutions to meet the needs of higher education. Careful planning both nationally and in every state will be required to make sure that each existing institution is utilized to the best advantage and that new institutions are established with regard for the optimum location of each kind of institution and for their effective interrelationships. Certainly, it seems that it will be most difficult to establish a sufficient number of new post-high-school institutions in the near future to allow for small and manageable enrollments; those that are established should be carefully and soundly planned.

A further problem arising from diversity is that of mutual understanding and cooperation. A determined effort on the part of workers in every kind of college to understand the functions of their own institution and of the others will lead to more effective cooperation of all in the interest of the students and of society. In addition, intense effort is needed to help adults and youth understand the different purposes of available institutions. In this way, students may make more appropriate choices of colleges and, thus, improve the quality and the extent of their education.

As the most recent addition to this family of post-high-school institutions, the community junior college has so far failed to achieve from its elders full understanding or complete cooperation. Part of this failure derives from multiplicity of its functions, some of them not shared by other institutions. The community junior college does indeed offer two years of conventional higher education to some of its students. Yet it is not only a lower division. It adds to the college transfer curriculums other courses adapted to the occupational and personal goals of its students. This diversity of program and purpose is one of the most valuable aspects of the community junior college; at the same time, it increases the difficulty of fitting the institution neatly into the earlier pattern of higher education and of articulation of transfer curriculums.

# I. The Community Junior College as a Part of Higher Education

The community junior colleges of America are intimately concerned with all the current problems of higher education. They have become full partners, in many states, and will bear an increasing share of the burdens of higher education for all. In addition, they must meet several problems that are peculiar to their own expanded responsibility.

Some of these problems arise from their comparative newness in the arena of higher education. Even after some 70 years, their total function and the full scope of their responsibility are still evolving. It is not surprising, then, that they are misunderstood, even mistrusted, by some of the faculties of other institutions, who have had little opportunity to learn of the present quality and future potentialities of the community colleges. One of their problems is that of interpretation—helping faculty members in the schools and other colleges to understand their place in the total educational enterprise. In addition, they still have not mastered the technique of helping prospective students and the citizenry in general understand emerging educational needs and the programs that are developing to meet them.

It is clear that innovative programs must be developed with great care. The community junior colleges especially must provide a wide variety of curriculums, but each must combine demanding standards of student achievement with responsible and effective guidance and all reasonable fiscal economy. If unnecessary or trivial courses are organized, if students are enrolled in such haphazard fashion that they then withdraw in great numbers, if instructional standards are allowed to deteriorate—then the community junior college shall have forfeited its right to a share in the achievement of the most majestic educational ideal ever attempted by a nation. By their success in this high endeavor, on the contrary, these institutions can contribute significantly and enduringly to the preservation and enhancement of American democratic institutions.

## BIBLIOGRAPHY

Barzun, Jacques. *The American University*. New York: Harper and Row, 1968.

Caffrey, John (ed.). *The Future Academic Community: Continuity and Change.* Washington, D.C. American Council on Education, 1969.

Carnegie Commission on Higher Education, *A Chance to Learn.* New York: McGraw-Hill Book Co., 1970.

Harcleroad, Fred F. (ed.). *Issues of the Seventies.* San Francisco: Jossey-Bass, Inc., Publishers, 1970.

_____et.al., *The Developing State Colleges and Universities.* Iowa City, Iowa: American College Testing Program, 1969.

Hutchins, Robert M. *The Learning Society.* New York: Frederick O. Praeger, Inc., 1968.

Mayhew, Lewis B. *Colleges Today and Tomorrow.* San Francisco: Jossey-Bass, Inc., Publishers, 1969.

Newman, Frank (chairman). *Report on Higher Education.* Washington, D.C.: U.S. Government Printing Office, 1971.

Sanford, Nevitt (ed.). *College and Character.* New York: John Wiley and Sons, Inc., 1964.

_____*Where Colleges Fail.* San Francisco: Jossey-Bass, Inc., Publishers, 1967.

Taylor, Harold. *Students without Teachers.* New York: McGraw-Hill Book Co., 1969.

# 2 | New Economic and Social Needs for Higher Education

The total number of community and junior colleges in the United States increased in 70 years from eight in 1900 to almost 1100, including both private and public two-year colleges in 1971. This growth required conviction that these new colleges were needed, and unremitting effort on the part of many citizens to see that enabling legislation was passed and that support, buildings, and faculty were available as the new institutions were established. The generalization

19

that during the sixties "one community college was established every week" is almost an understatement for that decade.

What are the economic and social needs that have led so many communities to develop community junior colleges? Why have constantly increasing proportions of American youth demanded more post-high-school education? What developments of the seventies can be interpreted to indicate continuation or modification of recent trends? Chapter 2 indicates some of the educational consequences of recent technological, demographic, and cultural developments.

## A. The American Economy

One of the basic characteristics of America and one of her most important natural resources is her technology—the ability to make use of materials and processes both to develop more materials and processes of production and to provide a constantly increasing flow of consumer goods. At the time of its discovery and settlement by Europeans, the continent had all the wealth—in metals, in arable land, in petroleum and timber, and soil and waterpower—that it has now. Actually, since a prodigal nation has wasted so much of its natural wealth, there were more of all these resources then than there are now. Yet the land supported fewer than a million Indians, at a bare subsistence level. Now the same land supports more than 200,000,000 at the highest level of material consumption in history; even very conservative predictions of population growth indicate that before the year 2000 the population will reach between 260,000,000 and 300,000,000.

This increase in numbers of people and this rise in the standard of living are made possible by enormously complicated and interdependent techniques of production. These techniques free persons from drudgery so that they may achieve a high level of schooling; at the same time, the techniques could not operate without a high degree of literacy on the part of the citizenry. The community junior colleges and American technology have developed together most rapidly within a single human life span. Both also are on the verge of further extension.

The increase in population and the development of technology have contributed positively to the increases in numbers of colleges and of enrollments. At the same time, these trends pose problems, the solution of which depends on improved understanding of the effects of huge population and of advanced technology on the quality of life. Consideration of the achievements and of the dilemmas they bring with them will help to illuminate the reasons for the community junior colleges and the directions of its future development.

*Power.*    The most dramatic technical development of our day is one with great potential for evil as well as for good—the controlled release of atomic energy through the processes of fusion and fission. Limited at present to changes in elements at both ends of the periodic table, such reactions can be started in theory with any of the elements. The hydrogen in a cubic mile of seawater could provide enough energy for 300 centuries at the 1970 rate of use—if its release could be controlled. In addition, any of the elements existing in the earth's crust might be similarly transmuted—so that the day is in sight when electric power from atomic generators will be so easily available that it will not be worthwhile to meter it. In case, however, the problems of creating inexpensive power from atomic energy are not solved rapidly, there is promise of the practical availability of solar power before supplies of stored organic fuels are exhausted. The consequences of unlimited low-cost power are beyond imagination. Purification of ocean water for human use, electrified highways, truly automatic homes, and liberation from the tyrannies of weather—these are only a few of the possible developments that could follow on the discovery of a safe and economical source of great quantities of power.

Terrifying consequences accompany each of the presently known power sources. As atomic energy plants are brought into production, it becomes apparent that the disposal of radioactive wastes is a major threat to all kinds of life; and so far no satisfactory technique of decontamination or disposal has been discovered. Organic fuels have filled humanity's power needs since the discovery of fire. They, too, are used more extensively to satisfy demands for artificial comfort and convenience. As a result, they are being consumed at a rate that bodes exhaustion of their sources within a few decades, and at the same time, they contribute unbearably to the degradation of the atmosphere. The consequences of both trends have brought about the elaboration of studies in environmental sciences, with a hope that solutions short of despair can be discovered before catastrophe ensues.

*Transportation.*    Another aspect of technology concerns the use of engines for transportation. The automobile and the airplane have made long distance travel rapid and convenient. They have expanded man's communities, and they have shrunk his world. They have brought new dimensions of production and recreation to human life. Other applications of the engine are equally important—the tractor in farming, the bulldozer in mining and in roadbuilding, and the truck and trailer in rapid and economical distribution of goods.

Their drawbacks are perhaps more serious than the benefits are useful. In America each year, more than 50,000 lives are taken by our rush to get from one place to another. Automobile exhausts are a major source of the pollution of our atmosphere and the clouding of our vision; they contribute measurably to destruction of plant life in the vicinity of smog-filled cities. The debris thrown from cars and the useless carcasses of wornout cars desecrate streets and highways and make necessary countless manhours of cleanup. Legal and economic attempts to deal with the menaces of transportation will have unpredictable effects on the economy and on the labor force.

*Agriculture.*    Advances have been made in agriculture to the extent that an agricultural worker now feeds himself and 52 others whereas in 1900 he fed himself and only seven others. Agricultural workers number only 3.8 million out of the total U.S. population of 205 million. In addition, because of the use of machines and scientifically balanced foods and fertilizers, this increase in productivity is accomplished with fewer hours of work and fewer acres. In this area of the economy also, evil side effects accompany the provision of plenty. Chemical fertilizers leach from the soil into the rivers and lakes, destroying fish and fowl while encouraging the growth of algae and contaminating the water for human use. The pesticides that have helped to bring about abundance also accumulate in animal tissue and are contributing to the disappearance of several species of birds and wild life.

*Automation.*    In industry as well as in agriculture, new processes and new machines have combined to increase the hourly productivity of labor. This trend leads to greater accumulations of capital in huge corporations, forcing out of production the marginal small producer. The net result to the worker in the short run is greater leisure and higher real wages. In the long run, automation changes the makeup of the labor force. Fewer and fewer unskilled laborers are needed; skilled artisans are less and less in demand. The use of automation in mass production factories eliminates much of the drudgery of material handling and machine setup. Human muscle power is a most expensive form of energy, costing in the neighborhood of $30 per kilowatt-hour as compared with only a few cents for electric power. Any process that can substitute mechanical energy for human energy is not only economical but contributes also to a higher standard of living as well as to the ease of life. There are serious philosophical problems involved in this proposed elimination of muscular work, yet it seems unlikely that people will continue to demand the opportunity to perform arduous physical labor simply because they feel that they need the discipline of perspiration.

***Research.***   In scientific research, recent progress has been astounding. Edison tried 3000 substances in his search for a material suitable for a light-bulb filament. Now, materials are almost literally created to meet needs—whether the need is for a heat-resistant ceramic, a crease-resistant fabric, a lightweight insulator for frozen foods, a malleable alloy, or a cheap but indestructible plastic for childrens' toys. One major American industry is said to plan its future investment and personnel development on the premise that in 25 years 90% of its income will be from products not yet invented, whereas three-quarters of its present products will be outdated. The scope of the nation's research effort may be inferred from the fact that annual expenditures for research exceed $15 billion; two-thirds of this amount, or $10 billion, comes from Federal sources.

Pharmaceutical chemistry has kept pace with industrial chemistry. A dozen diseases which scourged America in 1925 have almost disappeared as major factors in public health statistics; pneumonia, tuberculosis, diptheria, typhoid fever, scarlet fever, syphilis, malaria, and poliomyelitis have been robbed of much of their terror by chemotherapeutic discoveries. Women are enabled to plan the number of children they shall have, and all mankind have been assured of longer average life span with greater freedom from pain and from loss of earnings due to illness. Moods, neuroses, and psychoses yield to chemical tranquilizers, so that both productive work and enjoyable leisure may be increased.

The mating of progress and problems continues. Drugs used properly can relieve pain; but in the hands of school children, they can lead to disease, unemployability, and even death. Contraceptive pills seem not to have reduced the number of illegitimate pregnancies; on the other hand, they may have contributed to a much greater sexual permissiveness in the total society. On the one hand, this permissiveness may be defended as an aspect of psychological openness and honesty; it is just as defensible to see it as self-indulgence and social irresponsibility.

Space research also has its positive and negative aspects. Certainly it is daring and courageous for men to explore the moon and reach for the planets. None of us has the vision to predict the possible benefits to humanity that may ensue from the penetration of space. Equally, none of us can be certain that catastrophe may not be the end result. Could the moon provide a dumping ground for terrestrial wastes? Might it provide some unknown resource that would contribute to health or wisdom or peace? And if any of these outcomes results, can man be sure that only in this area will there be solutions that do not entail further problems?

*Communication.*    Direct distance dialing, mobile telephone, television from the moon, automatic record keeping and billing, long distance transmission of news photos, and instantaneous worldwide news reporting—all compete for attention. It is no wonder that the amount of adult reading is decreasing annually. But the ease of communication leads to the accumulation and storage of much information of doubtful value and accuracy. It permits secret files to be accumulated in computer banks and to be resurrected at later dates to impugn a man's credibility or destroy his credit. It provides the news media with appalling power to determine what the world will hear. The man who cannot sift and evaluate for himself the masses of information with which he is bombarded must either blindly believe or categorically distrust most of what he learns.


*Distribution.*    Technological developments have been barely suggested to indicate the tremendous expansion in knowledge in the past 50 years. The application of this knowledge has resulted also in a new science of distribution, so that the consumer is made to feel in dire need of products which, two months ago, he did not dream existed. The entire process has educational implications. Graduates not only need to master the techniques by which machines are controlled and improved; more imperatively, they need to cultivate the wisdom to use creatively the wealth and the leisure with which machines have endowed them. They need to develop resistance, lest they smother under an avalanche of goods! In addition, unskilled tasks are disappearing from the economy; every worker needs a constantly increasing level of education.

In distribution, once more the theme is repeated: progress begets problems. It is true that America is at present an affluent society. It is also true that affluence is not uniformly available. Both in central cities and in wornout mining or agricultural areas, a hopeless cycle turns from unemployment to hunger, despair, poor education, poor health, and to unemployment in the next generation. The problem is underscored by the historical fact that most of the victims of the cycle have been Black.

An additional problem concerns the methods used by producers to dispose of their wares to the affluent consumer. Evidence accumulates that many of the products advertised in mass circulation media are positively dangerous to health, or at best simply useless. The list includes prepackaged foods, cosmetics, automobiles, drug products, tobacco, and alcohol. Community colleges can be expected to contribute more effectively than they have done to consumer education, to education for workers, and to civic education, so that some solutions to these problems may be more diligently pursued.

# B. Recent Social Changes

The explosive expansion of technology has been accompanied by—in some cases it has caused—equally important changes in the character of American society. Inspection of two or three of the more obvious manifestations will indicate the nature of their influence on higher education. The growth in population, the emergence of new patterns of employment, and the rise in average levels of schooling should demonstrate what has been happening to the quality of human life.

*Population Changes.*   The statistics of population growth in the United States are a rich source of insights into recent educational problems. Numerical growth in itself has created real difficulties for the school administrator, as he attempts to provide classrooms and teachers to care for more and more young people every year. Beyond that, changes in the age distribution of the population intensify his problems. Even without elaborate statistical tables, it is possible to summarize some of the more important qualities of America's present population with estimates of its tendencies over the next 20 years.

The population of the United States doubled in size every 30 years from 1800 to 1920, when it reached 106 million. By 1970, it almost doubled once more to attain 205 million inhabitants. This is a gain of 93% in 50 years; if the same rate were maintained, the population by 1980 would reach 242 million, and by the year 2000, there would be as many as 336 million. There are indications, however, that the rate of increase is slowing, and that the population may, under certain fertility assumptions, approach stability at about 275 million by the year 2037. If this were to happen, the median age of the population by 2037 would be about 37 years, compared with 28 in 1970. The implications for education of a population with a much smaller proportion of young citizens are apparent. In the near term, however, it should be realized that the college-age students of the seventies have already been born; in 1969, there were more than 39 million youths between the ages of 10 and 19 years—the group from which most college freshmen will be drawn during the seventies. During the previous decade, the same age cadre (20-29 in 1969) numbered a little less than 30 million, and yet college enrollment grew rapidly during the sixties.

The American population is a very mobile one. Economic opportunity draws people—or the lack of it pushes them—from the farms toward the cities and from the center of the nation toward the oceans. Increasing urbanization makes necessary higher levels of literacy, even though it has intensified the ghetto problems of inadequate schools and unemployability. In addition, urbanization points up the problems of interdependence, as the frustrations of slum dwellers erupt in violent protest that is countered by proposals of repression. Every state must educate large numbers of its youth for life and work in other states, even in other nations. Some of the states suffer a continuous drain of manpower through the processes of migration. The quality of education in every state is of concern to all the states.

*The Labor Force.* Changes in the makeup of the labor force have educational as well as economic implications. (Discussion is based largely on data supplied by U.S. Labor Department.) Table I shows the percentage change between 1950 and 1969 in components of the labor force. The size of the labor force (not shown) was 59,648,000 in 1950, and grew to 76,520,000 by 1969. In spite of this numerical increase in the total labor force, there was a net decrease in the number of nonfarm workers, private household workers, and farm workers—all occupations requiring comparatively little formal education. Professional and technical workers, requiring long periods of specialized education, more than doubled between 1950 and 1969 in numbers of workers and almost doubled as a percent of the labor force.

During that period, white collar workers and service workers had net increases in the proportions of the two groups in the total labor force, while blue collar workers and farm workers had net decreases. This was a period of very rapid growth in college enrollments and in the gross national product. The trends seem likely to continue, at least in the near future—increases in employment requiring higher education, net decrease in employment requiring secondary education or less. *Occupational Outlook Handbook* summarizes the trends:

> Industries providing services (such as education, health care, trade, government, transportation) offer more jobs than those that provide goods. Raising crops, building, mining, and manufacturing require less than half the Nation's labor force.

During the seventies, services, construction, and government employment will grow more rapidly than will finance, insurance, real estate, trade, manufacturing, transportation, and public utilities. Mining and agriculture will continue to decline in numbers employed.

Employment has shifted toward white collar and service jobs, away from unskilled and semiskilled jobs. More of the jobs in every category will require extensive education and training.

Unemployment rates are highest for young workers (under 25) and especially high (over 12%) among nongraduates of high school. Lifetime

TABLE I
Percentages of the Total Labor Force in the Major
Occupation Groups, 1950 and 1969[a]

|  | 1950 (%) | 1969 (%) | Net Change (%) |
|---|---|---|---|
| Professional and technical workers | 7.5 | 14.3 | + 6.8 |
| Managers, officials, and proprietors | 10.8 | 10.3 | - 0.5 |
| Clerical workers | 12.8 | 17.0 | + 4.2 |
| Sales workers | 6.4 | 6.0 | - 0.4 |
| TOTAL WHITE COLLAR | 37.5 | 47.6 | +10.1 |
| Craftsmen and foremen | 12.9 | 12.9 | 0.0 |
| Operatives | 20.3 | 18.6 | - 1.7 |
| Nonfarm workers | 5.9 | 4.3 | - 1.6 |
| TOTAL BLUE COLLAR | 39.1 | 35.8 | - 3.3 |
| Private household workers | 3.1 | 2.2 | - 0.9 |
| Other service workers | 7.9 | 10.4 | + 2.5 |
| TOTAL SERVICE WORKERS | 11.0 | 12.6 | + 1.6 |
| Farm workers | 12.4 | 4.0 | - 8.4 |
| TOTAL LABOR FORCE | 100.0 | 100.0 | ---- |

[a]Source: Derived from Statistical Abstract of the United States, 1969 (90th annual edition). Washington, D.C.: U.S. Government Printing Office, 1969. Table 322.

earnings are higher for educated workers; men with college degrees can expect to earn in their lifetime nearly three times as much as workers with less than eight years of schooling, twice as much as high school dropouts.

One other aspect of the labor force with educational implications is the contrast between white and nonwhite unemployment. In March, 1969, 3.1% of the white labor force, but 6.1% of the black labor force, were unemployed. A partial explanation of this difference can be found in the fact that 62% of black workers had less than a high school education, but only 38% of white workers (all age groups) lacked the diploma. Alan L. Sorkin reports that the unemployment rate for nonwhite teenagers is as high as 25-30%. It is clear that lack of education is not the only explanation for discrimination against nonwhite teenagers; but it is a contributing factor. More education can make an important contribution to employment opportunity for black as well as for white youth.

***Patterns of College Attendance.***    Partly as a consequence of high teenage unemployment, but also because of a belief that higher education facilitates social mobility, more and more youth from low-income families now aspire to a college degree. Among high school graduates from the lowest income quartile, 46% in 1966 hoped to attend college. In 1960, only 23% of this same group expressed a desire to continue their education. In contrast, high school graduates from the highest income quartile desiring higher education rose from 68% in 1960 to 74% in 1966. By 1966, almost 60% of all high school graduates hoped to enter college; about 55% actually did enroll. Family income was still an important selective factor, but not so controlling as it once was. Of the high school graduates of 1966, the 60% desiring to attend college comprised:[2]

   18.5% from the highest family income quartile;
   16.2% from the third family income quartile;
   13.0% from the second family income quartile; and
   11.5% from the lowest family income quartile.

Attendance at college has become part of the aspirations of a majority of American youth. In light of the wide range of aptitudes and ambitions of youth, great diversity of college curriculums is needed to accommodate the legitimate aspirations of youth. It is no longer realistic to plan college offerings on the assumption that most of the students share the scholarly interests of the faculty.

## C. Educational Implications of Social Changes

***Higher Levels of Skill.***    The changes in the makeup of the labor force indicate that all roads to occupational and social advancement lead through the college. The increase in the application of science and the decrease in the application of muscle in performing the work of the world combine to encourage more and more young people to seek higher education. Carried to its extreme, the increase in automation of production will lead to greater leisure for some classes of workers; but it leads as well to less need for numbers of workers and to longer and longer work weeks for those in the highest levels of responsibility. Those who plan the content of college education should recognize that a major objective for the majority of students will no longer be purely vocational. In addition to highest standards of scientific training, the colleges will need to recognize explicitly the role of study for the improvment of the nonmaterial aspects of life.

*Foreign Travel.*    Another kind of educational need arises from the new ease and rapidity of travel and communication, and from America's role in world politics. Aside from military service and college "years abroad," many college graduates will be spending some part of their working lives in foreign countries. Obviously, this degree of mobility requires that more people be trained to understand foreign cultures, to withstand foreign climates, and to speak foreign languages. In addition to the required occupational skills, this aspect of modern employment requires a completely new kind of general education.

*Personal Development.*    The human effects of technological progress are not entirely good. Less physical labor and more mental exertion are required by much modern work. At first glance, this may seem to be an unalloyed gain. Yet much of modern work causes strain and mental fatigue and is of such a repetitive nature that it is monotonous and boring. A double educational task arises from this fact—to provide students with the opportunity to cultivate broad interests, including some muscular tastes and skills, and to develop programs of adult education which stimulate the imagination and challenge the abilities of these workers. In this way, education can help people to achieve the full benefits of the new technology.

*The Custodial Function.*    A less idealistic, but nevertheless real, consequence of the developments in technology is the emerging custodial function of the college. The age of first full-time permanent employment for men has risen to about 22 years. The crime rate is higher in the 18-20 age group than in any other. These facts suggest to some thinkers the need for useful educational programs, both to prepare youth for employment and for a higher quality of living and to occupy them wholesomely rather than destructively.

Several writers point out the high drop-out rate from college and the fact that some high-school graduates do not desire higher education as evidence that greater numbers of young people should not, or could not, achieve more education. In a static society of vintage 1850, their conclusion might be acceptable. In the light of the facts about population and the developments in technology presented earlier in the chapter, this attitude is indefensible. It is not too much to say that unless colleges and community junior colleges can develop *useful* educational programs and meaningful instructional techniques, civilization may decay simply for lack of humans competent to control it.

# D. Obstacles to College Attendance

The increase in the amount of schooling attempted in America since 1900 has been truly remarkable. No nation in history has ever invested to such an extent in mass education. In the college sector alone, enrollments have risen from 4% of the college age population (18-21) to well over 50%— although this statement conceals the fact that many of the students are over 21 years and that more than half of those who begin a college education drop out before completing it. Responsible analysts suggest that even more youth should be encouraged to attend college, although there are obstacles in the way of further enrollment increases.

One of the most important barriers is cost. Even attendance at a tuition-free community college is not entirely without cost. Clothing, books, and foregone earnings can amount to a frightening sum to a youth whose parents are barely making ends meet. Transportation to a college outside of one's own immediate community is an added burden. If tuition and board at a private college are included, even moderately well-off parents will find it difficult to support all of their children through college. Working one's way has a long and respectable tradition in America, but it usually requires high motivation, excellent ability, an extended stay in college, and considerable support from one's family.

Three aspects of obstacles to increased enrollments are worth mention:

1. It is necessary to plan curriculums that are responsive to the real educational needs of new types of students and that are available to greater numbers of students with wider ranges of abilities than earlier college student bodies exhibited.

2. Guidance plans are needed that will assist students and their parents in learning about the true nature and outcomes of higher education and about their own abilities and interests and ambitions. With this information, the student will be able to choose wisely both an educational goal and the appropriate institution to attend. Such guidance, of course, must be an integral part of the secondary school program, beginning in junior high school and continuing until the student has adopted a realistic set of life goals.

3. In addition, students must be helped to overcome the financial barriers to college attendance by means of adequate scholarship and loan plans and opportunities for part-time work, as well as by the establishment of community junior colleges to provide low-cost local opportunities for higher education.

If these three tasks can be accomplished, America can finally attain the dream of a higher education that makes possible a fully human quality of life. The community junior college can become an indispensable part of the realization of that dream.

## FOOTNOTES

1. *Occupational Outlook Handbook* (1970-71 edition). U.S. Department of Labor Bulletin No. 1650. Washington, D.C. U.S. Government Printing Office, 1970, pp. 11-19.
2. Froomkin, Joseph *Aspirations, Enrollments, and Resources.* Washington, D.C.: U.S. Government Printing Office, 1970, p. 2.

## BIBLIOGRAPHY

Binning, Dennis W. "Open Letter on Open Admissions," *College and University Business,* 48, No. 5 (May, 1970), pp. 53-55.

Caffrey, John (ed.). *The Future Academic Community: Continuity and Change.* Washington, D.C.; American Council on Education, 1969.

Froomkin, Joseph. *Aspirations, Enrollments and Resources: The Challenge to Higher Education in the Seventies.* Washington, D.C.: U.S. Government Printing Office, 1970.

Hirsch, Werner Z., et al. *Inventing Education for the Future.* San Francisco: Chandler Publishing Company, 1967.

Jencks, Christopher, and David Riesman. *The Academic Revolution.* Garden City, N.Y.: Doubleday Company, Inc., 1968.

Lerner, William (ed.). *Statistical Abstract of the United States, 1969.* (90th Annual Edition). Washington, D.C.: Bureau of the Census, U.S. Department of Commerce, 1969.

Lowe, Jeanne. "The End of the Line: Race and Poverty in Cities," in Alexander, B. Callow, Jr. (ed.). *American Urban History.* New York: Oxford University Press, 1969, pp. 519-540.

McGrath, Earl J. (ed.). *Universal Higher Education.* New York: McGraw-Hill Book Company, 1966.

*Occupational Outlook Handbook,* 1970-71 edition, U.S. Department of Labor Bulletin No. 1650. Washington, D.C.: U.S. Government Printing Office, 1970.

"Population Estimates and Projections," *Current Population Reports,* Series P-25, No. 448 (August 6, 1970). Washington, D.C.: Bureau of the Census, U.S. Department of Commerce, 1970.

Sorkin, Alan L. "Education, Migration and Negro Unemployment," *Social Forces,* 47, No. 3 (March, 1969), pp. 265-274.

# 3

# Philosophical Bases of the Community Junior College

Community junior colleges have been characterized by a willingness to recognize and to try to provide for new educational needs. Some critics profess to find in this adaptability a sign of weakness, a lack of direction, and a futile attempt to become all things to all men. The criticism arises from a failure of the critic to assess a completely new direction in higher education. The very first writers about junior colleges recognized this revolutionary concept, and referred to it as "popularizing higher education" or "democratization." One of the perpetual quandaries facing all community college teachers and administrators is how to adapt curriculum and instructional method so as to achieve this still unrealized ideal. The students are at the open door; but even with 50 years' warning, we have not prepared for them.

Democratization requires the elimination of barriers based on class, poverty, race, or cultural deprivation. The effective demand for it arises from the importance of education as a means to social mobility, and from the growing numbers of high school graduates. The social trends cited in the preceding chapter also contribute to the need for democratization of higher education. They diminish the nonschool alternatives for young people and set up educational attainment as the rite of passage from youth to adult status.

Under these conditions, the relation between college and student changes. The student is more mature, more impatient, and less willing to accept academic values that have no relation to his own perceived requirements. He does not settle for rewards long deferred. Even recent writers about this academic revolution have failed to recognize that the community college must be the prime mover in the adaptation of higher education to newly emerging kinds of students and to newly developing ways of educating them. For this reason, it is important to state clearly the basic principles on which community junior colleges are founded.

## A. General Principles

Junior colleges of all types are integral parts of the entire American educational enterprise. It is true that they have come into existence quite recently, but so have other portions of the school system—our entire sequence of educational opportunities is in many ways an indigenous development. Some parts have been copied from other countries and adapted to American conditions; other parts, such as the liberal arts college, the land-grant college, the public high school, and the junior college, are uniquely American. They share many common philosophical principles.

The first of these principles is that a democratic society cannot exist wholesomely without a well-educated citizenry. As the nation was established, it seemed to the founding fathers that two or three years of schooling would suffice to teach the citizens reading and ciphering and thus guarantee the perpetuation of constitutional government. Even so little schooling for all citizens in those days represented an impossibly idealistic goal. Yet learning, like avarice, grows by what it feeds on. And so each move to extend the learning of the American people has led to a demand for more educational opportunity and to the means to satisfy that demand. Three quarters of our younger people now complete the twelve-year course and graduate from high school. The next and inevitable step is universal availability of public education through the fourteenth year. The worldwide political responsibilities of the United States, its complicated technological economy, its ideals of social as well as political democracy, the serious problems arising from population explosion, the deterioration of the natural environment, and the lengthening of life expectancy—all of these point to a social need for more and more education for more and more people.

Throughout our history, this social purpose of education has been paralleled by an individual purpose. The nation was founded on the concept of the worth of the individual; it follows that every effort must be expended to help each person make the most of his abilities. American policy has been to afford higher education to each individual somewhat in proportion to his natural ability. This commitment faces the fact that many able young persons are denied education beyond the high school because they cannot afford to leave home to attend college. In addition, it recognizes varieties of valuable abilities which need development. The local community junior college, with little or no tuition charges and with a broadly diversified instructional program, complements the work of the high school, the technological institute, the college, and the university. It attempts to provide appropriately for the education of all citizens who desire and can profit by further study. In this way, American communities have moved to create opportunity for citizens of all varieties of high ability, of all social and economic classes, to develop their talents for the service of society and for their own self-interest.

It follows that the community junior college must be much more than the lower half of a college or a university. The junior college does duplicate one of their functions: it does provide lower division, preprofessional or prebaccalaureate courses of parallel scope and quality for similar student bodies. Here the similarity and the duplication end. The colleges and universities accept those who complete appropriate lower-division study on their own campuses or in the junior colleges and carry them with ever-increasing specialization toward the bachelor's degree, the master's degree, and the doctorate. The community junior college, meanwhile, welcomes other students who do not need or desire advanced degrees. It studies its community continually to learn the educational needs of its constituency and provides any course of two years or less that will accomplish socially desirable results. It intends to serve the whole population; students of technical subjects are no more entitled to the exclusive attention of the junior college than are the college transfer or the preprofessional groups.

This multiple function is difficult for the traditional academician to understand; the difficulty is compounded by the limitations of some existing public community colleges. Yet many other institutions serve several purposes. The university educates poets, artists, engineers, and physicians without questioning its own competence in each field. In exactly the same fashion, the community junior colleges provide both traditional and newly-developed courses of study—for both kinds are needed by their students.

Within its structure of diversified curriculums, nevertheless, the community college must recognize the basic individuality of every student. Instructors, counselors, administrators, planners, and legislators must stop thinking of groups or categories and focus on persons who need education. The initial task is not that of assigning a label that implies an educational limit. Instead, the first step must be a realistic assessment of where this young citizen stands educationally at entrance, and how far he can be encouraged to go in pursuit of his maximum development of skills and understandings. When it is recognized that certain performance goals are appropriate for all adult American human beings, efforts can be concentrated on developing the education that each one needs to get there. Hours spent and units earned become less important; goals attained by each student will be the unit of accountability.

Because of the breadth of their purposes, few community junior colleges should aspire to four-year status. A true community junior college, basing its offerings on known needs of its region, will find that it has an exacting and rewarding task; it has an individuality and a prestige which its faculty would not willingly jeopardize for the opportunity to become a four-year college of more limited scope.

## B. Admission Policy

The basic admission policy of many community junior colleges is starkly simple: "Any high school graduate, or any person over 18 years of age who seems capable of profiting by the instruction offered, is eligible for admission." Such a welcoming policy is required by the roles of the community junior college in American education. One of its primary functions is to give substance to the ideal of equal opportunity for appropriate education for all citizens. In carrying out this obligation, the community junior college is keenly aware that it is not possible to predict college success with anything approaching perfect accuracy; hence it plans to provide a chance for any applicant who, after competent counseling, insists that he would like to attempt a given course. It does not, of course, guarantee that every student will succeed. Its purpose is to make sure that every person is granted the opportunity to succeed or to fail by his own efforts. The responsibility for choice, for success, for failure, should rest with the student, not with a standardized test nor with the decision of an admissions counselor. A corollary of this position, obviously, is that the student with ability but without specific preparation for success in his chosen field of study must find educational options that will permit him to prepare to succeed. So-called remedial or developmental courses are an integral consequence of the open-door admission policy.

For decades, colleges have recognized somewhat unwillingly the need for additional preparation of many of their middle-class applicants. Courses in "bonehead English" have been offered to as many as half of the freshman class. The admission policy of the community junior colleges, however, is increasingly recognized as applicable to the educational needs of Blacks and Mexican-Americans. Their preparation for college success often requires a complete acculturation, as well as changes in the college offerings. In the academic world, it is as if they were visitors from a foreign nation. They need assurance that they are welcome, that success is possible, that success is worthwhile, and that they are accepted as persons of value in their own right. The college curriculum until quite recently was built on the assumption that all freshmen knew these things, and it has not been adapted rapidly enough to the flood of freshmen who do not.

This task of adaptation is most appropriately one for community junior colleges. They must actively recruit able youth who have never seen themselves as "college material." Then they must develop unconventional methods to prepare their recruits psychologically and academically for the struggle to develop their talents. The community junior college, located often in the heart of disadvantaged communities, can relieve the four-year institutions of these tasks. They can present to the four-year college at the junior level certified performers. At the same time, they can develop two-year curriculums that provide many of their students with more immediate preparation for life and for work.

The welcoming admission policy embraces also several categories of adult students. Some are part-time special students; their objectives are mainly cultural rather than vocational. They feel an effective curiosity to know more about their world and so register for classes in daytime or in evening sessions, as their leisure permits. Others are moved by advancing technology to bring their occupational skills up to date or perhaps to learn new skills so that they may qualify for advancement in their work. A third group of adults consists of mothers, their children grown to high-school age, who wish to renew their skills in clerical work or to learn a new skill such as teaching or practical nursing. Increasing numbers of such mothers are reentering the labor force in order to supplement the family income and to prepare for the added expenses to be incurred when the children start to college.

In many communities, the retired senior citizens constitute another important clientele for the adult programs of the community college. Here is a group, freed of the pressures of vocationalism, immediacy, and practicality, who are truly ready for liberal education. They bring to the classroom experience and often wisdom; they seek not credits but learning. Frequently the discussions of one class session provide them a focus of interest and a topic of conversation until the next meeting. Nor can it be argued consistently that, since they do not plan to use their late-won education productively in trade and in industry, they are not entitled to it. Worthy use of leisure time has long been one of the goals of American education, and for many retired persons the organized pursuit of learning for its own sake provides an absorbing interest which keeps them alert.

In the first volume of the *Junior College Journal,* William H. Snyder indicated some of the values of the policy of unrestricted admission when he pointed out that we had provided for the gifted in the university and for the "manually-minded" in vocational schools but that we had left the average boys and girls to shift for themselves. He suggested that:

"They need skill in order that they may make a living, but they need sufficient knowledge of the history of the world and the intellectual achievements of mankind to give them the power of orienting themselves to life. They must have both vision and skill, neither of which can be given intensively in the time allotted to junior college but each of which can be given with sufficient scope to enable students to earn a living and to adjust themselves to the progress of the world."[1]

## C. Diversification of Curriculum

Section B suggests that appropriate education should be made available to those who desire it. The suggestion implies that different kinds of post-high-school education may be appropriate for different people.

The community junior colleges believe that nearly all men are educable, that very many men need more education than that represented by their high-school graduation, and that it is economical and appropriate

for society and for men individually to attempt to provide effective
further education for a sizeable proportion of those who need it. The
community junior colleges realize that traditional college programs are
neither effective nor appropriate for a great many potential students. The
community junior colleges themselves have not yet solved entirely the
problems of designing courses that will be appropriate, but they have
made many excellent starts in that direction. In the process of seeking
solutions, they have progressed from the limited programs of the early
junior colleges toward the diversified offerings of the community junior
college.

One aspect of diversification has reached only the early stages of
realization. This is the development of techniques of introducing students
to the life of intellect. Much has been written about the wasted talents of
able youth from the cultures of poverty, whatever their color or ethnic
background. When these talented youths are brought into the colleges,
however, there is little adaptation to their primary educational needs.
The attempt is usually made to remedy their substandard speech or
reading or calculation, using the same sterile techniques that drove them
from the schools initially. The skills of communication surely are
essential; but a prior need of these new students is a rebirth of self-
concept, a renaissance of individuality. For years they have experienced
the lessons of social defeat, and until these lessons are unlearned, they will
be able to see no point in standard scholarship. Instructors may object
that this education is a task of the lower schools, not of college
curriculum. These students, though, are a present responsibility of the
colleges. The community college has the burden of educating them,
rather than of administering one more defeat.

A second area of curriculum diversity is education for transfer. Every
community junior college tries to include in its offering those courses
required by nearby colleges and universities as preparation for upper-
division work in the various fields of study. The survey of these
requirements is comparatively simple. The college administrator needs to
work with the officers of these institutions to determine accurately what
courses must be offered in order to provide fully acceptable preparation
for the various baccalaureate specialties. Then he needs to ascertain as
accurately as can be done the number of prospective students who hope to
transfer to each college and "major" in each field. It may become
apparent, for instance, that no student will desire to prepare in the
community junior college for transfer to the university school of
architecture. In that case, the college is justified in omitting from its
offerings those courses that prepare for architecture and for no other

major. If only one or two students express a need for such specialized lower-division courses, they may be advised to transfer to the university before their junior year, to attend a nearby community college which offers the courses, to take the courses through correspondence study, or perhaps to enter the university directly from high school. The small community college must not try to offer every possible course in its early years but only those which can be economically and prudently justified. As it grows, it can employ faculty to enable it to expand its offerings year by year.

Another aspect of curriculum diversity is the occupational field. In developing these courses, the community junior college depends upon continuous study of the locality. Several possibilities for occupational courses may be suggested by interested individuals. The decision to offer certain ones and delay others can be justified only by careful and intensive study of the community. The administrator will need to ascertain annual employment and turnover in each field, pay scales, growth trends in the industry, training requirements, equipment needed for a course, extent of student interest, and the attitude of employers and workers toward a college training program in the occupation. In addition, he will find that the series of interviews through which he learns these facts will provide him with excellent opportunities to explain the college to citizens of his community and thus to enlist support for the entire enterprise.

The educational needs of the part-time adult student, a fourth area of diversity, are likely to be satisfied by a more fluid organization than those of the occupational student; probably also the request for an adult course will develop more rapidly and be satisfied more often with a short-term class. Whereas the periodic survey of the educational and occupational needs of the entire community should concern itself with the needs of adults as well as of youth, this periodic effort must be supplemented by continuous sensitivity to suggestions for new adult offerings. Only by this process of constant scanning of the community can the community junior college administrator accomplish his task of providing for the post-high-school educational needs of his community.

Before establishing any course, the administrator will want to inform himself about practice in other colleges similar to his own. This is not to suggest that he will expand his curriculum only by imitating others; he cannot escape his responsibility for the creative solution of his problems. On the other hand, it would be foolhardy for him to ignore the experience of others when he might so easily profit from their successes and avoid their errors.

## D. The Responsibility for Guidance

It follows from the two principles of generous admission policy and diversified curriculum that students will find it difficult to choose courses appropriate for their abilities and their opportunities. While college faculty members sometimes feel that they could very successfully assign students to the proper courses, experience shows that this procedure is not usually effective. In a culture which values the concept of individual responsibility and personal freedom, we must protect as far as we can the student's right to choose for himself and to take the consequences of his choice, right or wrong. But such insistence on student choice is a travesty of freedom unless the student has adequate information about the nature and purpose of the several available curriculums, about his own personal and educational qualities, and about employment opportunities for those who complete the various courses. The provision of this information is the task of the guidance program.

Perhaps the most difficult long-range task of the guidance counselor is that of informing the student and the population at large about community junior college offerings. Semiprofessional college education is a comparatively recent development which requires explanation, and many students are misinformed about the success of junior college transfers in four-year college study. If the student is to choose his college course wisely, he needs to have accurate information and interpretation presented to him—and to his parents and to his high-school teachers—time and again. Only by such repeated exposure can young people and their parents overcome the stereotypes that lead them to ascribe value only to the four-year degree, to consider community junior college occupational education as the equivalent of trade-school training, or to esteem the local community junior college as an institution of last resort. Students, parents, and high-school teachers must be helped to learn the growing importance of the community junior college in American higher education by visitation and by exhortation over a period of years. If the preparation for college enrollment consists only of a catalog and a letter to parents handed to high-school seniors during the last month of high school, they will make many unfortunate mistakes in registration. Too often such mistakes lead to withdrawal from college and abandonment of higher education where complete and careful counseling might have led to a successful college experience.

The community college that concentrates on providing effective introductory and acculturative courses for the disadvantaged student intensifies its need for preregistration counseling and for continous face-to-face guidance during the early months of the student's attendance. It has been a boast of the community college from the earliest days that small classes facilitated a close student-teacher advisory relationship, but in recent years as the need for such relationships has grown, the size of classes has made them almost impossible. Recruitment of disadvantaged students to register is only a mockery unless counselors and instructors are enabled to supplement educational guidance with developmental personal contacts that encourage the recruits to remain and help them to succeed. The fact that these efforts are more costly, both in finances and in faculty time, is not a compelling argument against them.

In addition to the developmental aspects of counseling, students also need accurate information about themselves so that they may make effective occupational and educational choices. To some extent, this self-information is a task of the high school. Yet many students enter college either with exaggerated ideas of their intellectual stature or seriously underestimating their powers. Either mistake can lead to waste of effort and the development of a partially educated and unhappy citizen instead of an effective, well-educated one. The counseling service, therefore, collects information about the students from previous school records, from their own application forms, from tests, from their college instructors, and from observation. It is an important responsibility of the counselor to interpret this information tactfully but conscientiously to the student in order to assist him to reach decisions about his future education and career choice.

In the course of educational counseling, many problems will come to light that interfere with the student's optimum achievement. Personal or family worries, inadequate study skills, slow reading, substandard health, lack of finances, neurotic or psychotic tendencies, and excessive outside work are only a few of the problems that come to a junior college counselor's attention during an academic year. He will not solve them all; that is not his function. He will try to assist the student to find effective sources of help and to encourage him to make use of them. It happens quite frequently that such information makes the difference for a student between withdrawal from college and successful completion of a course.

# E. Standards of Teaching

The community junior college philosophy places great stress on excellent teaching. As early as 1921, Koos sampled the quality of teaching in colleges and universities and in junior colleges, and concluded that classroom procedure in junior colleges was on at least as high a plane as instruction of freshmen and sophomores in the universities. Several writers have emphasized that the chief function of the junior college instructor is always his teaching, whereas the university faculty member is expected to concentrate on research and publication in addition to teaching.

The nature of the student body of the community junior college would seem to underscore the importance of instructional technique. In comparison with freshmen and sophomores in the colleges and universities, the students tend to be older, they cover a broader range of abilities, and their background of secondary school study is more often undistinguished. Especially in the city community college, the number of disadvantaged students will be greater. It is fair to say that most community college students are able to learn but are relatively unpracticed. Under good instruction they can succeed admirably, whereas pedestrian teaching is more likely to discourage and defeat them than it would the more highly motivated freshmen and sophomores in the universities.

For all these reasons, teaching is the prime function of the community junior college and deserves every encouragement. Careful preparation and selection of teachers and encouragement to employed teachers to be constantly alert to improve their classroom effectiveness are essential elements in discharging this obligation. Experimentation will be needed in the coming years to devise ways to maintain inspired teaching even as class sizes are forced upward by the combination of a scant supply of teachers and a plentiful supply of students. Universities may become great through research, through publication, and through opportunities for graduate study, but the community junior college can attain its local renown and the affectionate esteem of its alumni only through the effectiveness of its educational program. Either it teaches excellently, or it fails completely.

## F. Standards of Student Achievement

Educational standards can be defined only in relation to objectives. The question for students as for teachers is, "How well did you achieve what you intended?" A recognition of this relationship leads inexorably to the realization that there is a double standard in assessing college achievement.

The older and more usual standard is expressed in disciplinary or vocational terms. Accurate performance is the only acceptable standard for the physician, the engineer, or the television repairman, A high level of knowledge of a subject or skill in performance of a task may rightly be demanded of the professional in any field. This is the meaning of standards in most discussions of the outcomes of university education.

Recently, however, there has been a tendency on the part of both faculty and students to reject these specialized and professional objectives of higher education. Instead, their emphasis is on growth of the student in more personal and individual ways. Increase of interpersonal sensitivity, acceptance of responsibility for the political and ecological consequences of one's acts, deepening of aesthetic insights, and development of a coherent and explicit system of values are examples of the objectives that are emphasized in the student culture.

The double standard poses several questions. Can both sorts of objective be attained through the same courses? Must each student decide to seek only one set of objectives because the two are antagonistic? Can they be attained serially, first personal development and then technical competence? Is either one really inappropriate in higher education? Is the professor's dedication primarily to his discipline, or to the humane development of his students, or to both? Answers to questions such as these are essential as a basis for a rational discussion of standards of student achievement. Perhaps the true nature of standards may be found in a middle ground— that the complete curriculum, and the complete set of student objectives, will encompass the greatest possible attainment of both sorts of goals by each student in his own way.

The community college seems destined to espouse the eclectic approach. Much of its effort will be spent in areas of personal development for students who are newcomers to higher education, the first of their families to attempt it. At the same time, occupational education is a major part of their purpose, as is preparation for transfer to senior institutions. In these fields, the standards are necessarily external. Performance of specified tasks is the criterion for completion of the course.

This duality of objective explains in part a recent trend in college evaluation. Some courses continue to be graded, with units of credit and grade points. These are usually courses associated with a specific occupation or with preparation for graduate study in a discipline. Other courses carry an option of accepting a report of pass or fail, or perhaps credit-noncredit. In some colleges, moreover, the student is permitted to withdraw from a course without any penalty or record on his transcript as late as the date of the final examination. The student may choose at the outset of the term the basis on which he wants to be judged. These plans are intended to allow the student to set his own goals in the course, and also to encourage him to explore fields outside his major without imperiling his grade point average.

These schemes are a step toward accepting student interest as a fundamental factor in learning, placing the responsibility for his education or lack of it on the student rather than on the institution. To the extent that these patterns of evaluation spread in the community colleges and also in the universities, the relationship between students and faculty will be shifted from the parental to the fraternal. At the same time, judgment as to the level of quality of instruction will become more imprecise. Success of the college will be judged by the success of its graduates in life rather than by the number of failing grades it assigns. In essence, flexible standards will make rigid evaluations almost impossible. The college will be judged by its students and alumni rather than by its peers. In the long run, both types of standards may benefit from this eventuality.

Such then are the principles underlying the community junior college: to make higher education available to qualified students of all ages, all social classes, all varieties of ability; to develop a sufficient variety of curriculums to meet the educational needs, at this level, of the community and of the individual students; to provide counseling and guidance services to help students choose appropriately from the available offerings; to devote concerted attention to effective teaching; and to encourage the highest levels of achievement of its students. To the extent that the community junior college makes these principles realities, it will justify its growing importance in the structure of American education.

### FOOTNOTES

1.    Snyder, William H. "The Real Function of the Junior College," *Junior College Journal,* **1**, (November, 1930), pp. 74-80.

### BIBLIOGRAPHY

Agnew, Spiro T. "Toward a 'Middle Way' in College Admissions," *Educational Record,* **51**, No. 2 (Spring 1970), pp. 106-111.

Bowles, Frank. "The Democratization of Education—A World-wide Revolution," *College Board Review,* No. 73 (Fall 1969), pp. 11-13.

Brunner, Ken August. "Historical Development of the Junior College Philosophy," *Junior College Journal,* **40**, No. 7 (April, 1970), pp. 30-34.

Carnegie Commission on Higher Education. *The Open-Door Colleges.* New York: McGraw-Hill Book Co., 1970.

Furniss, W. Todd. "Racial Minorities and Curriculum Change," *Educational Record,* **50**, No. 4 (Fall 1969), pp. 360-370.

Gleazer, Edmund J., Jr. *This Is The Community College.* Boston: Houghton Mifflin Company, 1968.

Henderson, Algo D. *The Innovative Spirit.* San Francisco: Jossey-Bass, Inc., Publishers, 1970.

Jencks, Christopher, and David Riesman. *The Academic Revolution.* Garden City, N.Y.: Doubleday and Company, Inc., 1968.

Knoell, Dorothy M. *People Who Need College: A Report on Students We Have Yet to Serve.* Washington, D.C.: American Association of Junior Colleges, 1970.

Moore, William, Jr. *Against the Odds.* San Francisco: Jossey-Bass, Inc., Publishers, 1970.

O'Banion, Terry. "Rules and Regulations: Philosophy and Practice," *Junior College Journal,* **39**, No. 7 (April 1969), pp. 11-15.

Quann, Charles J. "Survey Shows Variations in Grading Trends," *College and University Business,* **49**, No. 3 (September 1970), pp. 78-79.

Roueche, John E. *Salvage, Redirection, or Custody?* Washington, D.C.: American Association of Junior Colleges, 1968.

Yarrington, Roger (ed.). *Junior Colleges: 50 States/50 Years.* Washington, D.C.: American Association of Junior Colleges, 1969.

# 4 | Historical Development of the Community Junior College

The emergence of the community junior college as an established element of the American system of education over the past 70 years provides an excellent case study in the sociology of institutions. Only a handful of two-year colleges existed anywhere in the world in 1900. Yet by 1970, the United States had established almost 1100 of such colleges, with over 2 million enrollment. This rapid growth can be attributed to three main factors, although a good many subsidiary explanations can be found.

First, of course, there was the idea. The

penetrating educational statesmanship of a succession of university presidents and deans stimulated discussion and gave the first impetus to the establishment of junior colleges in several areas of the nation. These ideas, in turn, could not have become real except for the constant increase in economic wealth in the United States. The rising productivity which enabled the country to support more students in college required at the same time a constantly increasing supply of workers with the education to control and to improve the productive apparatus. Both the idea and the economic possibility, however, might have been fruitless in higher education, had it not been for that social phenomenon known as "The American Dream"—the belief inbred in every stratum of society that education is a social and individual good and that society is obligated to provide as much of it as any individual desires and can profit from. The junior college is one of the practical results of the interaction of these forces.

The present-day community junior college has evolved in four major stages. The first and longest lasted from 1850 to 1920. During that period the idea and the acceptable practice of the *junior college,* a separate institution offering the first two years of baccalaureate curriculums, were achieved. Next, the concepts of terminal and semiprofessional education in the junior college, which had been described earlier, gained widespread currency with the foundation of the American Association of Junior Colleges in 1920. By the end of World War II in 1945, this idea was an established part of the junior college concept. The changes in post-high-school education brought by the war emphasized a third element of responsibility, service to the adults of the community, and so the period after 1945 has seen the development of the operative definition of the *community junior college.* During this period, the rapid growth in college enrollments emphasized once more the transfer function of the junior college and brought increasing recognition of the importance of the institution as a part of the total system of higher education. Finally, the period since about 1965 has seen the beginning of a movement toward the full realization of the open-door concept, with the spread of colleges into the inner city and their emphasis on seeking ways to provide for all the educational needs of that community.

# A. The Evolution of the Junior College, 1850-1920

Several names are associated with the earliest development of the idea that the first two years of the American liberal arts college were truly not collegiate at all but belonged more appropriately to the secondary schools.

These leaders felt that if the college and the university could be freed from the necessity to provide these capstone years of secondary education, they might then become, in the words of Henry A. Tappan, "purely universities without any admixture of collegial tuition."

At his inauguration in 1869 as President of the University of Minnesota, William Watts Folwell echoed the idea of Michigan's President Tappan:

> How immense the gain . . . if a youth could remain at the high school or academy, residing in his home, until he had reached a point, say, somewhere near the end of the sophomore year, there to go over all of those studies which as a boy he ought to study under tutors and governors! Then let the boy, grown up to be a man, emigrate to the university, there to enter upon the work of a man . . . (In a footnote to his published address, President Folwell remarked, "That [the proposal] was not openly and vigourously denounced, was due to the fact that it was not understood, or if understood, was not taken seriously.")[1]

Neither Tappan nor Folwell succeeded either in eliminating the "secondary" years of their own universities, or in encouraging the widespread development of extended programs in the high schools. It remained for President William Rainey Harper, in 1892, to separate the first and last two years of the new University of Chicago into the "Academic College" and the "University College." Four years later these titles were changed to "junior college" and "senior college"—perhaps the first use of the terms. In addition, President Harper is credited with strongly influencing the foundation of several of the public and private junior colleges (notably Lewis Institute in Chicago in 1896 and Bradley Polytechnic Institute in Peoria in 1897) and obtaining the addition of two years to the high school program in Joliet, Illinois in 1901. The Joliet Junior College is thus the oldest extant public junior college.

President Harper, in common with the other statesmen of this early period, conceived of the junior college primarily as a continuation of the high school. He proposed a plan for radical reorganization of the entire public system of education, which was studied at a conference in 1903 and favorably reported by three committees of faculty members from academies and high schools affiliating with the University of Chicago. President Harper's plan involved:

1. The connecting of the work of the eighth grade of the elementary school with that of the secondary schools. (The junior high school.)
2. The extension of the work of the secondary schools to include the first two years of college work.

3. The reduction of the work of these seven years thus grouped together to six years.
4. Making it possible for the best class of students to do this work in five years.

It is a testimony to the remarkable persuasive powers of President Harper that a committee of elementary school men, another of high-school and academy principals, and a third representing Midwestern universities all endorsed this revolutionary plan. The University Committee suggested five arguments against the plan:

1. The high schools were unable to do the work because of the inadequacy of their equipment, the incompetency of their instructors, and the fact that they were already too crowded with their four years of work.
2. Youth, to grow and learn, need the surroundings of colleges and the example of the more mature juniors and seniors.
3. Larger cities, which have universities, would certainly not adopt the plan.
4. The plan would do a great deal of damage to the American college.
5. It would inflict irreparable injury to the pattern of American life.

Nevertheless, the University Committee, with two dissenting votes, endorsed the plan, because it recognized that the first two collegiate years were essentially secondary; the plan would hold "scores, even hundreds," of young men and women for two more years of education; much technical and other special preparation for life work (i.e., preprofessional courses) would be offered; the plan would save expense for the student; and anyway, the plan would be adopted only in those localities where it was needed.

On the West Coast, two eminent spokesmen took up the junior college cause. At Stanford University, President David Starr Jordan reviewed the Chicago developments and ventured a prophecy and a recommendation:

> It is safe to prophesy that before many years the American university will abandon its junior college, relegating its work to the college on the one hand and to the graduate courses of the secondary school on the other.

> I ask your Board to consider the project of the immediate separation of the junior college from the university or the university college, and to consider the possibility of requiring the work of the junior college as a requisite for admission to the university on and after the year 1913, or

as soon as a number of the best equipped high schools of the state are prepared to undertake this work.[2]

Spindt reports, however, that a faculty committee disagreed with their president and uttered a complaint that has since been repeated over and over without regard to the evidence. The faculty committee decided that " . . . the successful establishment of six-year high schools is a problem of the future. Upperclassmen coming from six-year high schools and small colleges with limited equipment and endowment, would not be as well trained or as far advanced as those who begin their college work here."

During the second decade of the century, Dean Alexis F. Lange of the University of California focused attention on the need for postgraduate work in the public high schools; it was a theme on which he spoke and wrote at every opportunity. Each of his articles contains at least one quotable passage. Spindt has captured one of the most outspoken expressions of Dean Lange's viewpoint:

The frank recognition of the fact—it is a fact—that the difference between the first two years of college and the high school is one of degree only and has never been anything else, implies the remedy. The first step would be for the University to reduce its "swollen fortune" in freshmen and sophomores by actively promoting their distribution among federated colleges, normal schools, and the six-year high schools that are to be and will be. The second would be to give these grades, in and without the University, teachers specially prepared and experienced in secondary education, and to make the position of such teachers a worthy goal, inclusive of *salary,* of legitimate and worthy ambition and initiative . . . As for the University a number of its most vexing problems would pass out of existence.

It is interesting to speculate about the first successful and persistent junior college. According to Bogue, Lasell Junior College, Auburndale, Massachusetts, offered two years of standard collegiate instruction as early as 1852. The University of Georgia in 1859 resolved to abolish its first two years because it was felt that the students coming to Franklin College (the liberal arts division of the University) were entirely too young, and "the foundation of failure, if not of ruin, is laid in the Freshmen and Sophomore years of College life." The plan was begun, but its completion was interrupted by the Civil War, which finally caused the University to suspend operation. After the University reopened in 1866, the plan seems to have been forgotten.

Several other candidates for the honor of being the first junior college have been sponsored by historians; the search is made difficult by the fact that no early definition had been expressed, so that some of the institutions that offered two years of collegiate instruction during the nineteenth century did not realize that they were the forerunners of a national trend. After the title was invented, there seems to be full agreement that the first public junior college established in connection with a high school was that at Goshen, Indiana, later discontinued, and that the oldest public junior college still in existence is Joliet Junior College, Illinois.

The history of the degree granted by the junior colleges is worthy of mention. In 1900, The University of Chicago began to award the Associate in Arts degree to all students who successfully completed the junior college program of studies. In his recommendation to the Stanford University trustees on abolition of the University lower division, President Jordan suggested "that on and after August 1, 1910, in addition to the present entrance requirements, two years, or sixty units, of collegiate work, the equivalent of the requirements for the degree or title of 'Associate in Arts' as granted in the University of Chicago, shall be required for entrance to the University."

Thereafter, however, some confusion entered the picture. In its "statement of standards" of 1915, the Association of Colleges and Secondary Schools of the Southern States prohibited the granting of degrees by accredited junior colleges. In 1930, William H. Snyder proposed that the newly established Los Angeles City College grant the degree of Associate in Arts, and the California Junior College Federation in that year passed a resolution asking that the degree be authorized and be conferred upon all the graduates, irrespective of whether they had completed the certificate course or the semiprofessional course. In 1934, however, Campbell reported forty-nine different titles, each granted by at least one junior college. Twenty-six different kinds were found in public junior colleges and forty-one in private junior colleges. In 1956, Colvert reported that "recognition of the associate's degree has gained wide favor in educational circles. It is now authorized in all states where there are junior colleges, with the exception of Virginia, and granted by junior colleges and many senior colleges . . . The granting of the associate's degree places the official stamp of approval on junior college education as definite collegiate accomplishment."[3]

In his pioneering dissertation, published conveniently just at the end of the evolutionary period, McDowell summarized the conditions tending to further the development of the junior college idea. He suggested four main influences. First, the university was moved to encourage the development of junior colleges because of its own rapid growth and unhealthy tendency to large classes, because it felt a need to divide secondary work from that of the university, and because a junior college allows for closer contact with and control of youthful students. Second, the normal schools of that day wished to offer collegiate work in addition to purely pedagogical subjects, so many of them became junior colleges. Third, the extension of the high school seemed to be "an additional step in the evolution of our system of public education." Finally, according to McDowell, there was the problem of the small college, too weak to offer a strong four-year program and practically forced by the developing pattern of accreditation to concentrate its efforts on a more attainable objective.[4]

The junior college, proposed and initiated both as an extension of secondary education and as an amputation from the university or four-year college, grew and prospered until in 1921 there were 207 such colleges: 70 public and 137 private. In that year, also, the enrollment in public colleges surpassed for the first time that in the private institutions. There were 16,000 students enrolled in all, of whom 52% (8349) were in public and 48% (7682) were in private colleges. In the minds of their administrators, however, these 207 institutions were not secondary schools; they felt that they were truly collegiate, as evidenced by the first definition of the junior college adopted by the newly formed American Association of Junior Colleges in 1922: "The junior college is an institution offering two years of instruction of strictly collegiate grade."

## B. The Expansion of Occupational Programs, 1920-1945

The original definition of the American Association of Junior Colleges, however, was already out of date. Passage of federal vocational education bills during World War I had attracted attention of public junior colleges desirous of sharing in the grants provided. One result was the second statute in California concerning junior colleges, passed in 1917. It provided that:

> Junior college courses of study may include such studies as are required for the junior certificate at the University of California, and such other courses of training in the mechanical and industrial arts, household economy, agriculture, civic education, and commerce as the high school board may deem advisable to establish.

Similar forces in other states led to similar authorizations for vocational courses. By 1925, the American Association of Junior Colleges felt impelled to expand its definition:

The junior college is an institution offering two years of strictly collegiate grade. This curriculum may include those courses usually offered in the first two years of the four-year college, in which case these courses must be identical, in scope and thoroughness, with corresponding courses of the standard four-year college. The junior college may, and is likely to, develop a different type of curriculum suited to the larger and ever-changing civic, social, religious, and vocational needs of the entire community in which the college is located. It is understood that in this case also the work offered shall be on a level appropriate for high school graduates.

This concept of occupational education had been enunciated much earlier, and some efforts had been made to include it in the curriculums of the junior colleges. In one of his most quoted utterances, Lange concisely expresses the basic essentials of junior college semiprofessional training. After pointing out that both general education and training for specialized efficiency must be provided, he states,

"The junior college cannot make preparation for the University its excuse for being. Its courses of instruction and training are to be culminal rather than basal . . . The junior college will function adequately only if its first concern is with those who will go no farther, if it meets local needs efficiently, if it enables thousands and tens of thousands to round out their general education, if it turns an increasing number into vocations for which training has not hitherto been afforded by our school system." *With characteristic candor, he admits that* "It is, of course, an inevitable phase of growth that as yet not one of the junior colleges I know about has fully found itself."[5]

Dr. Merton E. Hill, who was at that time principal of Chaffey Junior College, claimed for that institution the probable distinction of offering the first terminal courses in California public junior colleges. In September, 1916, Chaffey was established as a junior college in connection with the high school and offered terminal vocational courses in art, manual training, home economics, commerce, music, library training, general agriculture, farm mechanics, and soils.[6]

One of the strong advocates of semiprofessional education during this period was President Snyder of Los Angeles Junior (now City) College, founded in 1929 and almost immediately the largest of all the junior colleges. During its first year, Los Angeles Junior College established 14 terminal semiprofessional curriculums. Although convinced of the need for occupational courses, Snyder saw the total function of the junior college quite clearly. In another article, he objected to the "secondary school" characterization of the junior college, saying, "Why not keep it in the American college classification and give to it the standings and traditions which have for centuries been developed in our own distinctly American educational unit, the college?" Furthermore, he pointed out that at least 50% of junior college graduates do not continue their studies and that semiprofessional courses were needed just as much as transfer courses. Yet, "If the junior college is to be really collegiate, it cannot allow itself to become merely a vocational institution. It must have well-established courses which embrace both cultural and utilitarian subjects."[7]

These trends of thought, leading to the establishment of occupational courses in junior colleges over the nation, firmly established the concept of terminal education. In 1940, the American Association of Junior Colleges announced the receipt of a grant of $25,000 from the General Education Board of New York City to finance a series of exploratory studies in the general field of terminal education in the junior college. As an outgrowth of these exploratory studies, the General Education Board in December, 1940 granted an additional sum of $45,500 to support a cooperative study of terminal education in the junior colleges. Four volumes were published under this grant, discussing in some detail the concept of semiprofessional terminal education as a function of the junior college.

Several influences seem to have contributed to the rapid expansion of occupational education in the junior colleges. The leadership of state agencies for vocational education, set up under the Smith-Hughes Act and related federal legislation, was especially effective in the states that considered the public junior colleges to be part of secondary education. The widespread unemployment during the depression of 1929-1937 encouraged the spread of occupational education; it was realized that specific training beyond the high-school level would give an applicant a competitive advantage in the job market. During the 1950's, increasing automation required workers with higher levels of technical skills, and the junior colleges were quick to organize classes to train them.

The Vocational Education Act of 1963 recognized the junior colleges by removing the restriction to courses of "less than college grade" that had appeared in earlier federal vocational legislation, and by concentrating on the training needs of people rather than on preparation for specific occupations. Finally, the emphasis of many of the public junior colleges on a close working relationship with their communities encouraged groups of employers or of workers to request the establishment of additional occupational courses. Through these developments, the junior colleges branched into activities which were neither secondary education nor higher education; they began to achieve a separate identity and a unique set of purposes.

## C. The Community College Concept, 1945-1965

Although the addition of college-level occupational curriculums to the lower-division offerings brought an entirely new complexion to the junior college, the institution still had not achieved its full stature as a community college. This development required the further addition of adult education and community services. Once again, this expanded scope of operation had been dimly foreseen by some of the early advocates of the junior college and steps toward its realization had been taken in several cities prior to 1940. The drop in enrollment in day classes after the outbreak of World War II and the nationwide emphasis on training for defense work stimulated the colleges to engage in community action as a temporary measure. The offerings proved so valuable to so many segments of the population, however, that the colleges continued and developed them after the war, and thus with these offerings completed the development of the community junior college.

In 1930, in the first issue of the *Junior College Journal*, Nicholas Ricciardi gave a definition of the functions of the community junior college which has served as model for several later definitions:

A fully organized junior college aims to meet the needs of a community in which it is located, including preparation for institutions of higher learning, liberal arts education for those who are not going beyond graduation from the junior college, vocational training for particular occupations usually designated as semi-professional vocations, and short courses for adults with special interests.

In 1936, Byron S. Hollinshead essayed a restatement of the same principles:

That the junior college should be a community college, meeting community needs; that it should serve to promote a greater social and civic intelligence in the community; that it should provide opportunities for increased adult education; that it should provide educational, recreational, and vocational opportunities for young people; that the cultural facilities of the institution should be placed at the disposal of the community; and that the work of the community college should be closely integrated with the work of the high school and the work of other community institutions.

By 1939, the community junior college concept was sufficiently clarified that an article appeared in the *Journal* entitled "The Junior College as a Community Institution." In January, 1940, the first "fundamental principle" of the Commission on Terminal Education was "The Junior College is essentially a community institution." When the Report of the President's Commission on Higher Education, *Higher Education in American Democracy,* described the community college fully and favorably, using that term, the full task of these institutions was recognized by all who were concerned with them. Thus the concept of the community junior college has been fully developed, and the need for it has been established in all parts of the nation.

## D. The Period of Consolidation, 1965

The tasks of the community college have been widely accepted as they have developed over the years. Yet there has been a continuous realization that these tasks were being only partially fulfilled. Although the door was open, many of the guests did not come—they did not even know they were welcome. Of those who did enter, a high proportion dropped out. Occupational education was stressed in the literature, but three-fourths of the students stated a transfer goal. Fewer than half of these actually transferred. Guidance and counseling were proud boasts of the institution, even though fewer than a third of the colleges provided trained counselors in defensible proportions to the enrollments. Better teaching was a goal, but far too many teachers felt constrained to mimic the course outlines and the techniques of the university. Since 1965, emphasis in legislative enactments and in program development seems to have been concentrated on improving performance rather than on expanding the responsibilities of the colleges.

The open-door concept has been critically examined. As a result, several recent events give promise that community colleges can carry out more effectively their obligations to able persons who need more and better education. One sign is the recognition by the federal government of the potential contributions of the community college, through explicit allocation of funds for building, for technical education, and for faculty development. Districts with large populations or covering large areas have begun to recognize that distance from a college is a real deterrent to attendance by disadvantaged persons. As a result, opportunity is being provided where the people are. At least 39 community college districts (not including university two-year centers) now operate two or more college sites, bringing higher education into the communities and enabling each campus to develop programs appropriate to its own clientele.

Recruitment of minority students has also been undertaken by several community colleges and will spread to more of them. This is perhaps the most crucial development of the period of consolidation. As Gleazer suggests, the task is not to adapt the student to an existing and inflexible curriculum; rather it is to meet the student where he is and to develop a curriculum that will move him toward educational goals that are acceptable both to him and to society. "For every person in the classroom of the community college today, there is another whose needs are just as great and whose options are more limited. Those 2 million people are in community college territory."[8]

Occupational education is being reexamined and modernized. The growing needs for professional, technical, and service personnel are bringing about courses that substitute scientific skills for the largely manipulative skills of the vocational period. This trend was given impetus by the broader provisions of the Vocational Education Act of 1963, with its emphasis on persons who needed employment preparation rather than primarily on trades that needed workers. The movement toward technical education brings about a renewed need for definition of skills required for entrance into the courses and for opportunities for students who lack those skills to achieve them.

Transfer education also achieves new status in the higher education system as state after state has limited admission to public four-year and university education, asking the community colleges to accept the responsibility for lower-division education. This trend is an ironic return to the proposals of over a century ago; it becomes apparent from the statistics that more than half of the first time degree-credit enrollments are now in the community colleges. The trend is emphasized further by the fact that an increasing number of state universities enroll more junior students than they do freshmen.

Pressure of fully qualified transfer students for admission to the community colleges can have several consequences. The range of aptitudes in the student bodies will be even greater than in the past. The college faculties will need to resist the temptation to cater to the degree-credit student at the expense of the occupational student. Financial needs increase, bringing pressure for more state aid as compared with local support, and perhaps for more state coordination as well.

It is possible that curriculum can become more innovative, less imitative of university practices. If community colleges become the agencies that specialize in education of lower-division students, they may gain sufficient confidence to define their own tasks, to give up overemphasis on counting credits and hours, and to recommend for university acceptance graduates who can demonstrate mastery of prerequisite subject matter, no matter how it was achieved. Responsibility for most lower-division education presents real challenges to community colleges, for they must become truly comprehensive in their services to all sorts of students.

Guidance and counseling will be the keys to success in all of these efforts. If the basic goal is defined as the optimum development of each student's aptitudes toward self-determined ambitions, more emphasis on individual diagnosis and instruction are needed. Budgets will have to reflect this goal by providing personnel, trained and interested in guidance, in sufficient numbers to provide the service. The guidance worker will see himself as the hub of the entire educational system. He will bring into articulation the high schools, the universities, the faculties of his own college, and the curriculum, all in service to the students as he knows them and interprets them to the rest of the system.

In effect, it is possible to suggest that history has developed a workable concept of the true community college. The task during the consolidation period is to give concrete reality to the ideals that have been elaborated.

## E. The American Association of Junior Colleges

On June 30 and July 1, 1920, 34 junior college representatives met in St. Louis at the call of United States Commissioner of Education, P. P. Claxton. At this meeting, it was decided to organize a national association, and in Chicago, on February 16-17, 1921, a constitution and a name, "The American Association of Junior Colleges," were adopted. The constitution defined the objectives of the Association thus: "To define the junior college by creating standards and curricula, thus determining its position structurally in relation to other parts of the school system; and to study the junior college in all of its types (endowed, municipal, and state) in order to make a genuine contribution to the work of education."

Since that time, the Association has served as a spokesman for the interests of junior colleges of all types and has contributed beyond measure to their establishment as an important segment of American higher education. Among its outstanding achievements have been the continuous publication since 1930 of the *Junior College Journal*, the preparation annually of the *Junior College Directory*, and the compilation of the eight editions of *American Junior Colleges*, published by the American Council on Education. Association membership numbers 857 colleges, out of the total reported of 1091. There are 645 publicly supported member colleges and 202 independent colleges. The Association conducts a yearly convention, stimulates research, provides consultant services, carries on a broad public information program, engages in studies, and publishes monographs and newsletters on specific aspects of junior college education. It lists eight major objectives of its services:

1. To make additional, substantial efforts to raise the level of administrative competence in junior college education.
2. To assist in establishment of strong junior college teacher preparation programs, in-service workshops and institutes, to stimulate and to find ways of inviting promising people to the field of junior college teaching.
3. To stimulate and assist junior colleges to develop comprehensive curricula where appropriate, with special attention to technical education and community services.
4. To clarify and promote public understanding of the functions of junior colleges.
5. To assist the states in developing sound and orderly systems of junior colleges to serve the major part of the population in each state, and to provide at the national and state levels adequate information regarding the appropriate services of junior colleges so that legislation involving these institutions will be realistic and constructive.
6. To promote more effective relationships between junior colleges and high schools on one hand and senior colleges and universities on the other.
7. To assist in strengthening state and regional organizations of junior colleges and to encourage a closer relationship between their activities and those at the national level.
8. To adopt measures to promote greatly improved student personnel services with particular regard to counseling and guidance.

## FOOTNOTES

1. Folwell, W. W. *University Addresses.* New York: H. W. Wilson Co., 1909, pp. 37-38.
2. Spindt, H. A. "Establishment of the Junior College in California, 1907-1921," *California Journal of Secondary Education,* **32** (November, 1957), pp. 391-396.
3. Colvert, C. C. "Development of the Junior College Movement," Chapter 2 in *American Junior Colleges* (Fourth Edition). Jesse P.

Bogue (editor). Washington, D.C.: American Council on Education, 1956.

4.  McDowell, F. M. *The Junior College.* U.S. Bureau of Education Bulletin, 1919, No. 35. Washington, D.C.: U.S. Government Printing Office, 1919.
5.  Lange, Alexis F. "The Junior College as an Integral Part of the Public School System," *School Review,* **25** (September, 1917), pp. 465-479.
6.  Hill, Merton E. "History of Terminal Courses in California," *Junior College Journal,* **12** (February, 1942), pp. 311-313.
7.  Snyder, William H. "The Distinctive Status of the Junior College," *Junior College Journal,* **3** (February, 1933), pp. 235-239.
8.  Gleazer, Edmund J., Jr. "The Community College Issue of the 1970's." *Educational Record,* **51**, No. 1 (Winter 1970), pp. 47-52.

## BIBLIOGRAPHY

*American Junior Colleges.* 1940 edition, Walter Crosby Eells (ed.). 1948, 1952, 1956 editions, Jesse P. Bogue, (ed.). 1960, 1963, 1967, and 1971 editions, Edmund J. Gleazer, Jr. (ed.). Washington, D.C.: American Council on Education.

Bogue, Jesse P. *The Community College.* New York: McGraw-Hill Book Co., 1950.

Brick, Michael. *Forum and Focus for the Junior College Movement.* New York: Bureau of Publications, Teachers College, Columbia University, 1964.

Brunner, Ken August. "Historical Development of the Junior College Philosophy," *Junior College Journal,* **40** (April, 1970), pp. 30-34.

California State Department of Education, *The Junior College in California.* California State Department of Education Bulletin No. G-3. Sacramento: 1928.

Eells, Walter Crosby. *The Junior College.* Boston: Houghton Mifflin Co., 1931.

Gleazer, Edmund J., Jr. "The Community College Issue of the 1970's," *Educational Record,* **51** (Winter 1970), pp. 47-52.

Greenleaf, Walter J. *Junior Colleges.* U.S. Office of Education Bulletin, 1936, No. 3. Washington, D.C.: U.S. Government Printing Office, 1936.

*Higher Education for American Democracy.* The Report of the President's Commission on Higher Education. New York: Harper and Row, 1948.

Hillway, Tyrus. *The American Two-Year College.* New York: Harper and Row, 1958.

*Junior College Journal,* passim. The early volumes especially (vols. 1 to 10) contain notes on "Ancient History" as a continuing department. Washington, D.C.: American Association of Junior Colleges, 1930 — present.

Kelley, Win, and Leslie Wilbur. *Teaching in the Community Junior College,* Chapter 1. New York: Appleton-Century-Crofts, 1970.

Koos, Leonard V. *The Junior College.* Minneapolis: University of Minnesota Press, 1924.

Lindsay, Frank B. "California Junior Colleges, Past and Present," *California Journal of Secondary Education,* **22** (March, 1947), pp. 137-142.

McDowell, F. M. *The Junior College.* U.S. Bureau of Education Bulletin, 1919, No. 35, Washington, D.C.: U.S. Government Printing Office, 1919.

Proctor, William Martin (editor). *The Junior College: Its Organization and Administration.* Stanford, California: Stanford University Press, 1927.

Rogers, James F. "A Philosophy for the Junior College with Implications for Curriculum," *Junior College Journal,* **30** (November, 1959), pp. 125-131.

Sack, Saul. "The First Junior College," *Junior College Journal,* **30** (September, 1959), pp. 13-15.

Seashore, Carl E. *The Junior College Movement.* New York: Holt, Rinehart and Winston, 1940.

Spindt, H. A. "Establishment of the Junior College in California, 1907-1921," *California Journal of Secondary Education,* **32** (November, 1957), pp. 391-396.

# 5

# Accepted
# Functions of
# Community
# Junior
# Colleges

In the early days of junior college development, writers were much concerned about identifying the specific functions of the institution, as a step toward clear definition of its distinctive character.[1] In general, the many purposes listed were grouped under six or seven categories—preparatory (for further college study), popularizing or democratizing higher education, guidance, terminal education, adult education, general education, and community services.

Recent developments, including the growth in numbers and in enrollments of community colleges, have led to an implicit redefinition of the functional roles of the institution. First, the *preparatory* function has been expanded as overcrowded public universities reassign fully qualified high school graduates to the community colleges. Second, a stress on recruitment into college of able but under-educated students has been employed as part of the drive against poverty and racism. In effect, these two developments indicate a split of the original college transfer function into the two categories of educational skill improvement required by the open-door policy and the more traditional transfer functions.

A second innovation in the purposes of all higher education is the explicit and insistent introduction of development of the individual as a major goal of education. Autonomy and breadth of culture have often appeared in catalog lists of the outcomes of higher education; but as Nevitt Sanford suggests, professors "ask how such characteristics are to be produced, and, receiving no answer, they go back to teaching mechanics and thermodynamics." The demand for developmental education does not substitute for rigorous study in areas of professional specialization, but it does emphasize that mastery of a discipline is not the only purpose of higher education. Specialized study can be dangerous to society if it is not complemented by humanistic learning. Because of the broad ranges of abilities, interests, and educational and experiential backgrounds in its student body, the community college must be particularly effective in its efforts to provide developmental education.

For community colleges in the seventies, the total spectrum of functions may be listed under two headings—those dealing with the cultivation of the humane qualities of the student and those concerned with occupational or professional competence. The developmental functions of community colleges include educational activities that are complete in themselves; the activity itself leads to desirable changes in the personal aptitudes and behaviors of the students and is justified on that basis. Preparatory functions, as the phrase implies, are telic in nature. They are validated by success in later activities such as job placement or advanced study.

Among developmental functions of the community college are listed (1) improvement of learning skills for disadvantaged students; (2) general education for all students; (3) part-time education and community service for the entire post-high school population; and (4) counseling and guidance of students.

In addition, preparatory functions include (5) technical and vocational education of post-high school level; and (6) education for transfer to professional study. Each of these fundamental functions is defined briefly in the remainder of this chapter.

## A. The Development of Learning Skills

Educational disadvantage is not restricted to any identifiable social group. Young persons of good ability can fail to achieve no matter what their social or economic status, and quite without regard to their ethnic origins or their places of residence. As William Moore, Jr., points out, high risk whites outnumber marginal blacks. The development of learning skills for all high risk students requires a commitment to a quality educational program, not just to a specific target group. Furthermore, the solution is not just to redouble the efforts in remedial reading, writing, speech, and mathematics; this sort of effort has been defeating these youth in the lower schools for years. It is equally ineffective to suggest that the problem is not a collegiate problem and to say that the secondary schools ought to care for it. The marginal youth who need community college assistance are not in high school and will not return there. The community college task is to accept the student who needs and desires more education and to develop techniques to satisfy his needs.

Fundamentally, the educational barrier for most disadvantaged young people is lack of motivation. They see no value in school subjects, no relationship of study to their life goals, and no hope of success in the competition for scholarly attainment. All of life has taught them to distrust their abilities in this arena; their primary need is for restructuring their self-concept. Only when this is achieved will they begin to see point in the prerequisite studies that stand in the way of their registration in recognized college curriculums.

This reconstruction, this nurturing of a sense of worth and of potential, requires small classes with dedicated, competent, autonomous, and humane teachers. It requires more money per student than the education of the very able and self-accepting student, because it requires a much higher ratio of teachers to students. Counseling that opens doors of self-insight and of educational opportunity is essential; the counselor must be able to point out existing educational options in which the high-risk student has a chance of success. Omit from the program any of these conditions—teaching, counseling, financing, and diversity of curriculum—and another failure of the student and of the program is assured.

Remedial courses are still needed, but courses such as the "sub-freshman English" planned for the middle-class youth who is eligible for college admission are not the answer for marginal students. Imagination in course planning is needed, stressing meaningful objectives of overt behavior in packets small enough so that success may be achieved by the student and recognized by the teacher at frequent intervals. Colleges tend to assume that their students are independent and eager to learn. The assumption is even less valid for the marginal student than for the traditional one, but it is a worthwhile goal for college instruction.

As a function of the community junior college, development of learning skills involves:

Aggressive recruitment of the undereducated of all varieties.

An environment that stresses supportive interpersonal relations between the marginal student and several well-qualified and dedicated instructors.

Sufficient diversification of curriculum to permit students of all categories to find stimulating and relevant educational options.

A recognition that the high-risk student may have career goals other than the manual occupations. Neither the student nor the curriculum is served by assigning him to a course mainly because he lacks prerequisites for another course more suited to his interests and abilities.

A philosophy that seeks to create a curriculum to fit the marginal student rather than to adapt the student to an existing curriculum even at the price of his early disqualification. The standards of a college may be judged not by a high percentage of failing grades, but rather by the percentage of entering students who found there realistic preparation for the next stage of their lives.

## B. General Education

After self-confidence and motivation for learning on the part of all students are either recognized at admission or developed as suggested in Section A, general education is the second of the developmental tasks of the community college. Because it has been difficult to define in disciplinary terms, the practice of general education has fallen into disrepute both with students and with many professors. The basic concept is nevertheless a valid one.

General education is concerned with the fundamental similarities among all mankind. It seeks to develop insights and knowledge to assist every human in conducting the many daily activities that are common to all men who live in society. General education may be defined as a program of education specifically designed to afford young people more effective preparation for the responsibilities that they share in common as citizens in a free society and for wholesome and creative participation in a wide range of life activities. It attempts to clarify the focal problems of our times and to develop the intellectual skills and moral habits to cope with them.

The purposes of general education are not new purposes. What is new is the reaction against the overspecialization which characterized many college programs during the first half of the twentieth century. General education does not seek to replace specialization; most of the recent technical advances in our culture have come about because of the high quality of our specialized education. On the other hand, specialization is not a complete education for modern living. General education complements specialization through a recognition that although men differ in their abilities, interests, and accomplishments, they share many characteristics that demand common elements of education.

A partial answer to these newly realized needs has involved attempts to develop new organizations of instruction, emphasizing the utility of the subject matter to the student rather than the totality of the disciplinary field. At first such reorganized courses in any field were offered principally to college students who intended to specialize in some other subject field. More recently, the upsurge of adult and community college enrollments has led to a realization that in fact all persons share certain responsibilities in common and that all persons can profit from opportunities for general education. For this reason, the community junior colleges have become aware of their responsibility to include general offerings in their planning for all classes of their students. Adult students and occupational students and high-risk students face the focal problems of our times just as poignantly as those who plan to earn bachelor's, master's, or doctor's degrees.

A good many difficulties have retarded the efforts of the junior colleges in developing complete and coherent patterns of general education for all their students. The transient nature of the student bodies, the high rate of withdrawal, the externally imposed course requirements which transfer students must fulfill, and the shortage of qualified and interested instructors—all hinder the establishment of general education.

In spite of the difficulties and deterrents, the need persists for general education for all categories of students. Some progress has been made toward its solution. Further progress will continue as faculty members labor to select and organize experiences that will contribute to more abundant personal life for their students and which stimulate the students to work toward a more stable and more satisfactory society.

## C. Continuing Education and Community Service

In a civilization where no man's education may be considered sufficient and complete, people of all ages and conditions seek opportunities to continue their education while they work. America is becoming a nation of students, and the community junior colleges are increasingly active in providing courses for the fully employed part-time student. Part-time enrollments in several states exceed the number of full-time students; the 1971 *Junior College Directory* reports 1,064,187 part-time students, compared to 1,170,482 full-time students in the nation as a whole.

The category of adult students is difficult to define precisely; it is no longer possible to restrict the program of adult education to the hours after six o'clock, to include in it all students over 21 years of age, or to assign all part-time students to it. As many as 10% of the full-time students in some community junior colleges are more than 25 years of age; on the other hand, many of the students in evening classes are part-time "college age" persons working toward degrees. It is apparent that the term, "adult education," is no longer as limited in meaning as it was when Americanization was the main purpose; the term, "continuing education," is a more accurate description of the function.

The need for educational opportunities for persons employed full-time includes both credit and noncredit courses, courses paralleling daytime offerings as well as courses developed especially for this clientele, courses scheduled in daytime (for example, for mothers of school children) or during evening hours, and broadly cultural as well as specifically occupational courses. Under the influence of the Manpower Development and Training Act and the Vocational Education Act of 1963, the involvement of junior colleges in part-time education has increased.

Community junior colleges will continue to take the lead in studies of their communities to analyze needs for part-time education. Bogue's 1950 summary of this responsibility is still timely and apropos:

> "The Community College is in a strategic position from the standpoint of its basic philosophy, its relation to the community, its facilities either actual or potential, and by clear responsibility to provide for adult education on a far more progressive and inclusive scale than is the case at the present time. It would seem that every college, regardless of its size or method of control, should seek out and encourage adults in the community to improve themselves and their occupational status".[2]

The function of community services is the most recently developed of the tasks of the community junior college. Nevertheless, the scope and adequacy of these services determine whether or not the college merits the title of "community" junior college; to an important degree, they determine also the extent of community understanding and support of the several functions of the college. Because of the recency of the concept of community services, the experience of junior colleges in performing them has been limited.

Because the community junior college, in many areas, is the only conveniently available "community of scholars," citizens in all walks of life look to it for such services as scholars traditionally provide. Thus the chemistry instructor may be asked to perform an analysis of soil or water samples for a farmer; the biology teacher, to consult on techniques and feasibility of plant hybridization; or the language teacher, to translate a letter from abroad. Local civic organizations will look to the community college for speakers and consultants on a variety of problems. Performances of college musical and dramatic groups will be open to the public. Community groups are encouraged to use college dining rooms or classrooms for their meetings. Colleges provide cultural activities such as concert series, subscription dramatic seasons, and lecturers. They organize workshops and short courses for special-interest groups in the community. In a word, the community junior college actively seeks ways in which it can contribute to the intellectual and cultural activity of its communities.

## D. Guidance

The community junior college functions of occupational education, general education, transfer education, and continuing education will attract students with many different ambitions, with varying backgrounds, with extended ranges of abilities. If such students are to make effective use of the curriculums of the college, they must be assisted in choosing appropriate courses of study. Because of the richness and variety of offerings implied by the multiple purposes of community colleges, unaided selection by the student is almost impossible. The guidance function of the community colleges has been developed to aid the student in making appropriate choices.

The student who is about to embark on a career of college study needs to make many important decisions before he enrolls or very early in his period of attendance. Each unfortunate choice or omission will delay his attainment of his goal; often his resources of time or money are used up, and such mistakes prevent him from ever attaining it. Wise choices depend upon adequate information, and it is the task of the junior college guidance worker to help each student obtain and understand such information so that his educational choices may be made wisely. Four basic categories of information are essential for educational guidance: data about the student, about educational and personal requirements for occupations, about availability of educational opportunity, and about employment prospects in many fields. When such data are well understood by the student, he can choose his course of study with confidence that it will lead him toward his goal. At the same time, he will be made aware of the fact, which so often comes as a surprise to students, that not all college courses are equally valid for all objectives and that a radical change of goal may require a radical and time-consuming change of course.

As early as possible, and certainly not later than his first college enrollment, the student should be helped to face reality in the form of some facts about himself. His scores on aptitude tests serve as predictors of success in further study and in occupations: such scores should be available to the guidance worker and should be interpreted carefully to the student. In like manner, his pattern of interests, his record of previous school work, his family status, his financial resources, his personality, his determination, his ambition, all are relevant to the self-understanding which will help him choose an educational goal and an occupational one.

Facts about the world of work are equally pertinent. Each person may have an interest in several varieties of work and the capacity to succeed at several levels of training within each variety. Occupational trends, moreover, are increasing the opportunities for employment in some fields (for example, professional and technical fields), while diminishing them in others (for example, farming). Patterns of educational preparation for different fields are often a mystery to high-school graduates. The community college is obligated to make available to its students information and interpretation of this sort, so that they may relate their own realistically determined ambitions to the facts of vocational opportunity and choose appropriately from the diversity of offerings at the college.

But the guidance task is not completed when the student has planned his course. Throughout his college career—indeed, throughout life—crises in personal relationships can interfere with a student's success in his endeavor. During the college years, the guidance worker stands by to assist in the resolution of such difficulties. Personal difficulties may concern the student's management of his own perplexities in such fields as vocational choice, finances, health, use of time, efficiency of study, or understanding and acceptance of his strengths and limitations. In other cases, the need for assistance will arise from difficulties with others— classmates, instructors, parents, sweetheart, or wife. Although the counselor must not attempt to be all things to all students, he still must realize that misunderstandings can interfere with a student's achievement; his function is to assist the student in working out his problems, so that the college and the student may move on with their primary task of education.

Because of its greater spread of educational offerings and because of the greater diversity of its student body, the community junior college seems to need a complete and effective guidance service even more than other colleges. There are many important difficulties which have kept these colleges from achieving their goals in this field, such as cost of the service and shortage of qualified workers. None of the difficulties is insuperable, once the need is clearly recognized.

# E. Occupational Education

At the community junior college level, occupational education includes courses of two years' duration or less, combining the development of skills required for entry into a locally important occupation with related knowledge and theory calculated to help the student progress on the job. Such courses of study include also the general education calculated to prepare all students to assume responsible roles as citizens, as family members, and as individuals. In many institutions, occupational courses are planned as far as possible with an eye to the rapid changes that characterize the labor market. Emphasis is placed on preparing the student for families of related occupations rather than for a single job; fundamental abilities are developed so as to contribute to the student's adaptability as employment opportunities change.

It is probable that community junior colleges will develop more and more of these programs of two years or less, designed to prepare their students for immediate employment on completion of the program. Several reasons may be adduced for the rapid development of occupational education. The high rate of withdrawal of students from college is one cause for concern. Students of the problem of dropout realize that most of the students who enter junior colleges will not go on to further education, although they classify themselves in most cases as "transfer" students. If those students who terminate their full- time formal enrollment with two years or less of college are to be properly accommodated, the colleges must develop courses of two years' duration which are complete and valuable. Otherwise the withdrawing student leaves with an uncompleted portion of an education and a feeling of defeat rather than of having completed a self-assigned task.

Recent employment trends emphasize the need for community college occupational education. The age of initial full-time career employment is rising, and the skills required are increasing. Technical and scientific training is needed in the kinds of jobs that are growing in number in the labor force. There is also a rising trend in the dollar value of productive equipment per worker: each employee in many occupations is responsible for thousands of dollars worth of capital goods, and the employer wants some assurance of maturity and preparation in those he hires.

A further reason for the development of occupational courses arises from the "democratization" or "popularizing" of higher education. As greater man-hour productivity and higher standards of living free a continually increasing proportion of our able young people from the labor market, more of them will seek higher education. For some of these increased numbers, education of practical and immediate value is required. Numbers of Blacks and Mexican-Americans may find in these courses access to economic and social participation in the life of the majority. Occupational education must not come to seem for them a last resort assignment, even though in the past it has too often been used that way for school failures. Rather, every student should be helped to reach a realistic assessment of his own aims and potential and to choose and qualify for the kind of course that offers the best chance in life for him. If the counseling staff can succeed in this kind of effort and still keep open avenues to further education as the student's goals mature, occupational education will attain a dignity and status that it has lacked until now in the prestige-conscious academic world.

Until recently, there has been some resistance to the establishment of such occupational education, so that even though 70–75% of entering students are in fact terminal students, only about one-third of the course offerings in junior colleges are terminal—and a fraction of these are occupational. One reason for this disproportion between educational need and educational opportunity is the feeling that choice of a terminal or occupational program of courses "closes the door" of further study to a student who later decides to work toward a bachelor's degree. This objection is only partly valid. Students who change from occupational to baccalaureate courses are a small minority of all entering students. Occupational courses should certainly be planned to accommodate primarily those students who will graduate and enter the occupation for which they trained. For the student in an occupational program who does decide to attempt a baccalaureate program, it should be possible to demonstrate (1) that all his study is of value to him, even though he has to spend more than the conventional four years in earning his bachelor's degree, and (2) that some part of his junior college courses, as they meet the required or elective provisions of his four-year college, will be evaluated appropriately there. Certainly any student in any college who changes his objective in midcourse (as from medicine to engineering, architecture to law, or petroleum technology to geology) will find that he has neglected certain prerequisites of his new course which must be completed before he can go on. As community colleges become the preponderant source of upper-division university students, admission decisions for all juniors will come to be based on demonstrated ability to do specialized university study rather than on simply passing core and prerequisite patterns. The mature transfer student from the community college will then be freed in part from detailed course requirements. The Associate in Science degree graduate with good grades and acceptable aptitude test scores will be permitted to prove himself in competition, rather than being required to make up a standard list of required courses.

## F. Education for Transfer

Preparation for further study at the four-year college or university is the traditional task of the junior college. It was the primary purpose envisaged by Tappan and Folwell, Harper, Lange, and Jordan. This was the objective adopted by the earliest established junior colleges, both private and public. It is the goal which the junior colleges have accomplished most extensively and most successfully and for the greatest numbers of their students. Yet it also the source of a considerable amount of misunderstanding of the junior colleges on the part of the universities, the students in the junior colleges, and the general public.

The multiplicity of purposes in the community junior college, only partially clear to workers in other fields, is one source of this difficulty. The community junior college has purposes limited in time, for the most part, to the first two years of study after high school. The university and the four-year college also offer courses appropriate for this range of educational background and for this age group. To this extent the functions of the university and the community junior college overlap. Yet the community junior college is much more than half of a university. While it must achieve the aims of the first two years of university study for some of its students, it has other worthy purposes which are no part of the idea of a university and other worthy students who do not desire and should not work toward the baccalaureate degree.

In its "university-parallel" programs, the community junior college performs many important educational services. It enables many able young people to complete their first two years of college while living at home and thus aids them in conserving some of their funds for upper-division and graduate study. Thus it contributes both to equality of educational opportunity and to the development by some young people of specialized talents which might otherwise be neglected. It helps to fill the junior and senior classes of the four-year institutions, replacing some of the dropouts who entered those colleges two years earlier. It provides, moreover, a tried and tested student body for these upper-division classes. This function is a very important one in a society that needs all the trained talent it can get and that intends to afford every citizen opportunity to achieve his highest potential.

The later academic success of students from the junior college is important in relation to the success of students who entered four-year colleges as freshmen. This question has interested students of higher education since the establishment of junior colleges. In the most comprehensive study of transfer, Knoell and Medsker reported on the achievement of transfers from junior colleges to a sample of four-year colleges and universities in ten states. All junior college students who transferred in 1960 and who met certain other criteria were included in the study group. Their most general conclusion about success of transfer students was:

"A widespread tendency was noted for the first-term grades of the transfer students to drop below their cumulative junior college averages . . . The grades of most transfer students improved over the period of two years which they spent in junior college, declined in the first term after transfer, and then improved in successive terms, at least for those students who persisted to graduation . . . However, improvement beyond the second semester took place only in the grades of the graduates and the students who persisted to the end of the study."[3]

Several problems persist for community colleges in their exercise of the function of transfer education. Among these, one of the most important is that of developing proper relations with the upper-division institutions. The effective preparation of transfer students must be safeguarded, but too frequently this safeguarding has resulted in unnecessary and hampering restrictions on the right of the junior college to develop its own program for its own students. The question of advanced credit for technical courses is related to effective preparation for further study. A sizable number of students who complete terminal curriculums have applied for transfer, and evidence is accumulating that such students do succeed in bacclaureate programs.

A further problem for the community junior college is related to the fact that only a minority of those students who enroll as transfer students actually do transfer. The students who change their intention are among those for whom the occupational and other terminal curriculums of the community junior college are established. Yet it requires major attention of counselors and faculty to identify and reorient such students before they have failed too many courses or have decided finally to withdraw from college.

The definition and maintenance of proper standards of accomplishment in the junior college are further problems associated with their transfer function. Too often standards are defined solely by grade-point averages, without adequate consideration of the selection of students, the quality of instruction, or the purposes of the students or of the community junior college. Junior colleges are rated by some universities on the basis of their "grade-point differential"—a comparison of grade averages before and after transfer. It is true that grades in the junior college are one kind of evidence of the ability of a transfer student to continue college study. Yet it is possible for a faculty to concentrate on this recommending function of their grading policy to such an extent that they neglect their parallel responsibilities for excellent instruction, diversity of educational offerings, and careful guidance of all students. In considering standards, the community junior college faculty must remember that preparation for transfer is but one of several important functions. They must not concentrate so singly on success in one endeavor that they fail in several others.

It seems certain that preparation of students for further study will continue to be a major function of the community junior college. It is at least possible that increasing proportions of students will classify themselves realistically as "two-year" or "terminal" students, perhaps reversing the present ratios of transfer and terminal students. Even so, the expected growth in all enrollments in higher education will bring ever greater absolute numbers of transfer students to the junior colleges. It is not inconceivable that before many decades most of American lower-division education, with its implied selection of students for further education, will be completed in the junior colleges. Although such a development would increase the responsibility of these colleges, it might serve to improve their relations with the receiving institutions.

### FOOTNOTES

1.  Brunner, Ken August. "Historical Development of the Junior College Philosophy," *Junior College Journal,* **40,** No. 7 (April, 1970), pp. 30-34.
2.  Bogue, Jesse Parker. *The Community College.* New York: McGraw-Hill Book Co., 1950, p. 229.
3.  Knoell, Dorothy M. and Leland L. Medsker. *From Junior to Senior*

*College: A National Study of the Transfer Student.* Washington, D.C.: American Council on Education, 1965, p. 27.

## BIBLIOGRAPHY

Bogue, Jesse P. "Basic Functions of Community Colleges," *The Community College.* New York: McGraw-Hill Book Co., 1950, Chapter 3.

Campbell, Doak S. *A Critical Study of the Stated Purposes of the Junior College.* Nashville: George Peabody College for Teachers, 1930.

Cross, K. Patricia. "The Quiet Revolution," *The Research Reporter,* **IV,** No. 3 (1969), pp. 1-4.

Harris, Norman C. *Technical Education in the Junior College: New Programs for New Jobs.* Washington, D.C.: American Association of Junior Colleges, 1964.

Jennings, Frank G. "The Two-Year Stretch," *Change in Higher Education* (March-April, 1970), pp. 15-25.

Knoell, Dorothy M. *Black Student Potential,* Washington, D.C.: American Association of Junior Colleges, 1970.

Knoell, Dorothy M. and Leland L. Medsker. *From Junior to Senior College: A National Study of the Transfer Student.* Washington, D.C.: American Council on Education, 1965.

Koos, Leonard V. *The Junior College.* Minneapolis: University of Minnesota Press, 1924.

Willingham, Warren W., and Nurken Findikyan. "Transfer Students: Who's Moving from Where to Where, and What Determines Who's Admitted?," *College Board Review,* No. 72 (Summer 1969), pp. 4-12.

# II

# THE ORGANIZATION OF COMMUNITY JUNIOR COLLEGES

# 6 | Types of Junior Colleges

Junior colleges have developed in response to various local influences and are subject to the laws of the 50 states and to the guiding principles of their own governing boards. Their relationships to secondary schools and to colleges and universities vary from region to region and even within the same state. These facts explain some of the diversity of purpose and of organization which the colleges exhibit. Their rapid growth, in number, in enrollment, and in scope of educational program, has made it impossible to classify and to define them simply. Each of the terms used to name them, in this volume as well as elsewhere in the literature, is somewhat unsatisfactory.

The original title was "junior college." In its present usage in the literature, "junior college" has two distinct sets of meanings. In the first sense, it is used as a generic title to cover all the institutions that offer two-year college programs, regardless of what other education any individual college may provide. The term is used in this unqualified sense in the present volume. In its more limited usage, often carelessly contrasted with "community college," a junior college is a two-year college, usually privately controlled, which concentrates primarily on preparing its students to transfer to four-year colleges to pursue the bachelor's degree. In this limited sense, hardly any college in the *Junior College Directory* is a junior college. Nearly all the independent colleges offer some two-year courses of a terminal nature, and a good many of the publicly controlled colleges devote most of their attention to transfer work and offer only four or five occupational curriculums.

In recent years, some writers have objected to "junior college" as a term too limited in its connotations to be applied to a two-year college that fulfills all the functions described in Chapter 5. Because of the expansion of functions, colleges in Alaska, California, Illinois, Michigan, and New York, for example, have almost entirely deleted "junior" from their titles, although very similar institutions in Florida and Mississippi have retained the word. Even within a state, colleges with similar purposes may disagree on nomenclature, as with Cochise College, Navajo Community College, and Yavapai County Junior College in Arizona, or City College of San Francisco, Fullerton Junior College, and El Camino College in California. The national body has retained the title, "American Association of Junior Colleges"; in names and in the literature, there is increasing use of the word, "community."

As yet, no fully satisfactory and unequivocal terminology has been universally adopted to substitute for "junior college." The terms, "city college" and "community college," usually imply the concepts of service to the local community, public support, and two-year programs. Here again, however, misunderstanding is possible. There are community colleges and municipal colleges that offer programs of four years leading to bachelors' degrees; there are privately supported two-year colleges that perform community services. Even the newer terms, therefore, are not entirely unambiguous.

In most common usage and in the present text, "junior college" includes institutions offering general and specialized education to persons beyond high-school age, either to meet immediately their present educational needs or to prepare them for further study. "Community junior college" is a kind of junior college which is *usually* a public institution, draws *most* of its students from its supporting community, develops programs of study in response to needs of the local community, and is likely to offer a wider variety of courses than the "noncommunity" junior college, which intends to attract students from a much wider geographic area. The phrases, "public junior college" and "community college," are roughly synonymous, though not identical.

Junior colleges can be classified conveniently on the basis of their fiscal control as well as by reference to the comprehensiveness of their curriculums. "Independent" colleges are those not supported by public taxation and not controlled by a governing body elected by the community at large; "public" colleges are those established and controlled by legislative enactment, supported by taxation, and governed by boards that are either elected by their constituents or appointed by elected officers. The remainder of Chapter 6 is concerned with some of the statistics and descriptions of colleges within each classification.

## A. Varieties of Independent Junior Colleges

The 1971 *Directory* of the American Association of Junior Colleges[1] presents statistical information about 244 independent junior colleges. They enrolled 131,141 students in all classifications in October, 1969, and employed 9,377 faculty members. Of their students 48% were full-time freshmen, 31% were sophomores, and 20% were part-time students. These facts indicate, as might be expected, that the holding power for regular students is better in the private junior college than in the public institution, in which the freshmen were more than twice the number of sophomores. The part-time students in independent junior colleges account for about one-fifth of the total enrollment, whereas in the public colleges they amount to almost half of all enrollments.

Most of the independent junior colleges are coeducational, although significant numbers enroll only men or only women students. Of all listed private junior colleges, 181 are coeducational, 10 are for men, and 53 are for women. More than half of these are denominationally controlled, although a strong minority are listed as "nonprofit" colleges. The listings in the *1971 Directory* are grouped in the following manner according to their source of control:

| | | | |
|---|---|---|---|
| Nonprofit and proprietary | 116 | Lutheran | 11 |
| Catholic | 43 | Presbyterian | 8 |
| Baptist | 20 | Other denominational | 24 |
| Methodist | 22 | | 244 |

Geographically, independent junior colleges are found in each of the six accreditation regions of the United States, as shown in Table I. The majority are found east of the Mississippi, whereas very few have been established in the Western States.

In size of enrollment, the independent junior college tends to be smaller than the average public junior college. Table II sets forth the enrollment statistics for the independent junior college. In total enrollment, the median size of the privately controlled institution was 380 students, as compared with an overall median of about 1950 in public institutions.

**TABLE I**
**Geographical Distribution of Independent Junior Colleges, 1970[a]**

| Accrediting Regions | Number of Independent Junior Colleges | |
|---|---|---|
| New England | 39 | |
| Middle States | 69 | |
| Southern | 70 | |
| Eastern United States | | 178 |
| North Central | 55 | |
| Northwest | 5 | |
| Western | 6 | |
| Midwestern and Western United States | | 66 |
| TOTAL | | 244 |

[a]Source: Author's tabulation from 1971 Junior College Directory.

For full-time students, the arithmetic mean enrollments were 552 in the independent junior colleges and 2596 in the public. The independent colleges enroll a smaller proportion of part-time and unclassified students than do the public institutions. Only one-fifth of all independent college enrollments are so classified, while almost half of the public junior college students are either part-time or unclassified.

The independent junior college is an integral and necessary part of the entire American enterprise of higher education. By its nature, it does not concentrate so intently on service to the local community and part-time adult students as does the public junior college. For these purposes, it typically substitutes distinctive aims that can best be achieved within the framework of limited enrollments, residential campuses, recruitment of students from a wide geographical area, and concentration on excellent achievement of a limited set of educational objectives. In addition, the privately controlled junior college is sometimes better able to carry on experimentation in the development of special curriculums or improved techniques of instruction. It can, because of its limited enrollment, afford more opportunity for guidance and counseling and for informal association of students with faculty members than can the larger, nonresidential public community college. Bogue summarizes these specialized opportunities of the independent junior college by pointing out that:

> The good colleges, however, will do their share to pioneer new ideas, to maintain freedom from group pressures, to demand that personal achievement shall match native ability, to enrich educational experi-

**TABLE II**
**Distribution of Size of Enrollment in Independent Junior Colleges, 1970**[a]

| Enrollments | Number of Colleges |
|---|---|
| 1-99 | 22 |
| 100-199 | 43 |
| 200-299 | 49 |
| 300-499 | 54 |
| 500-999 | 46 |
| 1000-1999 | 23 |
| 2000-2999 | 3 |
| 3000-9999 | 4 |
| Total colleges | 244 |
| Median enrollment | 380 |
| Mean enrollment | 552 |

[a]Source: Condensed from the 1971 Junior College Directory.

ences through college community living, to emphasize the development of the whole person, to teach and exemplify democratic values and a high degree of flexibility in dealing with the problems of individual students. Moreover, the residential college, in contrast to the purely local community college, can lift its students into regional and even national association and thereby contribute to the breakdown of tendencies to provincialism. The faithful performance of these functions, however small in comparison to the total educational program of the nation, will contribute significantly beyond any measure of numbers or magnificence of plants.[2]

The innovative potential of the private college is realized at Bennett College in Millbrook, New York. *American Junior Colleges* (Seventh Edition)[3] — from which all quotations of descriptions of colleges in this chapter are taken — presents a brief description of some of the salient features of the curriculum:

This small college for women emphasizes liberal arts and offers transfer and occupational curricula in art, child study, design, and the performing arts. A special overseas service program combines two years at Bennett with a third year abroad to prepare students to meet the growing demand for personnel with secretarial skills, a broad educational background, and fluency in a second language. The college conducts a biennial field trip to New York City and sponsors, in alternate years, a three-day conference that brings authorities from a variety of fields to the campus to meet with students.

The private college under religious auspices may be represented by Clarke Memorial College at Newton, Mississippi. Established in 1907 by the General Association of Baptists and now sponsored by the Mississippi Baptist Convention, the school became a junior college in 1918. *American Junior Colleges* (Seventh Edition) reports its present program:

> This small coeducational school offers two years of liberal arts education and seeks to develop within its students a sense of Christian ideals and service. A division of subcollegiate studies offers courses for adults who require further preparation before undertaking college work.

In many cases, the private college does not intend to offer a comprehensive curriculum; it develops its own statement of purposes and attracts from any part of the nation students who are willing to pursue the course of studies leading to those objectives.

## B. Varieties of Public Junior Colleges

The *1971 Junior College Directory* lists 847 publicly controlled junior colleges, which enrolled 2,107,363 students in the previous year. These colleges accounted for 78% of all junior colleges listed; their total enrollments were 94% of all junior college students of all categories. A total of 99,968 instructors and administrators staffed the public institutions. Of the students enrolled, 33% were classified as full-time freshmen and only 14% — less than half as many — as full-time sophomores. An additional 32% of all students were part-time freshmen and sophomores. The extent of community service of the public junior colleges is indicated by the fact that 49% of all enrollments are either part-time or unclassified students. Nearly half of all public junior college enrollments, then, are part-time and adult students; of the regularly classified students, two-thirds are freshmen. These facts indicate that for many of their students, the public junior colleges are not in fact two-year colleges even though their organized curriculums are usually designed for completion in two years.

The median enrollment of the public junior colleges, as noted previously, is about five times as large as that of the private junior colleges. Yet in both types, there are wide variations in size, as shown by the distribution of enrollments shown in Tables II and III. Small classes and opportunities to know instructors, two advantages claimed for the junior college, undoubtedly exist in the 65 private junior colleges and the 11

**TABLE III**
**Distribution of Size of Enrollment in Publicly Controlled
Junior Colleges, 1970**[a]

| Enrollments | Number of Colleges |
|---|---|
| 1-99 | 2 |
| 100-199 | 9 |
| 200-299 | 30 |
| 300-499 | 78 |
| 500-999 | 174 |
| 1000-1999 | 217 |
| 2000-2999 | 93 |
| 3000-8999 | 191 |
| 9000 and over | 53 |
| TOTAL COLLEGES | 847[b] |
| MEDIAN ENROLLMENT | 1950 |
| MEAN ENROLLMENT | 2596 |

[a]Source: Condensed from the 1971 Junior College Directory.
[b]Total includes five colleges outside the United States.

public junior colleges that enroll fewer than 200 students each. These advantages may well be somewhat impaired in the 244 junior colleges that enroll more than 3000 students. On the other hand, it is possible to question whether the smallest colleges can usually provide the breadth of program and the quality of instruction that a fully adequate community junior college requires.

Geographically, public junior colleges are distributed throughout the areas of the six regional accrediting agencies, but whereas private junior colleges are concentrated in the Eastern and Southern sections of the nation, public institutions are found more frequently in the Central and Western sections. The distribution by accreditation areas is shown in Table IV.

Nearly all the public institutions are coeducational. There are still two or three military or technical junior colleges whose enrollment is limited only to men, but none of the public junior colleges offers instruction only to women.

Whereas control of the private junior colleges was distributed among religious denominations with about 45% undenominational and nonprofit colleges, the control of the public junior colleges is divided among several varieties of governmental agencies. Some are controlled by a state board, and others are campuses of state universities or state colleges. County governments, local school districts, and independent junior college districts are additional patterns of control.

During the decade from 1960 to 1970, some 420 public two-year colleges were established, almost doubling the number that existed in 1960. During the same period, enrollments almost quadrupled. Among the results of this expansion was the reorganization of the patterns of control of community colleges in many states. In addition, the several states that introduced community colleges into their systems of higher education during the decade adopted a variety of patterns of control. It is likely that continued interest of educators and legislators in the governance of community colleges will bring further changes in their organization; certain trends already seem evident.

*The unified district* control of community colleges is disappearing. During the early period of rapid establishment, the concept of the junior college as an extension of secondary education led city school districts to extend their school systems to include "grades 13 and 14." Under this concept, one locally elected board of education controlled all public schools from kindergarten through junior college, or in some districts, from grades 7 or 9 through 14. The determination, that community colleges are in fact higher education and that their size and complexity requires the primary attention of their governing boards, has led to the rapid disappearance of the unified district mode of governance in favor of separate local community college boards.

*Multi-college districts,* both urban and rural, have increased in numbers during the decade of the sixties; the growth seems likely to continue. In large cities such as Los Angeles or Chicago, the provision of community colleges available to all youth of the metropolis led early to the establishment of a number of separate campuses under the same governing board. More recently, suburban areas and extended rural areas in Arizona, California, Colorado, Illinois, Iowa, Michigan, Mississippi, Missouri, Ohio, South Carolina, Texas, and Washington have established multi-campus operations. The plan leads to economy in administration and coordination of extensive and diversified curricular offerings and encourages attendance by citizens in all parts of populous or extended districts.

*Centralized state control* of community colleges has been increasing. One pattern involves the introduction of a statewide board with limited powers over existing local community college boards, as in Arizona, California, Illinois, and New York, for example. A second pattern assigns complete responsibility for the development of statewide systems of community colleges to a new state agency, as in Alabama, Massachusetts, Connecticut, Rhode Island, and Virginia. A third innovation is the assignment of responsibility to Boards of Regents of the existing public university to assume control of developing systems, as in Alaska, Georgia,

**TABLE IV**
**Geographical Distribution of Public Junior Colleges, 1970**[a]

| Accrediting Regions | Number of Public Junior Colleges | |
|---|---|---|
| New England | 37 | |
| Middle States | 107 | |
| Southern | 252 | |
| Eastern United States | | 396 |
| North Central | 289 | |
| Northwest | 59 | |
| Western | 98 | |
| Midwestern and Western United States | | 446 |
| TOTAL | 842 | |

[a]Source: 1971 Junior College Directory.

Hawaii, and Kentucky. Whatever the agency for state governance of community colleges, centralized control requires deliberate plans to encourage and protect community service and community involvement. A centrally controlled and financed college can become in fact a community college, but such an outcome will ordinarily require the establishment of a local agency with real responsibility and autonomy for the cultivation of local policies and programs.

Trends that are at present more in the discussion stage than in actual development include the establishment of central city colleges to serve the educational needs of the poor and to upgrade the economic and social potential of the undereducated. Existing community colleges that require expensive daily travel for the inner-city dweller and that expect him to be already equipped for academic competition do not meet the need. Their shortcomings have been recognized, but so far few solutions have been established.

The rural community college that devotes explicit and imaginative attention to the special educational needs of its own clientele is another future development that has been defined but so far rarely realized. About one-third of all rural Americans live in true poverty and derive different educational disqualifications from their cultural isolation and distance from colleges. For the rural poor just as for the ghetto dweller, education is one of the keys to open the door of opportunity; but the traditional pattern of abstract and future-oriented higher education does not fit this particular lock. Money, staffing, instructional space, and appropriate curriculums — all are lacking in to too many of the existing rural community colleges; and in too many areas even the first steps toward supplying collegiate opportunity for the rural poor have not been undertaken.

The organizational achievements of the past several decades in the establishment of almost universal higher educational opportunity are impressive and unprecedented. It would be a serious mistake to assume, however, that existing patterns have fully met the need and that the period of establishment of community colleges has reached its peak. Although many of the obvious needs have been met, difficult problems in the establishment of institutions and development of curriculum still lie ahead.

## FOOTNOTES

1.  Harper, William A. (ed.). *1971 Junior College Directory*. Washington, D.C. American Association of Junior Colleges, 1971.
2.  Bogue, Jesse Parker. *The Community College*. New York: McGraw-Hill Book Company, 1950. p. 120.
3.  Gleazer, Edmund J. Jr., *American Junior Colleges* (Seventh Edition), Washington, D.C.: American Council on Education, 1967.

## BIBLIOGRAPHY

Bogue, Jesse P. *The Community College*. New York: McGraw-Hill Book Co., 1950.

*Community College Programs for People Who Need College*. Washington, D.C.: American Association of Junior Colleges, 1970.

Gleazer, Edmund J., Jr. (ed.). *American Junior Colleges* (Seventh Edition). Washington, D.C.: American Council on Education, 1967.

Hall, George L. *100,000 and Under: Occupational Education in The Rural Community Junior College*. Washington, D.C.: American Association of Junior Colleges, 1968.

Harper, William A. (ed.). *1971 Junior College Directory*. Washington, D.C.: American Association of Junior Colleges, 1971.

Kintzer, Frederick C., Arthur M. Jensen, and John S. Hansen. *The Multi-Institution Junior College District*. Washington, D.C.: American Association of Junior Colleges, 1969.

Knoell, Dorothy M. *Black Student Potential*. Washington, D.C.: American Association of Junior Colleges, 1970.

Yarrington, Roger (ed.). *International Development of the Junior College Idea*. Washington, D.C.: American Association of Junior Colleges, 1970.

_____. *Junior Colleges: 50 States/50 Years*. Washington, D.C.: American Association of Junior Colleges, 1969.

# 7 | Legal Controls of Community Junior Colleges

In the earliest period of rapid growth of public community colleges (approximately 1920 to 1940), local school districts were most often the founding agency. The new colleges were frequently housed in the same buildings that were used for the local high school, governed by the same board of trustees, taught by some of the high-school teachers, and referred to as "grades 13 and 14."

After World War II, the influx of veterans into the public colleges brought an emphasis on the collegiate character of the institution instead of on its secondary education beginnings. As a result, new establishments (during the period roughly from 1945 to 1965) tended to result in a completely independent junior college district, without ties to any other level of education. During the same period, older community colleges began to move from the high schools to their own campuses and in many cases to go through the legal steps involved in becoming independent from the local school district.

These trends contributed to the rapid growth in numbers of community colleges and in total enrollments and brought to the colleges the attention and concern of legislators and university administrators. As a result, the recent period of consolidation has seen a movement toward greater centralization of control and more adequate state support of community colleges. It is impossible to establish rigidly defined categories of control, because each state develops its system of higher education in relation to its own history, finances, and aspirations. Yet a study of the *1971 Junior College Directory* supports the conclusion that at least eight of the states have established state boards to control and distribute finances for community colleges; twelve have assigned their community colleges to one or more of their publicly supported universities; and ten others have moved to strong state coordination of the system of higher education while attempting to preserve a maximum of autonomy to the local boards of trustees that originally exercised almost complete direction of the community colleges.

Chapter 7 approaches the question of legal controls, first through a description of an organizational plan in each category, and second through an examination of patterns and problems of finance.

## A. Patterns of Control and Coordination

*The independent community college district* is still found in approximately 20 states, although there is a trend to remove the statewide supervision of budgets and curriculum from State Departments of Education and assign it to newly established boards with responsibility only for community colleges. In this pattern, a locally elected board of trustees is responsible for policy and operation of the community colleges that serve a limited geographical area — a city, a county, or some aggregation of lower school districts that constitutes a quasi-community. The trustees have the authority to adopt an annual budget and establish a local tax rate (plus other income from state sources and perhaps from tuition) to support the budget. The board employs the superintendent, decides on building plans and costs, approves curriculum and other academic policies, and issues contracts to instructors. It has no responsibility for or to other local school levels.

An independent school district derives its authority by delegation from the state and can exercise its functions only within limits established by the legislature and appropriate state officers. Ordinarily some part of its budget is provided by the state according to formulas that consider local taxable wealth per student and total attendance figures. Legal safeguards control the authority of the local board in such matters as expenditures, minimum standards, bonded indebtedness, and qualifications of instructors and administrators. Within these limits, the board has freedom to differ from nearby community colleges and to establish courses of study that seem especially appropriate for its own district. In general, the college board and its president will promote the interests of their own institution as opposed to statewide system interests or the interests of other systems of higher education.

*Strong state coordination* has been introduced in recent years both to curb the unilateral efforts of strong-willed community college boards and presidents and to provide a unified voice for these colleges vis-à-vis the universities and public schools. The very nature and recency of the dual system of controls lead to conflicts between centralization and local autonomy. When new coordinating or state boards are imposed over long-established local boards, there is usually a period of some years during which operating procedures are worked out. On the one hand, a new board that attempts to assume too much control too rapidly will encourage resistance and political attack from below; whereas a board that attempts to limit its staff to the minimum of workers for record gathering and reporting and to exercise only advisory powers will find it difficult to bring about true coordination.

Arizona may serve as an example of the combination of local districts with a strong state board. The state board has several powers and duties:

1. Enact ordinances for government of the colleges.
2. Set standards for their establishment and operation.
3. Arrange for certification of teachers.
4. Establish qualifications for teachers in vocational and academic subjects.
5. Fix tuition for resident and nonresident students.
6. Establish curriculums designed to serve the best interests of the state.
7. Determine the location of campuses within districts.

The district governing board, elected by the people of the district, has the following powers and duties:

1. To maintain the college for at least eight months annually.
2. Enforce the courses of study and use of textbooks adopted by the state board.
3. Employ officers and other staff as it deems necessary.
4. Determine salaries.
5. Award degrees, certificates, and diplomas.
6. Prepare a budget for operations.

*State Established Community College Systems.* Complete centralization of community college control has been established in several states; under this pattern local advisory boards are usually established to consult with the administrator of the local college and to safeguard the community's interest in its college. An example of the state system is Minnesota.

From 1915 to 1957, junior colleges in Minnesota were supported entirely by local funds and operated on high school campuses. Their programs were largely in transfer fields, and to that extent they were successful. Their financial needs, however, were subordinated to those of the lower schools; administrators recognized the validity of the comprehensive curriculum but could not afford it. In addition, several areas that needed community colleges were reluctant to assume the added local tax burden.

State involvement was approached in two steps. First, in 1957, state aid was granted on a per pupil basis. By 1963, conditions had improved but not as rapidly as numbers of students. Moreover, several local districts had not moved to establish community colleges. The legislature, therefore, in 1963 voted to set up a state system of community colleges, with total support from state sources. The eleven existing colleges joined the state system, and eight new colleges were established within five years.

The colleges are relatively autonomous, except that the state board presents budget requests and allocates budgets, both current and capital. Payrolls and purchases are centralized, as are building planning and establishment of new colleges. In Minnesota, centralized control has resulted in more rapid development of needed campuses, expansion of curriculum, and improvement of financial support for the colleges.

*University Systems of Community Colleges.* University systems of community colleges are found in several states, either as the only plan of control as in Alaska and Hawaii, or side by side with district systems as in South Carolina and Pennsylvania. From the standpoint of community college systems, there may be several disadvantages to unification with the university, as well as some advantages. The mere fact of legal control by the university does not determine whether the advantages outweigh the disadvantages, so much as the way in which the control is exercised.

The comparative prestige of the two institutions constitutes one of the major disadvantages of unifying the control of the university and of community colleges. Because of size, earlier establishments, and advanced studies, the university will certainly receive more attention from the governing board and president than any or all of the community colleges. In budget allocations during times of economic stringency, the colleges are likely to be cut soonest and most deeply. A more important danger, however, is that the removal of control of the colleges from the local communities makes it more difficult to match programs and needs. Moreover, university faculties and administrators are unlikely to place a high value on remedial education and occupational curriculums. With the best of intentions, they are still inclined to place first priority on the transfer function and, in so doing, to denigrate the kinds of courses that are most meaningful for a majority of the students in the community colleges.

Advantages of university control will be found largely away from the community college campus. Interchange of students and acceptance of their credits ought to be simplified; university traditions seem to lead to more careful architectural planning for the system's community colleges; consultation services and specialized courses for in-service training of faculty are readily available from university faculty. Carefully designed admission procedures may make it possible to assign students to the campus where they will find the most appropriate programs. In the experience and judgment of junior college writers, the university system seems to be in general less desirable than a plan that gives greater responsibility to the local community and autonomy to the community college in developing both its budget and its curriculum.

Since all community colleges are under the control of the single university, with no nonuniversity public community colleges, the University of Hawaii Community Colleges may serve as fairly successful examples of this pattern. The Board of Regents of the University of Hawaii controls (as of 1971) one University, one four-year college, and six community colleges, as well as the East-West Center and the Center for Cross-Cultural Training and Research. The six community colleges are coordinated by a Vice President for Community Colleges, who reports directly to the President of the University and through him to the Board of Regents. The Vice President has a separate staff for facilities planning, curriculum development, and student services. Members of the staff provide services to the community colleges but are not considered to be line officers.

Each of the community colleges is administered by a Provost, who is responsible most directly to the Vice President. Each college develops its own budget, and when necessary decides its own priorities in matching its requests to available funds. The provosts achieve coordination of their efforts by means of monthly meetings to discuss questions of specialized curriculums and matters of common concern. Coordination with University of Hawaii departments is carried on through the office of the Vice President. In this way, many of the possible disadvantages of University control are obviated, and the community colleges have attained within less than a decade a position of status and responsibility in the State. Before they reach ten years of community college existence, they will enroll more students than the University campuses. They will add two newly developed colleges; and they will bear major responsibility for lower-division education in Hawaii.

A recent dissertation at University of Southern California dealt with principles that should be observed in recodifying the community college provisions of the *Education Code* of the State of California.[1] The dissertation is based on studies of practices in other states and an extensive study of attitudes on the part of persons professionally engaged in community college work in California—professors, administrators, board members, legislators, and county attorneys. The results showed a high degree of agreement on a series of conclusions and recommendations. Principles from the dissertation that deal with control are summarized and renumbered as follows:

1. Respondents support the concept of local control of community colleges.
2. The community college should continue to provide tuition-free education "to all who may benefit from such instruction."
3. State developed minimum standards are approved, together with flexibility in applying these standards at the local level.
4. Community colleges should continue to provide opportunity to students who present unique educational problems.

As concerns the *Education Code,* the respondents were in agreement (among other points) that:

1. Statutes that deal with governance of the public community colleges should be designed exclusively for this unique institution of higher education and should not apply to any other level of public education in the state.

2. A separate state school fund should be created for the financial support of the community colleges.
3. A single apportionment should be enacted that applies regardless of (a) age of the student, (b) number of units attempted, (c) the type of class taken, (d) the length of the course, and (e) the nature of the program or service offered.
4. All senior colleges should accept certification by the two-year college of the completion of lower-division requirements.
5. A program of community services should be required of all public community colleges.
6. The local governing board should be empowered to levy a special purpose tax for special programs of remediation of educational deficiencies.
7. The local governing board should be given the primary power to develop standards, rules, and regulations in the governance of this institution.

## B. Elements of Community College Support

Funds for the support of community colleges come from tuition charges, from local property taxes levied for their support, from general state revenues in accordance with some measure of student enrollment, and from federal grants. A recent study of seven states with large community college enrollments indicates that the four elements of support vary markedly from state to state.

Nearly all of the states levy *tuition charges* for attendance at the community colleges, even though their legislative enactments and public pronouncements emphasize that the colleges should provide low-cost education to all of the people. It is apparent also that tuition charges have been increased during the past decade and introduced in some of the states that did not previously collect them. Most of the writers on the subject of community colleges—Eells, Proctor, Koos, Seashore, Medsker, and the President's Commission on Higher Education—have recommended free enrollment or low tuition charges. Their argument is that even a low tuition cost, when added to foregone earnings and the cost of books and equipment in classes, can operate to exclude some low-income students who could benefit from further education.

Loans and scholarships have been advocated as means to enable such young people to attain an education. Some loan legislation provides for deferred payments of the loan or for forgiveness of a certain portion of the loans for each year spent in a specified endeavor. Loan programs, however, have not been uniformly successful in supplying the need for financial assistance to students. The culture of poverty is reluctant to make long-term financial commitments, especially for a long-term speculation such as college attendance. If the loan is used for four years of attendance, the graduate enters life and marriage with a debt that should be paid at the very time in his working life when money is most scarce. If he drops out of college before graduation, he has the debt but only part of the benefit of it. Loans are more useful for the "good-risk" than for the "high-risk" student who needs them most.

Scholarship grants seem to be a more realistic method of providing education to the low-income student. So far, there have been limitations on the effectiveness of most scholarship programs. Requirement of academic achievement as a condition of the grant can defeat the purpose of the program, if it is intended primarily to permit poor youth to attend college. Too often the sums of the scholarships are too small to meet a major part of the costs of attendance. While it is in the American tradition to suggest that the student can always supplement his scholarship by part-time work, this solution requires good efficiency in study and high motivation for learning. These qualities may well be lacking in the very students for whom the scholarship program is intended.

The argument for low tuition is supported by the realization that in the past there has always been a positive relation between level of education and earnings. If this is so, it is reasonable to adopt the view that education is an investment of the commonwealth; the higher the level of education, the higher will be the taxes on later income. In this view, each generation will pay for its own education by providing a better education for the next generation.

*Local property taxes* were the preponderant source of support for community colleges in the early years of their establishment. They are still important in the states that retain the local district organization. For example, district taxes provide as much as 60% of community college support in California, but none in Washington. States that depend largely on local property taxation for the support of community colleges are finding it increasingly difficult to meet the requirements of rising enrollments and inflated costs of building and instruction. Although burdensome on the property owner, local support does encourage a high degree of community interest in the college; it justifies the retention of program control by the local board and permits a diversity of offerings to meet local needs.

The local owner of real property, however, is becoming progressively less able to contribute the major share of the cost of all local public services. Especially the home owner with a fixed income, such as retired persons, finds rising property taxes more burdensome. It seems inevitable that state and also federal sources of support will bear a greater share of community college costs in the near future. Almost every state legislature considers bills each session to authorize such increases.

*State support* provides a more stable source of funds for all colleges in a state than independent local taxation, since it draws revenues from a wider variety of taxes. The guarantee of a minimum expenditure per student by means of equalization formulas can safeguard quality in all of the community colleges. These benefits are countered by the possibility that state legislators are less responsive to local educational desires; they balance the priorities of one community against those of another and reach decisions at times on political rather than on educational considerations. State support in 7 states with highest enrollments varies from as much as 80% in Washington and 65% in Florida to about 33% in California. As state universities, with funds primarily from state sources, limit their enrollment of freshmen and sophomores, there will be an increase in enrollments at the community colleges; thus, the coming decade will certainly see greater state support of the community colleges in a greater number of states.

Simultaneously, pressures are mounting for coherent *programs of federal aid* to community colleges. Because in the past federal policy has supported grants for certain federally important categories of educational need rather than for basic assistance, federal grants have sometimes increased the inequalities among colleges in the several states rather than lessening them. "Categorical grants" are intended to encourage colleges (and schools of all types) to undertake specific educational programs identified by federal officials. Examples of categorical grants are the long-standing programs for vocational education and more recent ones under the Education Professions Development Act. Grants for construction also are limited to buildings that meet federal restrictions. Buildings planned and developed to meet the present urgent needs of community colleges may at times not meet these provisions. In such cases, the college may change its building priorities in order to qualify for the federal money. Because of the piecemeal nature of federal appropriations for education, any college may find itself dealing with as many as a dozen federal agencies in its proposals for federal grants and in the auditing of its expenditures. The net results of categorical grants, then, may often be the redirection of college programs, the establishment of programs that must be supported locally or abandoned after the federal legislation expires, and the construction of buildings that bring added maintenance costs not foreseen by the college when it requested the original grant.

A coherent scheme of support for community colleges would include a minimum dependence on student tuition charges. The principle of education for those who need and can profit from it would indicate that no more than 10% of current costs should be borne by the student. If the history and the political philosophy of the state permit, an even lower figure would be appropriate. Local taxation, in the states that retain the local college district organization, might well be held to approximately 20 to 30% of current costs. State sources then should assume (depending on the local organization pattern) from 60 to 80% of the burden. A federal share, now amounting to less than 10%, might more properly be appropriated for equalization of opportunity among the states, so as to recognize that mobility of the population makes it advisable to provide an adequate education where the students reside. Then their later migration to the wealthier states would not bring acute social problems of unemployability and dependency. The use of federal funds for basic aid to all levels of education, rather than to selected categories of need, would seem to make educational as well as fiscal sense. This policy has been recommended by national associations for more than half a century but so far has not been adopted at the federal level.

## FOOTNOTE

1.  Grande, John A. and Donald L. Singer. *An Assessment of and Design For That Portion of the Education Code Dealing with the California Public Community Colleges.* Unpublished Doctoral Dissertation, University of Southern California, 1970.

## BIBLIOGRAPHY

Altman, Robert A. *Summary of State Legislation Affecting Higher Education in the West: 1970.* Boulder, Colorado: Western Interstate Commission for Higher Education, 1970.

Henry, Nelson B. (ed.). *The Public Junior College.* The Fifty-fifth Yearbook of the National Society for the Study of Education, Part I. Chicago: University of Chicago Press, 1956. Especially Chapters XII and XIII.

Hurlburt, Allan S. *State Master Plans for Community Colleges.* Washington, D.C.: American Association of Junior Colleges, 1969.

Morrison, D. G. and S. V. Martorana. *Criteria for the Establishment of 2-Year Colleges.* Office of Education Bulletin 1961, No. 2, Washington, D.C.: U.S. Government Printing Office, 1963.

Morsch, William. *Seven State Systems of Community Colleges.* A Report Prepared for the Bureau of Social Science Research. Cambridge,

Massachusetts: The Author, 1278 Massachusetts Avenue, Cambridge, 01238.

Orlans, Harold. *The Effects of Federal Programs on Higher Education.* Washington, D.C.: The Brookings Institution, 1962.

*Principles of Legislative Action for Community Junior Colleges.* Washington, D.C.: American Association of Junior Colleges, 1962.

Ward, Charles F. *An Analysis of Selected Legal and Operational Differences Among  Public Two-Year College Systems.* Center Technical Paper No. 9. Raleigh, N.C.: Center for Occupational Education, North Carolina State University, 1971.

Yarrington, Roger (ed.). *Junior Colleges: 50 States/50 Years.* Washington, D.C.: American Association of Junior Colleges, 1969.

# 8 | Establishing the New Community Junior College

Between 1960 and 1970, the number of publicly supported two-year colleges doubled, growing from 431 to 842. As a result of this increase, several hundred administrators have had the privilege of nurturing a college from the moment of its legal establishment through its growing pains to the achievement of full accreditation. A very few of these, moreover, were active in their communities in urging the original establishment of the local junior college. Their tales of their first offices in barns, in barracks, in hotel rooms, in church buildings, or in momentarily unused corners of high schools and of their seemingly unsurmountable early problems are part of the growing folklore of the junior college movement. An excellent sample of their labors is found in Chapman's story of Cuyahoga Community College in Cleveland, Ohio, as it prepared to open in the fall of 1963.[1]

Although the number of community colleges established each year during the sixties varied from a reported net increase of 4 to a gain of 91 (1967 to 1968), the average number of new colleges per year during that decade was 40. During the seventies, each year will see a larger number of persons reaching age 18 than the year before. This annual increase in the cadre of new college-age youth encourages the prediction that by 1980 there will be as many as 1200 community junior colleges. To attain this number, the average rate of establishment per year must remain at about 40. Because of declining numbers of births after 1963, new establishments during the eighties seem likely to decrease in number. At least for a few years, new institutions will be founded in response to other social forces, not simply to increases in the age group to be served.

The present chapter outlines some of the principles, problems, and procedures involved in bringing a new community junior college through its very earliest stages. The first section will describe the steps from a local realization of the need through the legal authorization of the college; the second will present the work of the administrative officers of the college in bringing it to the point where the first students may be enrolled in classes.

## A. Securing Legal Authorization

There is a growing trend toward the establishment of state master plans for higher education. In states that combine their master plan with a high level of state financial support and program control, the share of the local citizens in deciding to have a community college is diminished. In most of the states, though, it is still usual for the primary impetus for a new community college to come from the local level. Someone in the community realizes a need and begins to press for additional educational opportunity. Such persons are not always educators—they may include newspaper editors, chamber of commerce leaders, PTA members, school boards, or any public-spirited layman, as well as the administrators in high schools or city school systems. Usually, such realization of need is not at first precise and clearly defined. Most leaders do not envisage at the outset the nature of the institution which they feel is needed. The existence of enabling legislation for junior colleges and of a number of successfully operating junior colleges in the state may help to focus attention on such colleges as an answer to the need. In general, however, some perceptive and responsible observer becomes concerned about opportunities for higher education and begins to interpret the need to others at the same time that he searches for an appropriate method of satisfying the need.

The existence of numbers of able high-school graduates who are not in college is likely to be noticed first as one of the evidences of the need for an additional college. Such a condition may arise from any of several causes. Thus, the effects of the depression led to the establishment in 1933 of the Palm Beach Junior College in Florida, and the imminent return of World War II veterans, whose education had been interrupted by military service, contributed to the founding of Montgomery Junior College in Maryland and of Orange County Community College in New York, as well as of some 60 other public junior colleges founded between 1946 and 1950. Since 1950, overcrowding of existing colleges, policies of establishing limits on the size of university campuses, rising tuition costs, and need for new kinds of less-than-baccalaureate education have all combined to bring the community college to the attention of community leaders.

In addition, local pride and desire for economy in higher education have always played a part in initiating new colleges. If neighboring communities have successful junior colleges to which local students must travel and to which they or the school district in which they reside must pay higher tuition, it is inevitable that sooner or later the desirability of a local junior college will be suggested.

*Preliminary Studies.*     After it has come to the attention of the community that a junior college seems to be needed by young people and that the state has established legal procedures to provide one, several additional factors need to be studied before further action is pressed. Some estimate should be made, first, of the number of students who might be expected to enroll in such a local college. Are there enough annual high-school graduates in the contributing area to assure that the new college will be of adequate size? Are there groups of adults in the community who will swell the enrollments permanently or temporarily? Is it likely that the number of youth needing education will grow or diminish in the foreseeable future? In various state laws, provision is made for either a minimum school enrollment or a minimum total district population before a junior college may be authorized. Early writers on the junior college, also, have suggested that a minimum prospective enrollment of 100, 200, or 300 students should be in sight to guarantee the success of a new college.

Such specific limitations seem unrealistic. Because so many variable conditions affect the desirability of founding a college, no concrete stipulations can apply to all areas. The need for a limited academic program in a remote area might justify recommending the establishment of a junior college for a prospective 100 or 150 students. In a more metropolitan area, with nearby junior colleges available, it would probably be unwise to plan an additional site unless at least 1000 day students, a comprehensive curriculum, and an extensive adult program were in sight.

*Gaining Support.*    Once the idea of a community junior college has been conceived, two early steps seem absolutely essential to its eventual realization. The first is consultation with the local school administrators and school boards. In this way unnecessary duplication of effort can be avoided; in addition, these sources can supply accurate information about legal procedures for establishing local junior colleges, estimates of probable enrollment, effect of such a development on the tax rate and on the educational opportunity of younger pupils, avenues of approach to other areas which should be included in the junior college territory, and other useful services and consultation. On the other hand, if local school authorities either refuse to support or actively oppose the establishment of a junior college, it will be in some states impossible and in all states unwise to proceed further with the proposal until those attitudes are changed.

The second essential procedure, which should be undertaken early in the elaboration of the plans for college establishment, is a careful presentation of the entire concept of community junior college education and of the possibilities so far apparent locally to the press of the area. Junior colleges have been established in the face of influential newspaper opposition; but the entire process of establishing the need, interpreting it clearly to the electorate, and securing authorization is facilitated if the editors of the region are fully informed of the progress of the idea. For this reason, it may be well to invite a competent authority on the junior college from the state department of education, a university, or elsewhere to meet with the editors and acquaint them with the community junior college concept and its local applicability, so far as it may be determined at this early stage.

*State Approval.*    As was suggested in Chapter 7, state involvement in community college planning and operation varies from total control to minimum procedures of approval and minimum support. Where a state board of control exists, the master plan is likely to determine the areas to be served and the sites to be chosen for each of the community colleges, reserving to local advisory boards some involvement in building planning and curriculum development. In states that will assign major responsibility for community college support and control to the areas to be served, a less formal procedure usually suffices.

Informal consultation by employees of the coordinating board for higher education may have established the fact that a community junior college is feasible in the area. Following this, the first formal action is likely to be a petition, either from a local school board or boards or from a number or percentage of qualified voters, requesting the established state agency to determine whether or not the area under consideration meets the criteria established by law for the approval of a public junior college. In accordance with the principle of local responsibility for public education, it is important that the first formal request be an expression of substantial local interest in the establishment of a college.

Following the receipt of the petition, the coordinating board will investigate the likelihood of successful operation of a college in the area. In accordance with specific legal provisions and exercising the responsibility for judgment legally delegated to it, it will survey the assessed valuation, the population, the school population, the availability of other educational opportunity, the economic future of the area, and the attitudes of representative bodies of citizens. On the basis of its findings, it will arrive at one of several conclusions. Such a survey might reveal that no real need exists for a community junior college, that the community could not support one in acceptable fashion, or that the imminent decline of the community would make it unwise to invest in such a college. Again, the survey staff might approve the idea set forth in the petition but recommend changes in estimated enrollment, in preliminary listings of possible courses of study, in suggested site, or in other elements of the original and tentative plan submitted to them. It is more probable, if the preliminary work has been carefully planned and carried out, that the state survey will confirm the conclusions of the local sponsors of the movement and that submission of the proposal to the electors of the district will be approved.

*Local Election.*   After approval by state survey authorities of the original proposal for the junior college, some states allow a local municipal or county school board to proceed with the establishment of the college. In some states the local authorities are required to submit the question of establishment of the new college district to a vote of the people in the area of the new college. This procedure, of course, is slower and more costly. In addition, it may result in defeat of the entire proposal. There are nevertheless several practical advantages to the popular-election procedure. It facilitates public discussion and public understanding of the nature of the college; it brings into the open any latent opposition to the establishment and requires the voters to commit themselves on the proposal before final steps are taken. Thus the new college, when it is established, will be more widely understood and more firmly supported. The citizenry who must support the college and who will benefit by its existence will have had a direct and positive voice in its founding.

*Governing Board.*    Independent community junior college districts must provide for a board of trustees after the voters have authorized the establishment of the district. When a state agency is the sponsoring body of the newly authorized community junior college, this step is not required; even so, the law may provide for the naming of a college advisory board to consult with the president and to approve certain matters before they are acted upon by the legally responsible school board. In other states, the laws provide for the appointment or the election of the board of trustees for the independent community college district. Upon their qualification, the first concerns of the new governing board must be to provide funds for the interim operation of the college until local taxes, state aid, and tuition fees are available, to provide space for the initial operation of the college, and to find a competent administrator to direct the development of the college.

# B. Establishing the Authorized Community Junior College

Late in July, a president was chosen for a newly authorized community junior college. By mid-August, he had come to the community to begin his work. Before the end of August, a suitable unoccupied building had been acquired and reconstruction had begun including a new roof, new exterior sheathing, new interior wallboard, and gallons of paint. At the same time, a dozen faculty members were employed, students were informed of the existence of the institution, and library orders were rushed to publishers. By mid-September, a basic program of lower-division courses was being taught to 180 students, about equally divided between full-time day and part-time evening registrants. The curriculum planning, the gathering of materials of instruction, the development of the college philosophy, and even the design of student record forms were completed at the same time as instruction was being offered. In its second year, the institution more than doubled its enrollment and was able to bring its borrowed building up to presentable status, while embarking on construction of its permanent campus on a nearby site.

Many school administrators would prefer to move more deliberately in preparing for the first year's instruction. The college described was independently organized and so was unable to make use of established facilities and of personnel who were already working in an allied secondary school or at another campus of a multi-campus district. Yet even in districts that are already in operation, a year or more of preplanning is very helpful to faculty, administrators, and students and to the initial quality of instruction.

In the separate community junior college district, a period of approximately a year between the legal authorization and the offering of the first full-scale program is not only useful but almost essential. A review of the tasks which must be accomplished will demonstrate the need for time. Again, it must be understood that in some of the organizational patterns for junior colleges, some of these arrangements may have been completed before the employment of the new chief administrator. The complete plan of procedure, however, is best described in relation to the supposition that an administrator is employed for a junior college district which is legally authorized, which has access to taxing power and to some initial appropriation of funds, and which has an enthusiastic board of trustees. Such a district would have no other employees and no property of any kind; the board might have been carrying on its business with borrowed offices and staff. The community has voted for and expects a college to be established but has made no final commitments as to site, staff, or educational program. Since state provisions vary so widely, it is further assumed that money for capital outlays will be provided as needed in the manner appropriate to each state.

*Time Schedule.*    One of the administrator's first concerns must be the establishment of a time schedule for operations, acceptable to his board of trustees, which can also be explained to the public through the press and in speeches. In such a plan, the most important date will be that agreed upon for welcoming the first full-time class to the college. College terms usually open in September; the administrator should, if at all possible, allow himself a minimum of nine months, and preferably a full year, to complete his preparations for that opening. With the target date in mind, he will schedule each of the major tasks that must be completed before then. Among them will be selection and preparation of a site, either temporary or permanent, detailed survey of educational needs of the community, decision on curriculums and courses to be offered, preparation of a catalog, selection of instructors and other college officers, interpretation of the institution to prospective students as well as to the public generally, preparation of a schedule of classes, procurement of books, equipment, and supplies, preopening orientation of the faculty, and registration of students.

A full description of the essential steps and the time sequence factors involved in establishing an actual new junior college is found in Benson's presentation of the use of computers in establishing "critical paths." In Benson's words,

> "An essential element of the (critical path) method is the necessity for explicitness in planning; it automatically requires the establishment of detailed plans as evidenced by the flow-chart network. The method provides management by objective as well as management by exception . . . It can be valuable aid to administrators faced with the task of establishing a new junior college."[2]

*Site Selection.*    Usually the studies that led to the legal approval of the college will have included some consideration of possible sites for the first classes. The administrator will find it necessary to become familiar with these sites and to determine what kinds of contractual arrangements are necessary and what physical changes need to be made. Since the provision of facilities, including architectural work, bidding procedures, and actual construction or reconstruction are most time-consuming, this entire process must be one of the first activities of the new president. Junior colleges only rarely offer their first classes in new buildings designed especially for them; local high schools, churches, military buildings, dwellings—any building with sturdy walls and a roof—are used temporarily while a permanent home is being provided. Even though the entire curriculum cannot be foreseen so early in the planning, it is necessary to make concrete arrangements for a home for the college, maintaining flexibility so that adaptation in space assignment may be made as the analysis of educational needs progresses.

The question of a permanent site also requires early attention; enough is known about the requirements of junior colleges to allow decisions to be made on the basis of availability, extent, accessibility, and adaptability of any proposed site even before the final details of vocational and academic curriculums are determined. Some colleges have found that bitter and extended public debate, especially between rival communities, may be aroused over choice between two sites. It is highly important that the new administrator become acquainted as rapidly as he can with the characteristics of each possible site and with the educational advantages and disadvantages of each, so that he may properly evaluate the claims of local boosters for each site and recommend wisely to his board.

*Survey of Needs.*    A general survey of educational needs, of course, was the basis for the establishment of the new community junior college. Yet it will be necessary for the new president to conduct a more detailed investigation as a basis for his later decisions. At the same time, the process of investigation itself can serve as a part of the interpretation of the college to the community and to its prospective students. One part of the survey will be directed at high-school students. From them it is possible to ascertain how many plan to go to college and specifically to the new college, what kinds of courses they think they need, what vocations they have chosen, and what activities they would want to engage in while at college. A good deal of informed judgment will be required both in the design of the questionnaire and in the interpretation of the answers. Certainly an interest of 127 boys in engineering courses, as an example, should not lead to immediate provision for that number of laboratory spaces. Such a study will be useful, even so, in indicating proportions of interest in the several possible fields of study; it serves, as well, to convince all students that the college is about to become a reality and intends to offer the courses they need.

A similar survey must be made of the business and industrial leaders of the communities. Employers, managers, labor union officials, chamber of commerce manager, placement officers, and any other knowledgeable persons should be interviewed about employment trends, training requirements, labor supply, and economic future of their specialty in the region in order that the college interviewer may form some judgment about feasible curriculums for the college. Here again, an opportunity is provided for the college official both to gain useful information and to provide interpretation of the college to its patrons.

After the results of these two surveys are tabulated and presented to the board of trustees, certain tentative decisions will be reached concerning educational opportunities to be offered, both for transfer to four-year colleges and for training for immediate employment. At this point, it will be useful to call a meeting of interested adults, including many of those interviewed in the survey as well as leaders in every kind of local organization, to present for their criticism and suggestions the present status of the planning for the college. From such a meeting can come four beneficial results: revision of the educational planning on the basis of discussion in the meeting, informed public support and loyalty to the program, a realization by civic leaders that their advice had been considered and applied, and a list of names of able and interested persons for assignment to the several advisory committees which will begin to help in developing details of curriculums, especially in the occupational fields.

Until this time, all decisions have been tentative and subject to revision. After the survey results have been presented to the college board and to the citizens' meeting, the tempo of events increases. The citizens' meeting may be considered as a "point of no return" in the planning for the college. Decisions reached in the light of all of the investigations to date are final; action on them is required.

Study of other colleges will be helpful at this time. Some of the curriculums adopted are planned to prepare students for transfer to parallel curriculums at nearby colleges and universities. For this reason, consultation is in order with admissions officers and deans of the institutions to which future students seem most likely to transfer, so that appropriate parallel courses may be established. Although the four-year institutions will not agree with each other entirely on course organization, they will probably all agree to accept any course which is equivalent in content and standard to that offered by any one of them. On the basis of study of their catalogs supplemented by conferences with each, decisions can be reached on the minimum essential offerings in each of the subject fields. How many semester courses in which foreign languages? How to arrange the sequence of courses in college algebra, analytic geometry, calculus? What topics in physics? In chemistry? What courses in history? In economics? In sociology? How to determine eligibility for freshman English? Answers to such questions are preliminary both to publication of the catalog and to employment of faculty members.

Existing community junior colleges should also be consulted at this point. The new institution will not wish to pattern itself identically after a neighboring college even if it is in the same district and under the same board of trustees. Yet the experience of other similar colleges can be invaluable in learning of special techniques, triumphs and failures, and successful and unhappy solutions to problems of all sorts. A neighboring college will share solutions to problems of transfer-course organization, of catalog and schedule preparation, of vocational-course equipment and planning, and even of necessary student accounting forms.

*Employing Faculty.* The preparation of a catalog and the employment of faculty can proceed simultaneously. Once decisions have been reached about the probable number of students in the first year and the scope of the courses to be offered for them, a table of organization can be drawn up to indicate what administrative, counseling, and instructional personnel will be needed, with qualifications and salary scale for each. It is possible that the search for qualified instructors will consume most of the time of the college president for several months. Even though he will know several persons whom he wishes to invite to join him without further search, he will find that in other areas he must interview seven or eight applicants before finding one with whom he is satisfied and who wishes to undertake the burdens of a pioneering venture. In addition, it is entirely possible that the local survey will lead to the decision to inaugurate an occupational curriculum for which it is almost impossible to discover qualified instructors. In such a case, it may become necessary to postpone the offering of the course.

The catalog will serve the entire district as one of the basic sources of information about the college. For this reason it should be prepared carefully, illustrated attractively, printed in quantity, and distributed widely. It is false economy and penurious public relations to prepare an inadequate number of official catalogs. It is especially important in the first year of the college to provide an impression of permanence and substance to all the patrons, and a well-prepared catalog can contribute measurably to this impression. It should present the history, the purposes, the regulations, and the educational offerings of the college in the clearest and most dignified fashion possible.

One of the first appointments the new administrator will make should be a librarian. Because of the time it takes for the selection, ordering, and preparation of the opening collection, a year is not too much time to allow for this work, even for an experienced librarian and a clerk-typist. Of course, there are packaged community college opening day collections that can be ordered all ready for the library shelves. But additional selections must be made that will provide learning materials for the special emphases of the individual institution. And nonbook materials must be included which involve serious decisions about how they will be cataloged, shelved, and circulated in the new library or instructional resource center.

*Equipment.*    A new independent public junior college, of course, will have no backlog of equipment or of books; everything must be acquired. For this reason, every instructor, as soon as he accepts the offer of employment, should be asked to develop in detail a list of equipment, supplies, and library books that he will need for his courses during the first year. If possible, he should be informed of the total sum available for his courses; in any event, his lists should be segregated to indicate the items that are absolutely essential, those that are highly desirable, and those that could be deferred to a later date. Since many items in the requests of instructors will duplicate each other, it will become a full-time job for a competent clerk to keep track of materials already ordered, to make certain that unnecessary duplicates are not ordered, and to distribute the incoming books and materials to the proper recipients.

*Informing Students.*   Simultaneously with the development of other aspects of the college—site, program, faculty, and equipment—attention must be paid to the prospective student body. Among the high-school seniors of the district will be many who had planned to go elsewhere to college and some who had given up hope of college because of expense or because they knew of no courses that would meet their needs. Some members of each of these groups must be recruited for the new college; a continuous program of information and interpretation is required. The high-school newspaper can aid in these efforts by announcing the various achievements in developing curriculum, acquiring site, and employing instructors. The cooperation of the high-school principal and teachers of seniors will be very helpful, especially if a program of college aptitude tests or a series of talks to senior classes can be arranged. The distribution of the catalog, the schedule of classes, or a letter to parents of high-school students can be followed by preregistration interviews in the high school before graduation day. Unless the students are informed early and continuously of the progress of the college, they will not be able to plan to attend it. On the other hand, such energetic efforts to inform high-school seniors and to enlist their support during early planning of the college instructional program and of student activities help to create a favorable spirit and a positive enthusiasm on the part of the first students.

*In-Service Training of Faculty.*   The newly employed faculty should be brought to the campus well in advance of the first day of classes. They will need to complete a good many routine tasks which only they can do, such as storage of chemicals or specimens for laboratories or assembling of complicated specialized equipment and arrangement of their classrooms to suit their purposes. Equally important are the orientation sessions by which they become acquainted with each other, with the administration, with the college, and with the community. In these sessions, also, they can begin to develop agreement on some elements of the college philosophy. Since students will be gathering for final registration in the days before the opening of instruction, the instructors will be needed to help in advising them.

It is apparent from the description of the tasks to be completed in preparing for the opening of a new college that a considerable period of time, at least nine months to a year, is desirable for their successful completion. Certainly their accomplishment would seem to necessitate the employment of some help for the administrator; he will need a purchasing agent or business manager, certainly, and probably a dean of instruction to care for the surveys, the catalog, the schedule, and other details of establishing the instructional program. Colleges have been opened more rapidly and with less professional assistance. Yet if the college is to attain its full educational scope, stature, and quality at the earliest possible moment, it is important that it be thoroughly and soundly established.

### FOOTNOTES

1. Chapman, Charles E., "Ohio Joins the Club,"*Junior College Journal*, **35** (October, 1964), pp. 8-12.
2. *Establishing Junior Colleges.* Occasional Report No. 5, Junior College Leadership Program, School of Education. Los Angeles: University of California, 1964, p. 34.

### BIBLIOGRAPHY

Benson, Ellis M. "A Time Sequence Analysis of Critical Steps in the Establishment of California Public Junior Colleges." Unpublished Doctoral Dissertation. Los Angeles: University of California, 1963.

Brumbaugh, A. J. *Guidelines for the Establishment of Community Junior Colleges.* Atlanta: Southern Regional Education Board.

Gleazer, Edmund J., Jr. *This is the Community College.* Boston: Houghton Mifflin Co., 1968.

Johnson, B. Lamar *Establishing Junior Colleges.* Occasional Report No. 5, Junior College Leadership Program. Los Angeles: University of California, 1964.

Johnson, B. Lamar *Starting a Community Junior College.* Washington, D.C.: American Association of Junior Colleges, 1964.

Kintzer, Frederic C. *et al. The Multi-Institution Junior College District.* Washington, D.C.: American Association of Junior Colleges, 1969.

Morrison, D. G., and Martorana, S. V. *Criteria for the Establishment of Two-Year Colleges.* Washington, D.C.: U.S. Government Printing Office, 1963.

*A Primer for Planners.* Washington, D.C.: American Association of Junior Colleges, 1967.

Roueche, John E., and Boggs, John R. *Junior College Institutional Research.* Washington, D.C.: American Association of Junior Colleges, 1968.

# 9 | Administration of the Community Junior College

Previous chapters have described some of the variations in size, in objective, and in legal support and control of community junior colleges. No single chart of administrative organization could include appropriate officers and lines of responsibility for all these kinds of institutions. Even in colleges that are similar in size and type of legal control, local considerations may lead to substantial differences in the names of the various administrative officers and in the grouping of their duties. Moreover, it is important to realize that the arrangement of

**113**

administrative titles and assignments according to one scheme or another does not in itself achieve any purpose; it merely makes it more convenient for the responsible officers to work harmoniously. The most sophisticated organization will not assure effective functioning of inept or uncooperative staff members, whereas a primitive and haphazard arrangement may yield good results if it is manned by devoted and able administrators. Nevertheless, a clear statement of administrative responsibilities and lines of authority can help to eliminate duplication or conflict of effort and to provide each officer with a secure understanding of his relation to other workers and to the total task of the college.

In spite of the diversity of their organization and control, community junior colleges of all sizes share many common objectives. The attainment of these objectives by the teaching faculty and the students requires leadership, planning, coordination, financing, housekeeping, supervision, and evaluation. It is the task of the administrative staff to carry out these functions in such fashion that the instructional staff may work smoothly, without unnecessary difficulties, and with high morale at the fundamental job of the college—instructing students. The present chapter discusses some of the administrative functions necessary in any type of junior college. An initial section discusses changing concepts of the administrative task. Thereafter, the purposes and functions of the college board of trustees are considered; analysis of administrative tasks closely related to instruction and of supportive or secondary functions follows. The final section of the chapter presents a pattern of organization for a sizable community junior college which may be adapted quite simply to other varieties of junior colleges.

## A. Conflicting Concepts of Administration

Traditional administrative practice may be contrasted quite briefly (and somewhat unfairly) with emerging techniques. In its beginnings, the American college administrator was considered to be *in loco parentis*, to some extent for the faculty as well as for the students. Students were considered to be inherently undisciplined, and it was the purpose of the college to provide discipline through instruction and punishment. The president, and later the dean, had as much right as the parent to inquire into the activities of the student and to forbid or to chastise without concern for inherent rights of the young persons entrusted to his care.

Faculty members, too, were subject to close direction and control of the president. Even well into the twentieth century, the typical college president was completely autocratic, deciding on appointments, tenure, salaries, budgets, and conditions of work without much consultation with individual faculty members. Many presidents were benevolent, scholarly, well-intentioned men of principle; it simply had not occurred to them that colleges were very different from businesses. It was natural, even theological, to concentrate authority in the few and to expect obedience from the rest in any sphere of life.

A more contemporary view of administration may be compared to the role of the hospital administrator. He cares for the managerial aspects of the hospital and establishes conditions that permit the physicians and the surgeons to treat their patients. Controls are established with the help of the staff to protect patients from gross malpractice; but in general, the administrator allows medical expertise to rest with the professionals. In somewhat the same way, the college administrator recognizes that his faculty are not simply employees in the classical sense, but are themselves experts whose training and competence in their own fields are comparable to his own in its field.

The relation of administration to students has also changed. It is no longer possible to consider students as "charges" or as unformed personalities who have been submitted to the college for molding. In their own minds, students probably never accepted this view. Their independence was demonstrated by rioting in the eighteenth century, by the establishment of literary societies to bring some meaning into their education during the early nineteenth century, and by their escape from the inanities of the curriculum through fraternities and athletics during the latter half of that century. It is only recently that college authorities have begun to recognize openly that most of the changes in college practice since the establishment of Harvard in 1636 have come in response to innovations and pressures by students.

The community junior college, often smaller than the university, more explicitly devoted to teaching, less complex in its organization into schools, centers, and disciplinary departments, and with a total history of less than a century, is more able to adapt to emerging administrative imperatives. It can become more rapidly a true educational community by encouraging the communication that is the prime requirement of a community. The community college president can begin to cultivate more effective ways of achieving alert foresight and advance planning, so that growing frustrations in the college experiences of faculty and students may be recognized and remedied, rather than being ignored until the subordinate members of the community decide that violence is the only way to achieve change.

A basic principle is that persons affected by policy should have a voice in developing policy. This is not to say that students and faculty have the only voices; it is to say that policy developed without input from them is likely to be shortsighted and eventually ineffective. The principle does not indicate that the carrying out of policy (administration) should be done by committees; once a decision is arrived at, the implementation of it can very well be centralized in one responsible agency. The principle does entail sincere, meaningful, and regular procedures for communication upward as well as downward. Elements of the community whose inputs are needed are the political community, the governing board, the members of the administrative staff, the total faculty, and the students. Techniques can be established to attain direct access (rather than through subordinate administrators) from each of these groups. Modern administration requires that the techniques be adopted.

## B. The Community Junior College Board of Trustees

Locally controlled community junior colleges are governed in much the same way as other elements of the public schools. A locally elected board of trustees establishes policies for the college or colleges in its district, under the laws enacted by the legislature and the regulations of a state board. Support is usually made up of a combination of student tuition, local real estate property taxes, and state allocations.

Community colleges that are units of a university system, on the other hand, and those operated as units in a statewide system of higher education will have only a remote relation to the Board of Regents or the State Board of Control. Although the descriptions of school-board functions found in the literature on public school administration might be adapted to serve as guides to statewide boards of control, they are intended primarily to apply to locally elected boards having responsibility for the operation and control of a single school district. Such districts almost never include more area than one county; frequently they are limited in area to a township, municipality, or other comparatively small unit. The board members of such a district are, therefore, residents of the community, acquainted with its people and its problems, and concerned about the optimum development of a program of education for the local people.

A local community college board is the liaison between the community and the college. It establishes basic educational, operating, and personnel policies for the college; it employs the superintendent of the college district; and it approves budget and determines the necessary local tax rate to support the college. In general, it is responsible to the community for seeing that the educational program is defined, established, and conducted in accordance with law and with the desires of the community at large.

In the execution of these responsibilities, school boards face many dangers. A board may see itself as an administrative rather than a policy-making body. In this case the superintendent, who should be the professionally trained executive officer of the board, administering the affairs of the district in accordance with the law and the established policies of the board, is reduced to the position of errand boy, with little opportunity to exercise judgment or leadership. At the same time, preoccupation with administrative detail prevents the board from devoting its attention to policy matters and to the development of the educational program. An example may be found in personnel practices. Some boards attempt to interview applicants for employment and to nominate candidates from their own acquaintances. In the days of the one-teacher rural school, this was a necessary practice; in the choice of a superintendent of schools, it remains one of the board's major responsibilities. In relation to teaching positions, however, the board's responsibility is to establish the number and nature of the positions to be filled for the next year. The superintendent then interviews candidates and recommends to the board those he considers most qualified. If for some reason, the board is unwilling to accept any of the recommended teachers, it does not seek a substitute, but requests the superintendent to recommend another applicant. The line between policy forming and its execution is sometimes a fine one, but it must be scrupulously observed in order to realize the values of the uniquely American combination of lay control and professional leadership of the public schools.

An equal and opposite danger, of course, is that the board will relinquish its duties of policy making and evaluation to the superintendent, so that the board becomes in effect only a rubber stamp. Although some critics of school boards have suggested that they be abolished in favor of completely professional management of the schools, most educators and probably most citizens would agree with the point of view of the American Association of School Administrators:

School board members represent the people who own and support the schools. They form a grass roots organization which is closer to the people than to any other form of government. They voice the wishes and aspirations of the parents and the children. They spend the local taxpayers' money and are responsible to their neighbors for the action. They are the trustees of a great public responsibility.[1]

In the exercise of their trusteeship, the board and the superintendent must work as a harmonious team. The superintendent reports basic information of all sorts that is essential to good policy making and recommends policies which he judges will be effective. The board considers all of these matters in the light of its understanding of the desires of the community, the financial ability of the district, and the basic wisdom of the several board members, and reaches its decision. It is a fundamental concept in many areas of American life that policies thus decided by a pooling of information, experience, and judgment will in a majority of cases be sounder than those arrived at authoritatively by an individual. The executive application of policy to concrete cases often requires immediate decision by the administrator; this is the role of the superintendent. The policy in accordance with which such decisions are made, however, should be elaborated in advance of crisis conditions, deliberately, cooperatively, and in the light of the best information available; this is the role of the board of trustees.

Among suitable areas for policy making by the board of trustees of a community junior college may be listed:

1. The adoption of a statement of the purposes of the college.
2. Policies affecting the admission, control, and graduation of students.
3. Personnel policies, including employment practices, salary schedules, working conditions, and fringe benefits.
4. Development, use, and maintenance of sites, buildings, and equipment.
5. Financial procedures in budgeting and expending funds.
6. Relations with other colleges and with governmental agencies.
7. Its own procedural rules.

*Board Rules.* The relationship between school board, superintendent, faculty, and the public may be safeguarded by the adoption and publication of "Board Rules and Regulations" in which policy decisions gathered from minutes of board meetings are codified and if necessary extended. Although in such policy statements, it is impossible and probably undesirable to provide for every contingency, the adoption by the board of a compilation of policy decisions as evidence of its present philosophy and practice facilitates mutual understanding and cooperation on the part of all who are concerned with the college. The board and the superintendent should review the rules and regulations periodically with the purpose of eliminating nonfunctional or outmoded provisions and including newly developed policies.

A *faculty manual* is a useful adjunct to the board rules and regulations. Such a volume sets forth the philosophy of the college and the responsibilities of various officers and of faculty members and establishes procedures in relation to employment, promotion, expenditures of college funds, relations with students, and similar matters on which instructors need to be uniformly and reliably informed. It also should be adopted by the board as a statement of board policy and revised periodically.

Because the *annual catalog* contains many statements of policy regarding courses of study and student progress, it is important for the board to be informed in advance of the changes of basic policy to be introduced into each annual edition. If it has approved, in advance of printing, changes in curricular descriptions, grading policies, graduation requirements, and other important matters, the board will be able to accept by resolution each successive issue of the college catalog. Such acceptance officially establishes the catalog statements as elements of board rules and regulations.

A public junior college board of trustees that clearly understands its own proper relationships to its community and to its college is a basic element in effective administration. If such a board chooses a superintendent of the district with similarly clear understanding and develops rules and regulations that clarify the relationships and duties of all employees, smooth running of the entire junior college is virtually assured.

## B. Instructional Tasks of Administration

Some aspects of the work of the college administrator have a direct effect on the nature and the quality of instruction in the college. Other administrative procedures may be considered as supporting instruction, but not directly affecting its quality. Among the former, continuing study of community educational needs, use of lay advisory committees, development of the curriculum, selection of teachers, scheduling of classes, supervision of instruction, in-service training of instructors, evaluation, and fostering of student government are considered in the present section. The supportive tasks of administration will be discussed in a succeeding section of the chapter.

*Community Surveys.* Every junior college serves its own selected clientele and succeeds or fails in the same degree that it understands and provides for the educational needs of that clientele. The community junior college has accepted as its clientele the supporting community and attempts to meet the educational needs, beyond the high school but short of the bachelor's degree, of young people and adults. Such a college is established only after careful surveys of the local community have demonstrated the need for it; its courses of study are elaborated after further detailed investigation of specific curricular possibilities.

But communities change. Educational needs emerge or wane. The junior college administrator must never assume that he has completed his study of his community and that he can establish his curriculum once and for all. Instead, he must provide both for uninterrupted continuous study of his community and for periodic intensive resurveys. Such constant concern provides the basis for the steady development of the college toward more and more adequate educational service. The day-to-day study of community trends will consist in part simply of alert observation of local developments such as the influx of new industries, the overcrowding of the lower schools, the gain or loss of population in the area, and general social or technological changes that require new emphases in the college program. More formally, a sizable district may assign a faculty member to devote part of his time to this continuing search for the facts on which educational decisions may be based. Sometimes a coordinator of vocational education, for example, will be requested to report periodically on such facts as trends in the area, ideas of employer and labor groups about needed offerings, indications of coming needs for more courses or different courses, evidences of satisfaction or dissatisfaction of employers with junior-college-trained employees, and similar data. Such observations are not likely to be well done if they are only by-products of the chief administrator's daily rounds; someone must assume the stated responsibility for them lest they be lost, and their educational meaning with them, beneath the bustling busynesses of operational tediums.

There is much value also in a periodic full-scale resurvey of the community, similar to that completed before the establishment of the junior college. In addition to the information such a resurvey affords for curricular planning, it can provide two very useful results. Instructors, who participate in such a survey, gathering statistics, interviewing citizens, and visiting offices and factories, will learn about their community in ways that will inevitably help them to become better teachers. At the same time, the citizens and graduates interviewed will gain a new understanding of the purposes of the college and an enhanced regard for the quality of its efforts. Primarily, of course, the purpose of the survey is to provide an up-to-date description of the educational needs of the college communities. It will consider such data as population change, business and industrial activity, occupational distribution and trends, characteristics of present students, follow-up of former students in universities and on the job, forecast of future enrollments, and evaluation of the educational program of the college. Other activities may seem to the administrator more immediately pressing than the careful study of his community, but surely this one is essential and fundamental as a guide and justification for all the other activities of administrators, instructors, and students.

*Lay Advisory Committees.* In the several specialized areas of the curriculum, additional effective information from the community may be gained by the use of lay advisory committees. Originally formed to assist in the design and development of curriculums in vocational education, such committees in any instructional field are useful adjuncts to administration. Thus a community junior college might well establish lay advisory committees for each of its operating or contemplated vocational and technical curriculums, for several specialties in business, in home-making, in engineering, in general education, or for any other area where details of the curriculum, placement of graduates, selection of equipment, opportunities for field trips and guest speakers, or any aspect of instruction might be appreciably improved by the practical advice of a group of informed laymen. The leadership of these advisory committees will ordinarily be exercised by the junior college administrative staff; they will meet on call to consider reports of progress in developing the program and to advise on methods of improving and extending it. Although advisory committees are always consultative rather than legistlative or policy-making groups, the college programs will benefit measurably from careful consideration of their suggestions.

Proposals for added courses and curriculums, of course, will come from instructors and from students as well as from the more formal studies described above. From time to time, also, consideration must be given to the elimination of courses which duplicate other offerings or which are no longer educationally useful or economically desirable. Not all suggestions for the installation of courses will be sound ones; the survey staffs, specialized lay advisory committees, or departmental faculty members may serve well in their respective areas but fail to consider all aspects of a complete curriculum. Such groups are quite unlikely to propose any fundamental reevaluation of the entire pattern of requirements for graduation or of general education courses or of any practices whose effects extend beyond their limited responsibility. For these reasons, after all possible facts and insights have been assembled from all sources, the fundamental responsibility of leadership in the development of the junior college curriculum rests on the administrative staff. If administrative organization and operation stress the importance of this function, the board of trustees, the faculty, and the community will be interested and effective in their several roles. On the other hand, if secondary factors are given priority by the administrative staff, the curriculum will fail to serve well the community's educational needs.

*Teacher Selection.* For this same reason, one of the most important tasks of administration is the careful selection of teachers. During each registration period, the president will gather data that will enable him to analyze past trends in enrollments by courses and to forecast with considerable accuracy his future needs for faculty expansion. He will request the board to approve new positions at the earliest possible moment, so that he may notify placement agencies and begin interviewing candidates. So important is this administrative responsibility that some junior college administrators budget considerable amounts of time and money for travel to interview applicants. In the final analysis, the classroom teacher is the embodiment of the effective college curriculum. He is the most important employee of the college. The administrator who fails to choose good instructors, fails.

*Class Schedules.* The same registration information that enables the administrator to forecast his needs for additional instructors is useful also in developing the schedule of classes. After a policy on class size in the various instructional areas has been calculated, the number of sections needed is determined by simple division. The scheduling of classes, however, requires perceptive judgment based on a balance of four factors. The most important consideration is the ability of all students who need a given class to fit it into their schedules. When multiple sections can be offered in most courses, this requirement is no problem. When only one section can be offered in each of several important courses, careful cross-checking of curricular patterns will reveal conflicts and ways to their resolution. The conscientious schedule maker will work out a trial student schedule for each of the major curriculums offered by the college, in order to discover cases in which two courses required of the same student in the same semester appear at the same hour in the preliminary draft. The availability of rooms is another factor in schedule making—if the college has only one chemistry laboratory, some of the laboratory sections must be scheduled at unpopular hours. On the other hand, even where there are enough rooms, it is important to arrange for a balanced offering throughout the college day. If 50 classes are offered at one hour and one hundred classes the next to the same student body, the first set of classes will have overlarge enrollments whereas the enrollments in the second set will be comparatively small. Finally, it is important in scheduling to consider as far as possible the convenience of the instructor. A free period before a laboratory class or two consecutive sections of the same course or the preservation of a reasonable block of free time for conference, correction, and preparation mean a great deal to the morale of instructors. Schedule making is the delicate art of harmonizing all these factors so that the instructional objectives of the college can be achieved with the greatest effectiveness and with economy of effort and of capital resources.

Many of the tedious tasks of schedule making and schedule checking can be performed by punched card computers. Cosand describes a process through which several "trial runs" even in advance of the opening of a college enabled the administrative staff to be sure of the number and capacity of classrooms needed. In addition, the computer simulation checked the projected schedule to make certain that faculty members were assigned without conflicts and that students in all majors would be able to register for the classes they needed.[2]

*Supervision of Instruction.* Supervision of junior college instruction is another administrative responsibility. It is carried on for one reason—to improve teaching and learning. In the pursuit of this goal, it cannot be denied that the administrator who visits classes is attempting to assess the quality of the instruction and learning and that he will base some of his judgments about reemployment of teachers on his observations. It is a mistake, though, for the administrator and the teacher to limit their concept of supervision only to classroom visitation or to assume that its only purpose is evaluation of the teacher. If the teacher and the administrator see themselves as partners in the educational process, class visits will be seen as one method to enable the administrator to serve the teacher better. It is the only way in which the administrator can maintain meaningful contact with classroom problems, gain a first-hand understanding of the full scope of the curriculum, reach a realistic appreciation of his faculty, and come to see the true relationship between the physical environment (the administrator's traditional concern) and the quality of instruction. Such visitation not only emphasizes that the administration is honestly interested in high quality of instruction, but it can also lead to stimulation of a college-wide desire for continuous improvement in an atmosphere of freedom. Supervision has been, in some junior colleges and in an earlier period, authoritarian and threatening rather than helpful. It need not be so; properly understood, it is the soundest approach to improved faculty status. It enables the administrator to speak with confidence and knowledge when he discusses the high quality of junior college instruction.

*In-Service Training.* Hand in hand with classroom visitation and consultation must go a program of in-service training for faculty members. Few junior college instructors have had the preservice training to help them understand the distinctive opportunities and requirements of teaching in this kind of college. Even those who have had such training can profit from a continuing study of their current problems. It is a responsibility of the administrator to develop plans for experiences which will add to the breadth and depth of faculty understanding and appreciation of their significant role in American education. Participation in the community resurvey has been mentioned as one step in this process of in-service training. Vacation-time workshops, with added pay, can help faculty members within an instructional division seek better answers to problems of the organization of courses and the development of instructional materials. Faculty meetings, before the opening of the term and during it, can be devoted to presentations by instructors of the work and objectives of the several divisions of the college or consideration of descriptive data about students. Addresses by competent outsiders on the topic of their competence—not necessarily junior college topics—can help broaden the horizons of the faculty. It will often be true that a faculty will appreciate and profit more from a presentation by their own colleagues of aspects of a college problem than they will from an "expert" presentation, yet both are needed in a complete program of continuing faculty growth.

*Evaluation.*   Improvement of instruction can be based only on accurate assessment of present status, and although it is very difficult to obtain adequate and accurate evaluation data, some meaningful indicators of quality can be gathered. Standardized examinations are one measure of some of the outcomes of instruction. If the examinations are truly appropriate for the subject matter and for the students tested and if the comparative norms can be accepted as proper bases for comparison, much can be learned from standardized examinations about the effectiveness of the instruction in the community junior college. Because of difficulties both in choice of examination and in interpretation of results and because the purposes of the community junior college transcend the transmission of information, other kinds of evaluation must be added to that of standardized examinations. The success of transfer students in later study provides an additional indication of the quality of the junior college. Preparation for transfer is only one part of the community junior college program, and certainly the college is not the only factor affecting the success or failure of its transferring students; within these limitations, however, transfer-student success adds to evaluative information.

Less frequently studied is the success of terminal students, employed in jobs for which they trained at the college. A further source of evaluative insight is the student who drops out of junior college before he completes his course. Sometimes he may represent a failure by the junior college and in others a real success. Too few community junior colleges have been able to study thoroughly their withdrawing students, either while withdrawing or after a period of time.

Because of the diffuse nature of the adult program with its many constituencies, it is even more difficult to evaluate this aspect of the program. Public opinion is perhaps the most accessible index to college performance in this area; the program is established to serve the needs of adults, who can surely be trusted to judge well whether or not those needs have been satisfied. From whatever source the information is gathered, evaluation serves as a fruitful starting point for improvement; an organized evaluative program is a constant concern of administrators.

*Student Government.*   Student government is also listed as an administrative task closely related to instruction, since student government is fostered in community junior colleges mainly for its contribution to the education of students. Some officer of administration must bear the primary responsibility for helping to organize the student government and for advising the student officers in carrying on their responsibilities and associated functions. In some community junior colleges, the board of trustees formally delegates certain responsibility to the student government. This practice not only clarifies the precise nature of student authority but serves as a reminder of the obligation of the faculty and the board to exercise supervision and at times even a veto power over student government.

# C. Supporting Functions of Administration

*Land and Buildings.*   The provision of land and buildings for junior colleges is a major concern in any public district. School administrators, particularly in our growing cities, must plan years ahead to provide adequate sites for their schools and junior colleges before all appropriate acreage is subdivided and built upon and before land costs skyrocket. This problem is intensified for the community junior college by the requirement of 60 to 80 acres for an adequate campus; if sufficient parking space for student automobiles is to be provided, enough land must be added to allow one parking space per student. Foresight is required on the part of the superintendent and of the board if the growing junior colleges in many states are to have suitable sites.

The development of building plans is another time-consuming aspect of the business administration of the college. After forecasts of probable enrollments over a 20-year period have been determined, it is possible to delineate the specifications for a desirable site. Next, a master plan for campus development must be drawn up by the cooperative effort of faculty, administrators, board of trustees, and architects. Certainly such a plan cannot be correct in all details, but it is essential to develop a concept of the final state of the college plant if hideous flaws in early building and major inconveniences in later developments are to be avoided. The public junior college that can find temporary quarters for its first several years of operation is fortunate. Then the master plan, the plan of finance for buildings, and the detailed plans for each building can be developed carefully and critically, with ample consideration by faculty members as well as by architects and administrators.

*Finance.*    The financing of the community junior college program, as well as the careful budgeting and expenditure of funds, is another area that the instructor may take for granted, although the administrator must spend a major part of his time on it. Publicly supported junior colleges receive stipulated sums from their local communities and from the state. In several states these funds are allocated in accordance with complicated formulas. The average daily attendance of students, the tax effort of the local district, the number of instructional units, the established minimum foundation program, and the indebtedness of the junior college district are some of the factors used in determining state support. In addition, state laws ordinarily require the development of a detailed budget for the expenditure of district funds which must be approved before monies are allocated; all records involved in the calculation, receipt, and disbursement of funds are subject to audit by designated authority.

*Research.* Research into all aspects of the college program is another function of administration. Wise decisions require adequate information. The regular assembling of such information will enable college officers to solve easily many questions of daily procedure, while also providing a firm basis for long-range planning by projection and adjustment of past trends. An example of the usefulness of such research is the annual report of the president of Cuyahoga Community College. The 1968-69 report, entitled Where We Are, is attractively printed and illustrated for wide distribution to the college community.[3] Fifteen thousand copies were issued in the spring of 1970. Major sections of the report were Students, Graduates, Curriculum, Faculty and Staff, Serving the Student, Physical Facilities, Relating to the Educational Community, and a Summary of Fiscal Operation. Information in each section is presented by photographs, charts, and narrative. Such a summary serves not only to inform the board of trustees and the entire community about the progress of their

junior college, but it also enables the administration to plan effectively
for the future in the light of recent trends.

*Public Interpretation.*    The superintendent's Annual Report also can
help in the interpretation of the junior college to its community, as do the
student paper, the annual, the catalog, the football programs, and printed
schedules and announcements of specialized curriculums. Printed matter,
however, is not the only means of cultivating public relations. Because of
the intimate dependence of the public junior college on its local
community, a constant stream of information and interpretation is
necessary. Every instructor and every student contributes daily to this
cultivation of relations, good or bad; in addition, many community junior
colleges are adding a full-time or part-time director of public relations.
Such an officer seeks to keep the patrons of the junior college fully and
continuously informed, so that the college may merit cooperation and
support, and the public will make use of its services. Although the
administration is responsible for the organized program of public
relations, all activities of the college and of its students, faculty, and
administrators contribute to the total impression of the college in the
minds of the public.

# D. Organization for Administration

All the instructional and supportive duties listed for administrators, as
well as others too numerous and too intricate for summary discussion,
require personnel. The appointment of competent officers for these
administrative tasks and defintion of their responsibilities and their
relationships is a major element of the success of the superintendent and
the board. Titles of officers will vary in the several types of community
junior college organization and control, but in all of them certain tasks
must be accomplished. Clear-cut assignment of responsibility can be
achieved only through analysis and description of the work to be done. It
is on this basis that administrative organization can be developed.

The executive head of a community junior college has four major areas
of responsibility. In the smallest junior colleges, he exercises all of them
himself; in the largest, he must subdivide and delegate responsibility to
such an extent that he will have only indirect knowledge of some facets of
the instructional program. In the simplest organization, the junior college
president is directly concerned with:

1. The board of control, whether it is a locally elected board of trustees

or a statewide governing board, and the public that supports the college.

2. Fiscal affairs of his college: planning, budgeting, and supervising expenditures.
3. Buildings and grounds.
4. The entire program of instruction and student services.

As the enrollment grows and the size of the faculty increases, each of these areas of concern will grow in complexity.

*Relationships with the Governing Body and the Public.* These relationships will always be a primary concern of the community college head. In state-controlled and in university systems of colleges, these are the concern of the chief state officer; in multi-campus districts also the district superintendent will retain charge of direct relations with the board. In these organizations, the campus superintendent's outward responsibility is directed toward the central office and in some degree toward his local constituency.

In separate junior college districts, the president, as the executive officer of the elected board of trustees, will serve as the direct channel of information and policy recommendation from the college to the board. He will add assistants to help him discharge his responsibilities but not through delegation of authority. He may need to add secretaries to keep board minutes and assist with preparing for board meetings and a public relations officer, possibly an instructor, to prepare press releases and to assist with the interpretation of the community junior college to the people. He will wish to secure the aid of his administrative staff and faculty in developing policies by means of executive councils or faculty committees which can be either permanent or appointed for specific problems. He will encourage all members of the faculty to consider themselves as interpreters of the college to the community; he may request subordinate officers to attend board meetings as resource persons and observers. In the final analysis, however, the president himself represents the community junior college to the board and to the public.

*The Financial Operation.* This operation of the community junior college is the responsibility which the wise administrator will delegate at the earliest possible moment as his college grows. The detailed and time-consuming work required in gathering data for budgets and in accounting for receipts and disbursements would interfere with other necessary work of the president. He will need to keep constantly informed of the state of finances of the college; he will devote considerable attention to the development and presentation of the budget as an instrument of educational policy; and he cannot abdicate his ultimate responsibility to see that the financial affairs of the college are capably and honestly managed. Nevertheless, the day-to-day accounting for income from tax sources, from tuition fees, from the several enterprises of the college or of the student body and their disbursement according to law and the policies of the board will be the responsibility of a comptroller or bursar, who will prepare periodic reports on all financial matters for the information of the president. His subordinates will include accountants and managers of such businesses as the bookstore or cafeteria.

*The Physical Aspects.* A third area of the administrative responsibility of the president of the community junior college is the physical aspects which will be delegated to a business manager. He will be responsible for preliminary analysis of new site needs and building requirements, for the maintenance of existing buildings and equipment, for the procurement of supplies and equipment needed in the instructional program, and for the transportation of students and faculty, if any is provided. The business manager, in turn, may be aided according to the needs of the college by a superintendent of buildings and grounds, a purchasing agent, or a transportation superintendent.

*The Educational Responsibility.* This responsibility of the president is the most important and complex and it requires the most extensive delegation of authority. Two major aspects are student personnel and instruction. A sizable community junior college might well employ a Dean of the College to bear most of the delegated responsibility for the educational program. He would be assisted by a Dean of Student Personnel, who would plan and supervise guidance services, student activities, student government, health services, registration, and records, with such assistance as those tasks required. The Dean of Instruction would participate in recruitment of faculty and care for the development of the curriculum, the preparation of the catalog and the schedule of classes, and the supervision of instruction. The division chairmen, the instructors, and the librarian would be directly responsible to the Dean of Instruction. This task of instruction may be further subdivided according to the functions of education for transfer, occupational education, and education of adults. In general, the educational program should be treated as a unit as far as possible, with unified planning and coordination. Too great a segregation of adult from occupational education and of occupational from general education, either in organization or in physical site, works against both quality and availability of educational opportunity.

The foregoing discussion of administrative organization might be expressed in the form of a chart. Samples of such charts may be found in the board rules or faculty handbook of almost every community college. Since every community junior college is the unique resultant of its own history, site, personnel, finances, and philosophy, no general chart is presented here. In each institution, the titles and responsibilities of the administrative staff will vary, but the four areas of responsibility must be cared for in every one.

## FOOTNOTES

1.  *School Board-Superintendent Relationships.* The Thirty-fourth Yearbook, Washington, D.C.: American Association of School Administrators, 1956, p. 27.
2.  Cosand, Joseph, and John E. Tirrell. "Flying a College on the Computer," *Junior College Journal,* **35** (September, 1964), p. 5-8.
3.  *Where We Are.* President's Annual Report, Cuyahoga Community College 1968-69. Cleveland, Ohio: The College (2123 E. 9th St.), 1970.

## BIBLIOGRAPHY

Atwell, Charles A. and J. Foster Watkins. "New Directions for Administration," *Junior College Journal,* **41** (February, 1971) pp. 17-19.

Bogue, Jesse P. *The Community College.* New York: McGraw-Hill Book Co., 1950, Chapter 11.

Cohen, Arthur M. *Dateline '79: Heretical Concepts for the Community College.* Beverly Hills, California: Glencoe Press, 1969.

Cohen, Arthur M. and John E. Roueche. *Institutional Administrator or Educational Leader: The Junior College President.* Washington, D.C.: American Association of Junior Colleges, 1969.

Colvert, C. C. "A Study of Official External Influences on the Curriculums of Public Junior Colleges," *Junior College Journal,* **31** (December, 1960) pp. 210-213.

Cosand, Joseph. "Flying a College on the Computer," *Junior College Journal,* **35** (September, 1964) pp. 5-8.

Gross, Neal. *Who Runs Our Schools?* New York: John Wiley and Sons, 1958.

*Institutional Research in the Junior College.* Occasional Report No. 3, Junior College Leadership Program. Los Angeles: University of California, 1962.

Johnson, B. Lamar (ed.). *The Junior College Board of Trustees.* Occasional Report No. 16, Junior College Leadership Program. Los Angeles: University of California, 1971.

Johnson, B. Lamar (ed.). *The Junior College President*. Occasional Report No. 13, Junior College Leadership Program. Los Angeles: University of California, 1969.

Kintzer, Frederick C. *Board Policy Manuals in California Junior Colleges*. Occasional Report No. 2, Junior College Leadership Program. Los Angeles: University of California, 1962.

————. *Faculty Handbooks in California Public Junior Colleges*. Occasional Report No. 1, Junior College Leadership Program. Los Angeles: University of California, 1961.

————. *President's Reports in American Junior Colleges*. Occasional Report No. 4, Junior College Leadership Program. Los Angeles: University of California, 1963.

Rice, A. K. *The Modern University: A Model Organization*. London: Tavistock Publications, 1970.

Shannon, William George. *The Community College President: A Study of the Role of President of the Public Community Junior College*. (Unpublished doctoral dissertation). New York: Columbia University Teachers' College, 1962.

*Statement on Student-Faculty-Administrative Relationships*. Washington, D.C.: National Association of State Universities and Land-Grant Colleges, November, 1969.

Thompson, James. *Administrative Theory in Education*. New York: Macmillan Company, 1967.

# 10

# Instructors for Community Junior Colleges

The crucial role of the teaching faculty is implicit in all that has been said about the nature and the mission of the community junior college. Unless qualified and effective classroom instructors are available in sufficient numbers, the purposes of the institution cannot be achieved. Chapter 10 presents estimates of the numerical requirements for teachers in community colleges. Qualities of present junior college faculties are discussed, followed by sections on preparation and in-service training of teachers, working conditions, and the extent of faculty participation in community college governance.

## A. The Need for Instructors

Studies of the projected need for community college instructors during the seventies may be summarized in a few brief statements. More teachers will be needed, because higher percentages of increasing numbers of high-school graduates will attend community colleges. The increase in numbers of teachers will not affect all instructional fields equally, however; the annual production of master's degrees in the liberal arts seems likely to exceed the effective demand for their services. The need for occupational teachers seems to be both growing in numbers and changing in emphasis. There is likely to be continuing shortage of well-qualified teachers for community college occupational courses.

In total number, high school graduates will increase during the 1969 to 1979 decade from 2.84 million to 3.77 million—an increase of one-third. In addition, it is very likely that the trend for higher average levels of education will continue, so that the total number of entering community college students will increase by much more than one-third. In response to this growth in enrollments, the total number of instructors is expected to rise during the same decade from 86,000 to 146,000, or 70%. The net

**TABLE I**
**Numbers of High School Graduates and Total Professional Staff Positions in Publicly Controlled Two-Year Institutions of Higher Education, Selected Years 1958-59 to 1978-79[a]**

| Years | Total High School Graduates | Total Professional Staff | Total Instructional Staff | Other Professional Staff |
|---|---|---|---|---|
| 1958-59 | 1,639,000 | 28,000 | 25,000 | 3,000 |
| 1963-64 | 2,290,000 | 41,462 | 37,365 | 4,097 |
| 1968-69 | 2,839,000 | 96,000 | 86,000 | 9,000 |
| 1973-74 (est.) | 3,408,000 | 127,000 | 115,000 | 12,000 |
| 1978-79 (est.) | 3,773,000 | 162,000 | 146,000 | 16,000 |

[a]Source: Simon, Kenneth A., and Marie G. Fullam, Projections of Educational Statistics to 1978-79. Washington, D.C.: U.S. Government Printing Office, 1969. Abstracted from Tables 20 and 36.

result of both of these growth curves will be that the current student-faculty ratios will remain at about the 1968 level of 20:1.

Newly emerging emphases may alter the makeup of instructional staff. The nature of occupational education is changing from craftsmanship to technology and from instruction in tools and artisanship to instruction in instruments and techniques. Employment opportunities for graduates are shifting from simple clerical skills to computer operation and maintenance and from manufacturing and repair skills to personal services. Masters of Arts in English, social sciences, and behavioral sciences are already in oversupply in the community college teaching market. Increased needs are apparent for teachers of courses of educationally disadvantaged students, of paramedical workers, and of paraprofessionals in science, engineering, and teaching.

The statistics permit certain deductions about the nature of the employment market. In the fields of oversupply, college employers will become more demanding and more selective. They will require the new instructor to have education beyond the master's degree, and will give preference to candidates who have had specific graduate preparation for effective community college teaching. It is also possible that student-teacher ratios in liberal arts courses may be reduced, with a consequent improvement in the opportunity for disadvantaged students to learn. In the shortage fields, it will continue to be necessary to recruit instructors directly from nonteaching employment. The colleges will need to provide more sophisticated opportunities for in-service preparation and more effective supervision and assistance to teachers in these fields. In the end, community colleges may realize more fully their goal of effective teaching.

At any rate, the task of recruiting fully competent instructors for all subjects is formidable. Substantial increases in faculty salaries will help to retain present instructors and to attract additional ones. Four further steps are necessary: strenuous recruitment activities for fully qualified instructors, improved preparation of would-be teachers in both pre-service and in-service programs, more efficient utilization of faculty talent through the provision of additional paraprofessional help, and the continued improvement of the social climate for the academic life. Certainly the need is sufficiently acute, and the task is sufficiently important to justify aggressive and vigorous campaigns to interest able and idealistic persons in preparing themselves for teaching in community colleges. It is unlikely that any advance in the technology of communication will relieve the need substantially by providing an adequate substitute for the personal influence of fine teachers on comparatively limited numbers of students.

# B. Qualifications of Community College Instructors

What are the qualities of community college instructors that can help to define the kind of person to whom efforts at recruitment should be directed? Although present practice does not always indicate an adequate standard, a description of employed instructors presents a helpful point of departure for a discussion of training and recruitment programs. Data are available regarding the extent of academic preparation of community college faculty members, as well as about some aspects of their attitudes and previous experience.

*Degrees.*     One of the standard questions in any evaluation of quality of faculties deals with the academic degrees attained. In light of the purposes of the community college, advanced degrees are preparation for only part of the total task of teaching there, but they are an important index of preparation. In addition to its applicability as occupational training and experience for the instructor in academic subjects, the degree must be recognized also as a desirable attainment for the teacher of skill subjects. It can be an element in his development as a teaching personality. In the same way, the community college instructor in philosophy, languages, social sciences, or any liberal subject can profit from working experience outside the schools; any evaluated experience can contribute to teaching effectiveness.

Studies of faculty education have been summarized in several sources. Kelly and Connolly list the distribution of degrees as reported in 11 studies since 1918.[1] On the basis of the studies they report for the 1960's, it can be estimated that about 9% of community college teachers have attained the doctorate; 75%, the master's degree; and about 16%, less than a master's degree.

Certain comments seem appropriate about the distribution of the several degrees. There will be a variation in academic attainment between instructors in the several disciplines; social science and natural science faculty will have somewhat greater proportions of doctorates than those in business, while trade experience is likely to be valued more highly than bachelors' degrees for teachers in industrial fields. In all fields, teachers with less than the doctorate are working toward the next higher degree. The smaller proportion of doctorates held by community college teachers than by college and university professors is appropriate, because their instruction is limited to lower-division courses. The comparisons of community college faculty training with that of instructors in advanced institutions shows a similar proportion of degrees for both groups. Whether increasing annual numbers of master's degree graduates will enable the community colleges to improve their standing in proportions of advanced degrees depends in part on the efforts of administrators to interpret the need and to encourage able graduate students to prepare for teaching.

*Previous Experience.*    The shift in emphasis of the community college from "post-secondary" to higher education is nowhere more clearly indicated than in the changes in source of new instructors. Until quite recently, the largest single source of new instructors was the ranks of secondary school teachers. Recently, however, studies such as those of Phair in California and Kelly in New York[2] emphasize that graduate schools and business and industry are important sources of new faculty. An encouraging trend is that more and more students are preparing for teaching in community colleges, many of them after graduating from such colleges themselves. College administrators are recruiting from programs specifically designed for this preparation, and more than 100 universities offer programs that include seminars about the community college and supervised teaching internships.

*Knowledge about the Community College.*    The majority of community college teachers are still recruited from other positions to the colleges, with comparatively little opportunity to study in advance its distinctive purposes and problems. They have had little opportunity to develop comprehensive and appropriate personal philosophy about it. They express a diffuse acceptance of the concept of the two-year college as a part of American post-secondary education but find it difficult to accept the implications of the open-door admission policy. Those who come directly from the university without specific consideration of community colleges are likely to see the institution only as a proving ground for later transfer; the terms "not college material" or "uneducable" are often a part of their vocabularies. Verbal agreement is given to the idea of technical and semiprofessional education; but the concept that dropouts and disadvantaged persons deserve a chance at and can succeed in higher education, if the teaching is effective, is more readily espoused by administrators than by the teachers who have to meet the students without adequate preparation for the problems they pose.

# C. Preparation for Community College Instructors

Certain realistic assumptions should form the basis for program planning for the preparation of community college instructors. One of these assumptions is that the prospective teacher is not—cannot be—fully prepared at the time he obtains his first position. Employers should be prepared to help the beginning teacher continue to learn in his subject field. For one thing, the demands of his teaching will force him to achieve greater breadth and depth over the years; for several years he should become annually a better teacher and a more mature personality. Personnel practices in junior colleges should be established in the light of this assumption to make certain that growth does continue after employment. Helpful supervision, well-planned programs of in-service training during the college year, and salary schedule provisions that encourage teachers to use their summers to improve their instructional competence can all combine to keep the faculty moving toward ideal competence.

A second assumption that should influence teacher training programs is that the junior college teacher may frequently be asked to teach in two or more subject fields. For this reason every prospective junior college teacher should, if possible, include strong preparation in a second field as part of his program. The student who decides to aim for junior college teaching during his undergraduate days will have little difficulty in achieving this breadth. The credential candidate who has already earned a specialized master's degree may find it more difficult to include such a second subject in his preparation. Colleges and universities, in setting up curriculums that are intended to prepare junior college teachers, must include provision for this breadth as a part of their basic plans.

A third assumption that should influence patterns of preparation is that every community college teacher will have some responsibility at some point in his career for the education of students who are unprepared, culturally different, older, unmotivated, or in need of guidance. Planned programs in universities should make explicit provision for discussion of the contribution that education might make to the solution of social problems, for consideration of techniques to achieve this contribution, and for extended exposure of every teaching candidate, no matter what his subject, to aspiring students from the cultures of poverty. Until this is a routine part of preparation, the gap between community educational needs and professorial self-image will nullify attempts to achieve the ideal of community college effectiveness.

*Curriculum Proposal.*    In the light of these considerations, it seems that the curriculum for training community college teachers should be planned to begin, if possible, with the junior year of undergraduate study. It should envisage steady progress by the student during not more than four years toward completion of the following educational elements:

1. A master's degree in a subject field.

2. A teaching minor, amounting approximately to one-fifth of the student's total college credits, in a field related to the master's degree major field.

3. Courses in higher education to equal about one semester's total, including

   a. Educational psychology—junior college student characteristics, principles of learning, guidance, evaluation, and counseling.
   b. A course in history, purposes, status, and problems of the community college.
   c. Methods and techniques of teaching, including instructional resources, in the community college.

4. A semester's supervised full-time internship in a community college, including an assignment to tutor students in remedial courses, even outside his own discipline.

If some of the courses in higher education could be completed before the bachelor's degree, it might be possible for a student to extend his experiences in teaching. A variation of this plan will appeal to candidates who have earned the master's degree before considering junior college teaching. A specially contrived semester of study in higher education is followed by a teaching internship in a junior college, in which the full responsibilities of a teacher are undertaken, with salary, for at least one semester with supervision provided on a cooperative basis by the junior college and the teacher-education institution. The seminars that accompany the student teaching and the internship expand the material of the education courses required under the more conventional pattern.

*Occupational Instructors.*   The pattern so far presented has concentrated implicitly on preparing teachers of academic and general education subjects. With suitable adaptations, the same principles may guide the preparation of instructors in the vocational and technical subjects that are such an important part of the total program of the public junior college. Since such instructors are more likely to teach in one subject field, not so much stress need be placed on the teaching minor. Instead, a pattern of preparation such as the following might serve to attract able persons from other employment fields to teach these courses:

1. Education equivalent to the Associate in Arts degree.

2. Successful experience in the occupation to be taught, equivalent to apprenticeship and three years of journeyman experience. In some fields, apprenticeship and journeyman status are not specifically

provided, but the principle of extended and meaningful successful experience can be applied.

3. Courses in higher education equal to about one semester's total, and including the same elements as suggested for the master's degree candidate.

Such instructors should be encouraged to improve their formal education as they are able to do so, but in many fields no graduate training program exists that is as effective as employment experience in providing the technical knowledge and skills essential to teaching the junior college technical course.

*In-Service Training.*   If the training curriculum assumes that further growth in teaching competence will be required of the teacher even after he is employed, carefully planned programs of in-service training are needed. Pre-college meetings of several days' duration, both for new and returning instructors, can be addressed to aspects of the community college in American education. During the year, regular faculty meetings as well as especially appointed committees and intensive workshop sessions may be devoted to topics that concern the entire faculty or subgroups of it. Carefully planned and structured visits to outstanding programs in other community colleges can be a stimulating and useful exercise for instructors. In every case, a workable program must be developed locally, through the cooperation of instructors and administrators, to meet local needs. Its purpose is to assist members of the faculty to understand better some aspect of their work in the college and ultimately to improve the instructional program. Community junior colleges organize their adult programs on the premise that citizens at large need recurring opportunity throughout life to learn new things, both occupational and avocational. The same principle applies to their instructors.

# D. Working Conditions

A basic factor in recruitment of community college teachers is the desirability of their work in comparison with other available opportunities. Such factors as total teaching load, salary, extra class duties, sick leave, tenure, and retirement benefits—all contribute to the attractiveness of one position in relation to others for which one may be equally qualified. In several of these areas, no national data are available; in others, fairly definite information has been provided.

*Teaching Load.*   Teaching assignments in community colleges tend to approximate 15 credit hours of teaching per term; there is some variation, both from one college to another and in some colleges between subject fields, between 12 and 18 credit hours. Because of different load values assigned to laboratory or performance classes, it is likely that shop, science, fine arts, and physical education teachers will have fewer credit hours and a greater number of assigned student contact hours.

The entire topic of teaching load is becoming complicated by the introduction of newer techniques of organizing instruction. When a lecture-forum building is provided to permit efficient lecturing to large groups, supplemented by imaginative use of audio-visual materials, the instructor at least is immediately aware that three credits with 300 students make a heavier load than three credits with 30 students. The assignment of paraprofessional assistants to the teacher, perhaps to take care of students who do most of their learning in a learning laboratory, introduces an additional complication into the traditional pattern of "15 hours in class, 15 in preparation, and 15 in office hours and committee meetings." The instructor who uses many hours during one semester in developing a series of excellent video tapes for his basic course will deserve some consideration of that effort not only during the developmental semester, but also in semesters when the mediated course is being presented and revised. The instructor who finds that much more learning results when he sees the class together only once a week, but spends hours of individual conferences with the students, is likely to resent the suspicion of his colleagues that he is not working simply because he is not lecturing the full 15 hours each week. No easy solutions to equitable assignment of instructors under these conditions have been found.

*Salaries.*    Community colleges universally assign salaries according to a salary schedule adopted by the governing board. Salary placement is ordinarily based on extent of preparation for teaching, with higher salaries assigned to advanced degrees or additional credit hours beyond a degree. Years of experience in teaching or in work that improves the candidate's capacity for the teaching position are also credited. Minimum salaries for the least acceptable preparation are stated as well as maximums attainable by the teacher with a doctoral degree and a given number of years' experience. Under terms of the salary schedule, there is little opportunity for a teacher to bargain individually for a better salary on the basis of his own special talents.

In general, community college teaching salaries have kept pace over the past two decades with inflation but have not increased markedly in relation to the salaries for other workers. A *Research Report* of the National Education Association[3] indicates that for the year 1969-70 median scheduled salaries in public institutions ranged from $7075 for beginning instructors with bachelor degrees to $9674 for beginning instructors with the doctorate. In each of the classes, minimum salaries varied according to the location of the college, its size, and its available resources.

In the same study, the mean number of annual increments in salary between the minimum and maximum for each level of preparation ranged from 9 to 13. The amounts of annual increment varied, but the medians in public institutions were about $360 per year. An application of these statistics may clarify the salary picture. Assume a beginning teacher with a bachelor's degree is hired at a college in Washington for $7300 and does not complete any additional study. After 14 years of successful teaching at that college, he would earn $11,500. At the same college, if that instructor studied in summer and at night to earn a doctor's degree, his salary after 14 years would be $14,300 annually.

The colleges studied in the National Education Association *Research Report* had nearly all increased their scheduled amounts over 1968-69; the median increase was approximately 10% for that period. The prospective teacher should be aware that public colleges attempt to remain competitive in their rewards to faculty members. Almost every college has a salary schedule that is open for inspection by applicants or other interested students.

*Academic Rank.* Of the 462 public two-year institutions reporting salary information to the National Education Association study, 147 based their schedules on academic ranks similar to those assigned in universities. This figure indicates that approximately one-third of community colleges award ranks to their teachers; this number has been increasing, especially since 1960. There is evidence of considerable lack of agreement among junior college administrators and faculty members on the wisdom of imitating the ranking policies of the colleges and universities. Those in favor of a system of rank argue that it provides a symbol of prestige and permits outward recognition of meritorious service. The titles of assistant professor, associate professor, and professor give status to the teacher in his contacts with the faculty of other institutions and in submitting articles to journals for publication. Rank also recognizes the professional competence of the junior college teacher and sets him apart from the secondary school teacher. It is a source of strength when he exercises the professorial responsibility of participating in policy formation for his college.

On the other hand, other writers see the introduction of academic rank as a peril. It increases the drive toward specialization that is not appropriate in junior college teaching; it ties the aspirations and the practice of the junior college more closely to the traditional and the academic, rather than to the experimental and the community-centered aspects of its task. The mere fact of rank, it is suggested, will distract junior college faculties away from their major task of effective teaching and turn them toward the kinds of publication and research that will win promotions.

## E. Faculty Participation in Policy Formation

"As far as faculty is concerned, the salient development of the Sixties was faculty militancy." The speaker is president of a community college, and perhaps his use of the word "militancy" exaggerates the nature of the change in governance that has taken place. Community colleges have been comparatively free of the disorderly protest that has troubled so many university presidents, but surface calm should not lead to the conclusion that few changes have occurred. Partly because there is typically less bureaucratic distance between the instructor and the president and board, problem solving in the community college can be accomplished more simply and more quietly than in the university. The most visible evidence of the growing faculty involvement in policy formation is the change from loosely organized and socially oriented faculty associations to chartered elected faculty senates.

Community college senates are established in recognition of the new competence and concern of instructors and of the principle that decisions openly arrived at are likely to be more successful in operation. Three major areas of responsibility are typically assigned to senates:

1. determination of policy in curricular matters;
2. recommendation of policy and procedures in selection, retention, and promotion of all professional staff, including both colleagues and administrators; and
3. consultation in such areas as college organization, budget, building plans, and long-range development of the institution.

Several hazards inhere in the expansion of faculty influence in policy determination. One is the difficulty of respecting the fine distinction between policy formulation and administration. In the early stages of their establishment, senates often attempt too much and try to be both legislative and executive bodies. Another hazard is that of partisan control. A senate is a time-consuming body; it is easy for instructors to shrug off their responsibility to participate and so to allow other instructors with limited special objectives to control the policies of the college. A third effect of senate involvement is that policy decisions are often delayed. As a consequence, the complaint is voiced that democracy is inefficient. The charge is only partially true at most. A good decision responsibly arrived at is surely more efficient than a quick poor one. In a college community, a policy widely understood and accepted is far more effective than one announced administratively without adequate widespread consideration. The charge of inefficiency can hold only if the deliberative body adopts too many unsound policies.

An outgrowth of increasing faculty participation in governance is a rising demand for accountability for educational results. The same forces that lead instructors to demand a share in administration lead students and the community at large to seek evidence that objectives are being stated, striven for, and evaluated. If militance characterized the 1960's, it is likely that overt and formalized evaluation of faculty performance will characterize the 1970's. Faculty and the college as a whole will be held accountable for their outputs in well-prepared graduates. Explicit recognition of the attainment of results will have profound effects on all aspects of faculty recruitment, preparation, promotion, salary, and retention. It may well revolutionize practices in higher education within the decade.

## FOOTNOTES

1.   Kelly, M. Frances and John Connolly. *Orientation for Faculty in Junior Colleges*. Washington, D.C.: American Association of Junior Colleges, 1970, p. 5.
2.   Kelly and Connolly, *loc. cit.*
3.   *Faculty Salary Schedules in Community-Junior Colleges, 1969-70*. Higher Education Series Research Report 1970-R11. Washington, D.C.: National Education Association, 1970.

## BIBLIOGRAPHY

Brown, James W. and James W. Thornton, Jr. *College Teaching: A Systematic Approach* (Second Edition). New York: McGraw-Hill Book Company, 1971.
Cohen, Arthur M. and Florence B. Brawer. *Measuring Faculty Performance*. Washington, D.C.: American Association of Junior Colleges, 1969.
*The Education Professions: An Annual Report on the People Who Serve Our Schools and Colleges—1969-70*. Washington, D.C.: U.S. Government Printing Office, 1970.

Estrin, H.A. and D.M. Goode (eds.). *College and University Teaching.* Dubuque: William C. Brown Company, 1964.

*Faculty Salary Schedules in Community-Junior Colleges, 1969-70.* Higher Education Series Research Report 1970-R11. Washington, D.C.: National Education Association, 1970.

Garrison, Roger H. *Junior College Faculty: Issues and Problems.* Washington, D.C.: American Association of Junior Colleges, 1967.

*Junior College Teachers of Science, Engineering, and Technology, 1967.* (National Science Foundation) Washington, D.C.: U.S. Government Printing Office, 1969.

Kelley, Win and Leslie Wilbur. *Teaching in the Community-Junior College.* New York: Appleton-Century-Crofts, 1970.

Kelly, M. Frances and John Connolly. *Orientation for Faculty in Junior Colleges.* Washington, D.C.: American Association of Junior Colleges, 1970.

King, Francis P. *Benefit Plans in Junior Colleges.* Washington, D.C.: American Association of Junior Colleges, 1971.

Minter, W. John and Patricia O. Snyder (eds.). *Value Change and Power Conflict in Higher Education.* Berkeley: Center for Research and Development in Higher Education, 1969.

Office of Program Planning and Evaluation, Office of Education. *Education in the Seventies* (Planning Paper 68-1). Washington, D.C.: U.S. Government Printing Office, 1968.

Phair, Tom S. *A Profile of New Faculty in California Community Colleges.* Berkeley: University of California, Field Service Center, 1968.

Richardson, Richard C. "Needed: New Directions in Administration," *Junior College Journal* (March, 1970) pp. 16-22.

Simon, Kenneth A. and Marie G. Fullam. *Projections of Educational Statistics to 1978-79.* Washington, D.C.: U.S. Government Printing Office, 1969.

# 11 | The Community College Student

The student body of the community junior college is completely different in composition from any stereotype of the college student. Most students are high-school graduates, but they bring a wide range of tested aptitudes and all levels of grade attainment. Those who were school dropouts prove that school success or failure is not a wholly reliable indicator of innate aptitude. Mature students of all ages substitute the lessons of life for the classroom instruction they had missed earlier and learn along with the youth who has spent his whole life in school. Matriculants from every sociological class bring a diversity of backgrounds of preparation, experience, and ambition. Instructors are sometimes shocked to realize that their cultural and ethical values have not been validated at all in the lives of many of their students.

Because of these diversities, each college must develop a clear, unsentimental, factual understanding of its students to serve as a basis for program development. The instructors need such realistic awareness so that they may adapt their methods to the facts of student abilities and purposes. Patrons and students of the community college can profit from accurate information in attempting to square their expectations for the institution with its actual tasks. Writers on educational subjects especially need this understanding in order that their recommendations for the development of higher education may be appropriate and workable.

Chapter 11 describes some of the qualities of the student body, academic and personal, especially in comparison with the student bodies of four-year colleges. Section C deals with the unprepared student, and the final section presents some considerations about the emerging role of the student in the governance of the community college.

## A. Academic Aptitude in the Community College

Studies at individual colleges and organized sampling research uniformly agree that the average academic ability of the two-year college student is lower than that for four-year college students. The community colleges welcome students who represent all levels of tested academic aptitude and all segments of the socio-economic life of their communities. Their freshmen classes present aptitude test averages very like the averages of high-school senior classes. The range of scores, on the other hand, is different. The community college attracts more students from the middle ranges of ability, and

> "fewer from the very low- or very high-ability students. Low-ability high-school graduates do not continue their education, and high-ability graduates are more likely to enter four-year colleges. Ability differences between occupational and transfer students within community colleges are mixed, attributable primarily to sex differences. There appears to be general agreement in research that men in occupational curricula score significantly lower on tests of academic ability than men in the college-parallel program. For women, there seems to be little difference between college-parallel and occupational groups."[1]

Sample distributions of total scores on the *School and College Ability Test* (SCAT) are compared in Figures 11-1 and 11-2 with the distributions of national "norm" or standardizing groups of freshmen. The norm sample includes freshmen from four-year colleges and junior colleges; by definition, 10% of their scores fell within each decile. In the two figures, junior college distributions may be compared visually with the national distribution. It is readily apparent that both junior colleges have students at the top level of ability, as measured by SCAT scores; that the median scores for both junior colleges are lower than the medians for the norm group; and that the two junior colleges serve populations of differing aptitude. If an assumption were made that 70% of all college freshmen (as represented in the norm group) have sufficient "college aptitude" to do well in achieving baccalaureate degrees, then as many as 63% of the students from the junior college in Figure 11-1, and 43% of those in Figure 11-2, have that degree of tested aptitude.

The SCAT data from the college in Figure 11-2 were reported separately for transfer students and terminal students. Even though the two categories are difficult to define, with a great deal of student shifting

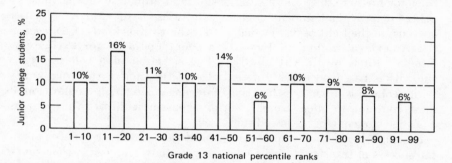

**FIGURE 11-1.** **SCAT total test scores, 4398 junior college students, compared to national percentile ranks (grade 13). If the junior college student body included abilities identical with the national group of college freshmen used for test standardization, 10% of the junior college group would score in each decile group, or in each bar of the graph. The variation above or below 10% in each decile shows how this junior college population differs from the national group of college freshmen.**

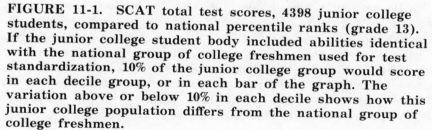

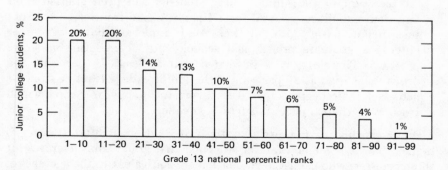

**FIGURE 11-2.** **SCAT total test scores, 827 junior college students, compared to national percentile ranks.**

from one to the other, they did represent the expressed intentions of these students at the time of registration. The students were very evenly divided between the two categories. Of the terminal students, 36% scored above the thirtieth percentile and might be assumed to have sufficient aptitude for senior college success. The transfer group, as might be expected, scored higher on SCAT: 56% of them scored above the thirtieth percentile score of the norm group.

It is apparent that although average test scores of junior college freshmen are lower than average scores of liberal arts college freshmen, the range of scores in both kinds of colleges is equivalent. Recommendations for further study and predictions of later academic success must be made for individual students, not for categories of students. It is further obvious, in the light of test evidence, that the various kinds of colleges in the American system of diversity are not operated for exclusively different kinds of student abilities. The selection of a college by its students is based on other differential qualities, and if the community junior college is to serve its function of democratizing higher education, it must continue to offer strong lower-division curriculums to prepare its qualified students for advanced study.

Research studies and reports from individual two-year colleges about the success of transfer students who go on to four-year institutions agree that the community college student does succeed in later study, although some qualifications must be attached to that statement. Findings of a careful and fully representative 1965 study of the transfer problem replicate those of other similar reports.[2] The basic question of the study was "What is the probability that a student who begins his baccalaureate degree program in a two-year college will complete it if he transfers to a four-year institution?" The answer, three calendar years after the date of transfer, indicated that by that time

> "62 per cent of the junior college students had been granted their baccalaureate degrees . . . At least 4 per cent had transferred to other institutions which granted them their undergraduate degrees or entered a graduate professional school before completing a degree program. Therefore, it is estimated that at least 75 per cent and probably as high as 80 per cent of the junior college transfer students achieved their degree objectives during the four-year period which began with their transfer to a four-year college."

Other conclusions indicate that the rate of dropout after transfer is higher than it is for nontransfer students; that grade point averages for those transfers who persist to graduation are equivalent to the averages of "native" students at graduation; and that attendance at community colleges has made the bachelor's degree possible for many students who would otherwise have been unable to attend college at all. The success of the transfer student is only a partial measure of the success of all students, but it is one important measure. Data on the occupational aptitudes and successes of nontransfer students would be equally valuable but have not been studied with the same care as transfer performance.

## B. Other Qualities of the Student Body

"To develop a college for the diversified student body that presents itself at the open door of the community college is a formidable task. The array of talents and goals is great. There is the average student who is not quite sure he can make it at the university; there is the bright one who can't afford to leave home and a job to go away to college; there is the poor student who lacks even the basic learning skills but who recognizes the importance of preparing for a career; and there is the student from a minority group who sees the community college as a bridge to equal opportunities. There is the housewife who seeks cultural enrichment and the technologically obsolete family man who wants job retraining. It is no wonder that community colleges have added the word 'comprehensive' to their titles."[3]

In almost any quality that can be measured, the community college student body will exhibit a greater range than other parts of the system of higher education. In age, approximately half of full-time students are under 20 years of age; about 40% are over 30; and some indeed are over 70. Part-time students, who often outnumber full-time students in community colleges, have a higher average age, since many of them are full-time workers, housewives, or retired persons.

The socio-economic background of the community college student is on the average lower than that of the university student. Fewer of them can claim fathers with any college education; their family income is lower; and their fathers are less likely to be in professional or managerial occupations. Their financial need is indicated by the fact that more than half of the full-time students are working for some or all of their college expenses; as many as one-fourth of the students in metropolitan areas report that they work full time while carrying a full-time schedule of classes. Clark's study of the student body of San Jose City College indicated that the socio-economic (i.e., occupational) distribution of the fathers of full-time students was almost an exact replica of the distribution of the city as a whole—that the College was in fact a "people's college," attaining the ideal of making college available to the children of all the people.[4]

Dropout and withdrawal of students are continuing problems of nearly all community colleges. The magnitude of the problem may be illustrated by national figures taken from recent issues of the *Junior College Directory*.[5]

|  | Full-time freshmen |  | Full-time sophomores | % |
|---|---|---|---|---|
| Fall 1966 | 528,336 | Fall 1967 | 255,679 | 48.3 |
| Fall 1967 | 584,122 | Fall 1968 | 293,663 | 53.8 |
| Fall 1968 | 659,583 | Fall 1969 | 336,500 | 51.0 |

The fact that half of the entering freshmen do not continue into their second year of attendance does not indicate that all of them failed to attain their objective. Some were in one-year programs, others desired only to prepare for a job, and others transferred to other colleges after one or two semesters. Still others will plan to return to college after a period of work and saving. These extenuations still leave room for concern about the 10% who drop out between registration and Christmas vacation. Few studies are available to suggest the real reasons for their disappearance, but it has been observed that a greater proportion of dropouts comes from the ranks of older students and first-semester students and that a high proportion of them leave for good reasons—health, family problems, financial need, permanent jobs, or family moving away. The growing emphasis on accountability in education will lead to more careful studies of pre-admission counseling and of the degree of college failure indicated by high rates of withdrawal.

## C. The Unprepared Student

A phenomenon of growing importance in community colleges is the enrollment of large numbers of students who are not yet prepared to succeed in academic pursuits. Failure to recognize and to accept this fact is a major stumbling block to efforts to attain the open-door purposes of the institution. All elements of the college hierarchy share this lack of insight, but faculty indifference to student realities has the most disastrous effects on the educational program. No matter how clearly the college administrator or the professor of higher education may explain the needs of students, instruction is in the hands of the individual instructor. If he denies the educability of any class of students or scorns responsibility for meeting student needs, the entire structure fails in its function. Instructors must be helped to gain an understanding and an affective commitment to these groups. There are at least two dimensions to the problem they pose: the recognition of the reasons for their lack of preparation, and the adaptation of curriculum and institutional procedures to the educational needs they present.

The problem of the unprepared student has been clouded by separate problems of access to education by ethnic minorities. There is a need for Chicano studies and Black studies programs, and some steps are being taken in community colleges to meet that need. Success of ethnic programs is hampered by the fact that some of the unprepared students are Afro-American or Mexican-American—but the categories are not coterminous. The unprepared student is one of any race whose previous education has seemed to him to be degrading, defeating, and pointless, and who is nonetheless convinced that access to economic competence requires him to achieve further education. From whatever ethnic group he comes, his goal is economic equality. He does not seek, he actively rejects, the middle-class concepts and values that the schools have so long exemplified. In the past, he accepted the evaluations of the schools and went away. More recently, he demands that the schools reexamine their practices and provide him meaningful access to economic rewards. It is ironic that he still accepts the schools as the avenue by which his "deprivation" can be overcome. His acceptance is a very special challenge to the community colleges to develop imaginative and innovative responses.

Many of the terms that have been used in discussions of this problem seem to these students to indicate a complete misunderstanding of it. The deprivation is not a cultural deprivation—there are fully developed and meaningful Brown and Black cultures in America that contribute to the strength, diversity, and richness of American life. Similarly, "disadvantaged" and "minority" seem to be condescending terms that overlook the fact that most of us are members of minorities. In a real sense, the deprivation of the unprepared student has been not cultural but material. He asks us to help him escape from poverty, not from his ancestral heritage. What he lacks most is quite simply money and the skills by which to acquire it legally.

Morgan categorizes part of this group of students as *The Ghetto College Student*. He summarizes the problem as follows:

1. Traditional teaching methods are not effective.
2. The ghetto college students expect equal treatment from institutions and from teachers.
3. They suspect that colleges do not accept them willingly, disparage their culture, and do not know how to become relevant to their needs.
4. They see poverty as the result of an impersonal, uncaring, elitist economic system.[6]

In response to this need, colleges too often establish "remedial" programs in writing, reading, speech, and arithmetic, in many ways repeating the same insensitivities that were so defeating for the students in their earlier schooling. Overcoming their lack of preparation for college study requires several other preliminary steps. First must come the establishment of a relationship of mutual respect and trust between instructor and students. This effort must be initiated by the instructor, and its outcome is uncertain. Yet without a climate of trust, the instructor who adopts a posture of impersonal and defensive reserve and dignity will doom his efforts and the students' progress.

A second step is to develop in the student a sense of personal worth and confidence. In the words of James McHolland, "We are in the self-esteem business." The building of self-esteem is a slow and delicate process that requires a small student-teacher ratio and a willingness on the part of the teacher to become personally involved. Not all good teachers can meet these criteria, and those who cannot should not be used for the beginning steps of the reeducation process. Only after the student becomes convinced that the curriculum will contribute to his personal goals and that he can succeed in mastering it may he be exposed to teachers whose major concern is their subject.

## D. Student Roles in Governance

The restlessness that has characterized student bodies at colleges and universities has not completely bypassed the community college, even though the protests at these colleges have been relatively peaceful. In a 1969-70 study of the subject, Gaddy found that 231 colleges, or 38% of his respondent group of 613 colleges, had experienced a total of 1586 "organized protests." Most of the protests were concerned with student-administration conflicts rather than with major issues of national or international policy, a sign that effective communication has been lacking between community college officials and their student bodies, but a sign as well that students do really care about the operation and the accomplishments of their college."Undoubtedly, some of these protests . . . could have been prevented had administrators been more accessible to the students and . . . more willing to participate in a 'meaningful dialogue.' "[7]

The techniques for communication are difficult to establish, perhaps more difficult in the community college than on residential campuses. As suggested earlier in this chapter, community college students are more likely than four-year college students to live at home and commute to school, to have demanding jobs, and to form most of their associations away from campus. Most of them remain at the college for less than the full two years. In addition, the history of "student government" at many community colleges leads the students to believe that it is meaningless, without real responsibility, and closed to all but a small group of activity-minded status seekers. It is viewed as a game for the elite, who are unconcerned about any real educational or personal issues of the entire student body.

Students with these attitudes, on becoming aware of conditions that need change, seek other avenues than student government to make their views known. They ask for more meaningful involvement in the initial discussions of policies, in line with the democratic principle that those affected by policy should have a voice in its determination. They seek actualization of the concept of "college community." Recent practice has seemed to emphasize the divergent interests of students, faculty, administration, and trustees. Each group forms its own caucus and strives for control at the expense of the others; in this contest, the most numerous segment, the students, have traditionally lost out in the "zero-gain" struggle. Confrontation has seemed their only effective technique for gaining entry into the system.

In an academic community, gain by one segment might be a gain for the entire community, rather than a gain at the expense of the other segments. This realization has led to suggestions for various systems of integrating students and faculty into the policy-making process at its beginning, not simply through dissent or approval after the decision has already been announced. One plan would have student representation on boards of trustees; another would assign specific areas of policy responsibility to trustees, to faculty, and to the students. Each of these plans is a partial solution to the need for active participation, but each tends to perpetuate the conflict of special interests. A pattern of fully cooperative deliberation would seem to require a unicameral college deliberative body.

McGrath suggests such a body when he writes:

> "A governmental structure which assembles all the constituent parties in some organization like a senate, including the board, the administrators, the faculty, and the students in policy discussion *ab initio* is better than one which provides for the reconciliation of opposing views after the constituent groups have taken independent action."[8]

Both faculty and trustees will find many arguments against meaningful involvement of students in academic governance—immaturity, transiency, lack of professional sophistication, lack of time for involvement, selfish interests, and greater numbers. It would be more appropriate for them to seek ways to make student (and faculty) participation more creative and effective.

As a preliminary proposal, perhaps a college senate could be made up of representatives of each constituency. It should be comparatively small to allow for communication and effective action. In most community colleges, a group including five students, five instructors, three administrators, and two trustees ought to be large enough for representation and small enough for efficiency. If community spirit allowed each member of the senate to see himself as working cooperatively for the good of the college rather than competitively for selfish interests, the senate could become a truly creative instrument for college development.

In the initial stages, each group of members would report back to its own constituency, both to inform them and to receive ideas and direction. The short terms of the student members would be a handicap to them but still far more satisfactory than no representation at all. Certainly students have a more direct and immediate stake in the quality of their education than the other segments of the community and are more currently aware of the quality of teaching. The task of the senate would need to be clearly defined as policy deliberation; executive decisions and administration would be reserved as at present to the board of trustees.

An example of operation will illustrate the proposed process. From any source a proposal comes to the college senate asserting the need for a gymnasium. This senate hears presentations of preliminary descriptions of its uses, its service to the entire community, its cost, and its relative importance in relation to other needs. During the process of these inputs, each senator consults with his own constituency and reports back to the senate the attitudes and information he has discerned. Eventually, the senate arrives at a resolution in favor of a gymnasium of specified functions and capacity, estimated cost, and a timetable for its construction. It then remains for the board of trustees to accept or reject the plan, to determine methods of funding, to employ architects, and to let contracts. The authority of the administration and board of trustees is not limited by senate participation in defining policy, but their effectiveness and responsiveness to their community is markedly enhanced. It is likely as well that the planned gymnasium will be a better and more useful building because of the involvement of the entire college community in the decision to build it. Is it also reasonable to expect that students, after participating in responsible decision making in college, will be more active participants in the political life of their communities?

## FOOTNOTES

1.  Cross, K. Patricia, "Occupationally Oriented Students," *ERIC Junior College Research Review*, **5**, Number 3 (November, 1970).
2.  Knoell, Dorothy M. and Leland L. Medsker. *From Junior to Senior College: A National Study of the Transfer Student.* Washington, D.C.: American Council on Education, 1965, p. 25.
3.  Cross, K. Patricia. "The Quiet Revolution," *The Research Reporter,* Vol. IV, Number 3. Berkeley: The Center for Research and Development in Higher Education, University of California, 1969.
4.  Clark, Burton R. *The Open Door College.* New York: McGraw-Hill Book Company, 1960, pp. 55-58.
5.  Data taken from totals in "Table II, Summary by States—All Junior Colleges," *Junior College Directory* for 1969, 1970, and 1971. Washington, D.C.: American Association of Junior Colleges, annually.
6.  Morgan, Gordon D. *The Ghetto College Student.* (Monograph Three) Iowa City, Iowa: The American College Testing Program, 1970, pp. 55-56.
7.  Gaddy, Dale. *The Scope of Organized Student Protest in Junior Colleges.* Washington, D.C.: American Association of Junior Colleges, 1970, p. 15.
8.  McGrath, Earl J. *Should Students Share the Power?* Philadelphia: Temple University Press, 1970, p. 105.

## BIBLIOGRAPHY

Cross, K. Patricia. *The Junior College Student: A Research Description.* Princeton, New Jersey: Educational Testing Service, 1968.

Dawson, Helaine. *On the Outskirts of Hope.* New York: McGraw-Hill Book Company, 1969.

Deegan, William L., Karl O. Drexel, John T. Collins, and Dorothy L. Kearney. "Student Participation in Governance," *Junior College Journal,* (November, 1970) pp. 15-22.

Fantini, Mario D., and Gerald Weinstein. *The Disadvantaged: Challenge to Education.* New York: Harper and Row, 1968.

Gaddy, Dale. *The Scope of Organized Student Protest in Junior Colleges.* Washington, D.C.: American Association of Junior Colleges, 1970.

Keeton, Morris, *et al. Shared Authority on Campus.* Washington, D.C.: American Association for Higher Education, 1971.

Knoell, Dorothy M., and Leland L. Medsker. *From Junior to Senior College: A National Study of the Transfer Student.* Washington, D.C.: American Council on Education, 1965.

Koos, Leonard V. *The Community College Student.* Gainesville: University of Florida Press, 1971.

Lombardi, John. *Student Activism in Junior Colleges.* Washington, D.C.: American Association of Junior Colleges, 1969.

McGrath, Earl J. *Should Students Share the Power?* Philadelphia: Temple University Press, 1970.

Moore, William, Jr. *Against the Odds.* San Francisco: Jossey-Bass Inc., Publishers, 1970.

Pentony, DeVere, Robert Smith and Richard Axen. *Unfinished Rebellions.* San Francisco: Jossey-Bass, Inc., 1971.

Trent, James W., and Leland L. Medsker. *Beyond High School.* San Francisco: Jossey-Bass, Inc., Publishers, 1968.

# III

---

# THE COMMUNITY
# JUNIOR
# COLLEGE
# IN OPERATION

# 12 | Developing the Curriculum

In the broadest sense of the term, the curriculum consists of all of the planned educational experiences provided by an educational institution. Since the clientele of the community colleges includes persons with all sorts of needs for education, curriculum development must be a continuous concern. As the needs for schooling change with social, technological, demographic, and economic trends, some courses of study become obsolete and others emerge. The charge of curricular irrelevance by students from minority groups has led to ethnic studies programs, and the increasing awareness of pollution has begotten ecological studies. Social security legislation combines with earlier retirement and better health care for the aging to emphasize the avocational values of education. The technological displacement of workers brings about programs for occupational reeducation. In the face of all of these pressures, reliance primarily on traditional determinants of the liberal arts curriculum would cause a community college to ignore some of the most vital and socially useful aspects of its responsibility.

159

Two broad aspects of curriculum development in the community junior college merit attention before discussion of the more specific elements of offerings. One is the definition of the breadth of the curriculum. Through what techniques can decisions be reached on the total program to be offered? The second aspect is the depth and quality of the program. After an adequate scope has been planned on the basis of community studies and thorough discussion, instructional changes must be effectuated in the classrooms by the instructors. The first aspect, it might be said, looks to external influences on the scope of the curriculum, whereas the second is concerned with procedures within the college that assure that purposes are achieved. Chapter 12 then, considers techniques of curriculum development within each of these two categories.

## A. Determining the Scope of the Curriculum

*College-Parallel Courses.*    Planning the college-parallel offerings of the community junior college is not a simple task. A competent faculty member should be assigned the responsibility and the time to keep informed of changes in university requirements. A fundamental principle of junior college transfer curriculums is that when the student decides to transfer to a specific four-year institution, he accepts almost his entire junior college course as defined by the accepting institution. The college must enable the student to know and to fulfill the requirements of the transfer college, so that he may be accepted there as a student in advanced standing and proceed to his objective without loss of time. The rigidity of transfer requirements is beginning to give way to a certification that the transfer student is prepared to succeed in upper-division study, but the newer freedom is by no means universal. Moreover, each major field in university study has certain prerequisite courses that must be completed in the lower division; careful planning of transfer student programs will continue to be necessary in the community college.

Several factors complicate the planning for individual students. Since colleges and universities and the schools and departments which they include are constantly studying and changing their own requirements, much effort is required to keep the junior colleges fully informed. But no community junior college sends transfer students to only one university—it is not at all uncommon for graduates of a junior college to be enrolled at as many as 30 or even 50 upper-division institutions in a given year. Each of these institutions, of course, has a pattern of lower-division requirements that differs slightly from all the others. The junior college student himself may further complicate the picture. Some lack the prerequisite courses from high school and must complete them before their lower-division work proceeds; some will drop a single difficult course from a carefully planned freshman program, thus causing a delay in the completion of their transfer requirements; and others will change their vocational objective or their choice of an upper-division college with an accompanying loss of time.

It is apparent that the junior college cannot duplicate every one of the lower-division offerings of even one large university, let alone of 40 or 50. The first step in establishing the transferable offerings is to analyze the requirements, for each major field of study, of each of the senior colleges to which a sizable number of students will be likely to transfer. A chart showing the exact lower-division requirements in social sciences of several nearby institutions in the fields of liberal arts, preteaching, premedicine, engineering, and other popular fields of study may well reveal a very considerable similarity among the institutions. Such a chart might indicate that the minimum program in social sciences for transfer purposes would need to include history of Western civilization, United States history, American government, and introductory psychology. In addition, one college might require specifically a course in economics, while another stipulates simply three (or six) semester hours in any of the social sciences. The single course in economics, then, could be made to satisfy both sets of requirements. Beyond the bare minimum initial offering, a list of priorities might be established naming additional courses to be introduced to satisfy the same requirements and also the divergent interests of students, as growth of enrollment and of faculty permits. In social sciences, this list might include, in order, such subjects as political science, philosophy, sociology, geography, and anthropology. The astute curriculum planner will strive to reduce the variety of courses while meeting the demonstrated transfer needs of his students. Quality of instruction and faculty load are improved, and scheduling of students is made easier, if two sections of one elective subject are offered in preference to one section each of two elective subjects. When growth permits the assignment of several instructors in the social sciences, of course, a greater variety of offerings becomes both feasible and educationally desirable.

The analysis suggested for the broad field of social sciences should be completed also for each of the other lower-division areas, such as English, foreign languages, mathematics, physical sciences, biological sciences, art, music, and home economics. It is not unlikely, in a small junior college, that it will seem impossible to offer a specialized course required in a specific major field at a single university, since only one or two students a year at most will want to enroll in it. An example might be Latin for Pharmacists. Students with this objective must be advised either how they may fulfill the requirement after they have transferred or to enroll immediately at the School of Pharmacy (or other school, as the case may be).

The list of offerings of college-parallel subjects should never be considered static and complete. Constant effort is needed to keep abreast of the changes in requirements of the several schools of the colleges and universities to which students transfer. The continuous development of the scope of subjects in this area of the curriculum is based on yearly review of the latest catalogs. In addition, it will be useful to send the interpretation reached by the junior college counselor, on the basis of this review, to the respective university admissions officers for checking and for suggestions about new or pending developments. A frequent report of transfer students is that they were not advised to fulfill one or another requirement of their senior college. It is the responsibility of the curriculum officer of the junior college to see that such courses are available, so that the guidance worker may include them in the student's class schedule.

It is not impossible, as junior colleges increase in number, in enrollment, and in educational quality and self-confidence, that the problems of curriculum for transfer may be simplified. At present, graduate schools of universities ordinarily admit students holding acceptable baccalaureate degrees from accredited colleges or universities and allow them to enroll in all courses for which they have completed the stated prerequisites. Junior colleges also, as they earn full accreditation, will eventually achieve the right to define the nature of their lower-division general education, so that their recommended graduates may enter the upper division of colleges and universities without restriction and with the right to continue their study in any field for which they have completed the stated prerequisites. Senior colleges will recognize that high achievement in any demanding course of study is better preparation for further study than average achievement in rigidly prescribed general subjects. Under these conditions, each junior college will be encouraged to develop a single general education program of high quality, supplemented by as much academic specialization as its own students need to prepare for their future study. Preparation for transfer will be evaluated in regard to its equivalence to that provided by the receiving college, rather than for its "parallelism." Fiscal economy, educational quality, and the best interests of transferring students—all reinforce the desirability of such a development.

***Occupational Curriculums.***    Other techniques are needed to develop the nontransfer elements of the curriculum. The entire process of curriculum development for occupational education is summarized in the first chapter of a community college survey:

> The Study is conceived to be an on-going program which essentially can never be fully completed. Involved at any stage are at least three phases which may be described as (1) research, (2) development of plans, and (3) implementation.

> This Report sets forth the initial findings of Phase 1. Answers to the following four questions were sought

> > a. What are the occupations for which training should be provided in the public schools of _____ County, and what evidence is there that this need exists?
> > b. What levels of skills and competencies are used in these occupations and what evidence is there that training in these skills and competencies is necessary for successful placement and advancement in the occupation?
> > c. What are the present educational practices in preparing for these occupations?
> > d. At what grade in the educational system should various levels of these competencies be developed, and what evidence is there that this is the most appropriate grade for their development?

> It will be clear to the reader that not all of the aforementioned questions are answered, even in part, for each of the occupational areas with which the Study is concerned. This is a report of progress upon which all concerned can commence to build programs of occupational education for the youth and adults of _____ County.

Phase 2 of the study, *Development of Plans*, will require immediate attention to problems such as the following:

> a. Which of the occupational curricula for which need is disclosed in the Study are feasible or defensible projects?
> b. What shall be the criteria of inaugurating occupational education programs for those curricula deemed feasible or defensible?
> c. What special facilities and personnel will be required to inaugurate such programs?
> d. What will be the costs for each program?
> e. What will be the time schedule?
> f. How can the curricula best be organized—e.g.,

1. Resident day programs
2. Evening or adult classes
3. Cooperative programs
4. Apprentice programs

g. How can occupational education programs best be coordinated with offerings of other schools, particularly junior and senior high schools?

h. How may an effective guidance program involving the junior and senior high schools and the Community College be developed?

Phase 3 will be concerned with *Implementation* of the plans developed in Phase 2, including such items as

a. Recommendations for new occupational curricula, additions to or modifications of existing curricula, and perhaps discontinuance of outmoded or unnecessary curricula.

b. Recommendations regarding

1. Personnel
2. Facilities, equipment, buildings, land, etc.
3. Costs

c. Provision for continuing study of occupational growth and development of the area served by the county secondary schools to the end that they may always be in tune with community needs and desires to the greatest degree possible and feasible.

The three phases described in this listing are essential parts of any junior college survey of its community. Such careful study of educational needs not only provides factual assurance to the governing board, the administration, and the faculty that their program of occupational education is soundly conceived; it has additional value in that the study involves large numbers of citizens from all walks of life. They become informed about the nature and purposes of their community junior college and adopt toward it an attitude of personal involvement that helps the college to accomplish its objectives of realistic education and later placement of its graduates.

When information gained from the educational–occupational survey indicates that a given series of occupational courses is desirable, the college general advisory committee will be informed at its next regularly scheduled meeting. Although it is purely advisory, having no legal authority or responsibility, the general advisory committee can serve the following functions:

1. To assist the college administration in interpreting developments in

the economy and the consequent educational needs of the community.

2. To develop community support and understanding of the educational program of the college.
3. To advise the college board and administration, in the annual meeting and individually thereafter, on problems of college policy submitted to them.
4. To help in interpreting the junior college to the many groups from which the general advisory committee's membership is drawn.

*Special advisory committees* have more limited functions, since they are formed to give advice in relation to a single course of study or to a closely related group of such courses. When data from the general survey indicate the possible need of an occupational course, the first step in its development is the appointment of an advisory committee. Several representatives of employer groups and several workers in the occupation will form the major membership of the committee. After the organization meeting, the chairman will usually be drawn from the lay membership. In addition, at least one responsible officer of the college and, if possible, one or more instructors from related occupational fields should be appointed to the committee; they will be able to carry on further investigations essential to the committee's work and to interpret educational policies and practices to the lay members.

Each advisory committee assumes a number of functions. After verifying that a need exists for employees with community college training, it will consider the overall scope of the course of training to be offered, including specific occupational classes, related instruction, and general education. When these decisions have been reached, the committee can turn its attention to needed classroom space, equipment, and supplies; it is very likely that members of the committee will be able to assist the college in acquiring some of these. The next concern will be the development of a description of desirable qualifications for the instructor, followed by assistance in screening of applicants. After he is employed, the new instructor will use the committee as a resource in developing his course outlines; he will ask them to contribute to instruction as guest lecturers or to suggest opportunities for field trips. After the establishment of the course, the advisory committee will continue to meet at least twice a year to consider problems as they arise, such as placement opportunities for students, criteria for selection of students, policies on student performance of useful production, interpretation of the program to unions, to employers, and to the community at large, evaluation of the program, new technical developments that require changes in the course requirements, development of cooperative work experience for students, and the selection of additional instructional equipment. In all its deliberations, the lay committee serves in an advisory capacity only; the agenda for each meeting should be presented in a way to stress the nature of the committee's function. Ultimate decisions rest with the college board of trustees and its responsible employees. In nearly all cases, however, the recommendations of a lay advisory committee will prove to be so soundly and so sincerely developed that the college officers will desire to follow them. That, in effect, is the purpose of the advisory committee.

Some curricular needs may not be discovered either through the survey of transfer courses, the community occupational survey, or the meetings of advisory committees. It is true especially in the area of adult part-time study that the first impetus for the development of a course may come from a group of persons interested in enrolling or from the personnel officers of a number of local industries who see a need that has developed since the last survey. In various community junior college areas, requests for adult courses may include such offerings as industrial supervision, animal husbandry, advanced mathematics, electronic technology, philosophy for the aging, physical education, or gems and mineralogy. College credit may be a minor consideration; the petitioners most often are interested in a single course, even of very short duration, rather than in a complete program of studies. The problem of the community junior college in relation to program development in these areas is to achieve a proper balance. On the one hand, the college desires to be truly and flexibly responsive to every legitimate educational need of its community; on the other hand, it is conscious of a need to maintain its educational integrity by insisting on a high quality of instruction. An additional advisory committee of public-spirited citizens, not restricted to any single trade, profession, or special interest, can be of service to the college administrator in elaborating the general policy to be applied in deciding upon such requests in the field of adult education.

Another important source of information on which to base the further development of the curriculum is the *follow-up study of former students.* Questionnaires and interviews with former students who are enrolled in upper-division curriculums can provide many insights into their estimate of the quality of their preparation. Their comments about instruction, counseling, student government, the activity program, or subjects offered may indicate aspects of the curriculum that need attention. Together with the grade achievement of transfer students, these comments are very useful indicators of the overall quality of the college-parallel program of the community junior college. Although it is easy to overemphasize the validity of these opinions, which can be no better than the experience and judgment of the undergraduates who hold them, they are still a necessary and useful part of the complete evaluation of the curriculum.

The graduate of an occupational course and his employer are additional sources of insight into the effectiveness of the curriculum. Are graduates employed in the fields for which they have been trained? What difficulties do they face for which the junior college could have prepared them in finding, keeping, and advancing on their jobs? Do employers feel that junior college graduates are better trained, more mature, and more effective, than workers obtained from other sources? What opinion have they formed of graduates' attitudes toward work? Are their shortcomings, when reported, due to their experience at the junior college, or to influences beyond the control of the college? Do they arise from the deficiencies in the occupational courses, or in the general education program? Students who drop out before completion of a course should be able to provide some penetrating suggestions for curriculum improvement. Their value in this respect is lessened, or course, by the greater difficulty of finding them after a lapse of time, by their reluctance to answer questions if the answer does not do them credit, and by the possibility that their negative attitudes at the time of leaving college still persist.

*Special Interest Curriculums.* In addition to college transfer and occupational curriculums, a number of special interest curriculums have been introduced in colleges of all types at the specific demand of students. Students have always influenced the curriculum of American higher education, but never before has their influence been so explicit and so insistent as in recent years. As a result of needs defined by enrolled students rather than by faculty or administrators, community colleges with significant numbers of ethnic minority students have introduced Afro-American Studies, Mexican-American Studies, and in a few colleges Asian Studies. The usual pattern has been a series of meetings (or confrontations) of concerned students with administrators, student definition of program content and nomination of preferred instructors, and acquiescence of college administrators to introduction and support of the curriculum.

A more sophisticated and foresighted approach has been usual in the introduction of developmental or remedial programs for unprepared students. In this area, the faculty and staff ordinarily define the need before the students become aware of it. They recognize that persons with ability are excluded from college or are reluctant to apply for admission because of inadequate skills of study or of communication. They are confident that the potential student and society will benefit if these learning handicaps can be overcome, and so they propose to offer courses that may be considered beneath the dignity of college professors but still are useful in salvaging undeveloped talent.

As both ethnic and developmental curriculums are offered in more and more community colleges, their planning is becoming more conventional. College authorities initiate program proposals, involve members of the target group in the planning, and seek out instructors who are qualified rather than simply available. The outcome will be that these new programs, initiated in response to student need, will be fully integrated into the purposes and the procedures of the community junior college.

*Statewide Influences.*    Not all external influences on the curriculum of the community junior college are local ones. State agencies exert both regulatory and advisory pressures. In some states, legislation requires the teaching of specific courses (such as physical education) or the organization of certain services (such as education for adults). A state board may exert leadership through organization of conferences on specific topics such as counseling or improvement of instruction or general education. Cooperation by several agencies is another avenue of curriculum development. The "California Study of General Education in the Junior College" was sponsored by the California Junior College Association, The California State Department of Education, The School of Education of the University of California at Los Angeles, and the American Council on Education. Similarly, state universities and other state agencies exert some measure of influence on the community college curriculum.

*National Influences.*    The American Association of Junior Colleges is an important stimulating force upon the junior college curriculum through the Junior College Journal, the Research Bulletins of the Association, and the Commission on Curriculum. The United States Office of Education employs a Specialist in Community and Junior Colleges to gather and disseminate information about these colleges and to provide consultative service to the states in relation to the establishment and the development of the junior college curriculum.

It is apparent, then, that the total process of defining the scope of the community junior college curriculum depends upon information and stimulation from many sources. In the process of this development, the community junior college receives requests for service from the community, studies the programs of other junior colleges, colleges, and universities, keeps abreast of the emphasis and proposals throughout its state and the nation, and actively searches for ways to fulfill its responsibility to provide for the post-high-school educational needs of its community.

# B. Maintaining the Quality of Instruction

The external influences described in the previous section help the administrator to decide which courses should be offered in each community junior college. These decisions are only the first necessary steps in establishing an effective educational program. Many further decisions about class schedules, about methods and materials for the various courses, and about selection of students and evaluation of instruction will influence the extent and the quality of the curriculum to which the students have access. A course in humanities, for example, may be approved after considerable study, and included in the junior college catalog. Yet it may fail entirely in its intended influence on students because teachers are unavailable or poorly trained or uninterested in it, because adequate classrooms or instructional supplies are not made available, because guidance workers fail to call it to the attention of students, or even because it is scheduled at an unattractive or conflicting time. Provisions that have been found effective in assuring the high quality of the curriculum include the appointment of a curriculum officer, often named the Dean of Instruction, the establishment of a collegewide curriculum committee, a continuous program of research and evaluation of curriculum, and the encouragement of faculty members to prize and to aspire to competent and enthusiastic instruction.

*Dean of Instruction.*    It is the responsibility of the Dean of Instruction to promote continuous review of the offerings of the college to the end that the quality of the faculty, the organization of the courses, and the auxiliary services of the college may all combine to provide excellent educational opportunity for all classes of students. His duties in relation to the instructors will include a forecast of needed additions and replacements each year, development of their assignments for each semester, and elaboration of plans for the induction of new teachers and for continuous in-service training of the entire faculty. One of his most important functions is the supervision of instruction. Through classroom visitation, he gains concrete acquaintance with the nature of the curriculum and refreshes his awareness of the daily problems of instructors; he is enabled to provide realistic help to them in improving their techniques of presentation, as well as in considering revisions of the course purposes or materials. In meetings with the staff of the several departments or divisions of the college, he is enabled to interpret to them such matters as university regulations or the meaning of college policies; at the same time, he keeps himself informed of the instructional problems which are engaging the attention of the faculty.

The Dean of Instruction is typically responsible also for the preparation of the college catalog, especially for the sections that present suggested programs of study for various objectives of students and for the descriptions of each course offered. The schedule of classes expresses all curricular research and philosophy as it joins the converging forces of instructors, students, time, buildings, equipment, and units of credit into a single educative process. Most of the decisions involved in the schedule, and not a little of the detailed cross checking, rest with the Dean of Instruction. As a basis for his decisions, he will need a continuous flow of information on matters such as past course enrollments, projected enrollments, trends in student demand, comparative student-contact hours of instructors, rates of withdrawal from classes, room capacity, faculty preferences, and classes that are likely to conflict.

*Curriculum Committee.* The Dean of Instruction will exert most of his efforts for the continuous development of the quality of the curriculum through the curriculum committee, of which he is typically the chairman. This committee is charged with the responsibility of considering all proposals for major changes in the curriculum of the college, from whatever source; the changes that it approves are recommended to the president and to the board of trustees for official action. In addition to its work as a review board for curricular proposals from all sources, the curriculum committee ordinarily assumes leadership in the development of plans for improvement in the college offerings and initiates and supervises needed studies of the instructional functioning of the institution. Its membership will include the Dean of Instruction as chairman; other administrative officers who are concerned with instructional matters, such as those in charge of summer session, adult education, vocational education, and other specialized offerings; representatives from the library staff and from counseling and guidance; the deans or chairmen of the instructional divisions of the college, and several representatives of the teaching faculty. Suggestions have been made that the curriculum committee should also include lay persons and members of the student body. Such representation is probably unnecessary if the functions of the curriculum committee are limited, as suggested, to instructional problems and if the pattern of general and specialized lay advisory committees is utilized to advantage. In addition, an effective curriculum committee will meet with comparative frequency; participation should be a part of the assigned load of the members. Lay persons should not be expected to contribute so much time to this professional function.

Within a given year, a curriculum committee might well achieve a series of projects such as the following:

1. *Routine review of the entire curriculum:* Each division of the junior college reports at a scheduled meeting, presenting its enrollment trends and its problems of schedule or equipment or student recruitment or instructional effectiveness together with recommendations for additions or deletions of courses.
2. *Curriculum studies:* (a) The committee considers and acts on results of a vocational survey, proposing a course in laboratory technician training. (b) Considers a proposal from an interested instructor for the inauguration of a course in children's literature for prospective elementary teachers.
3. *Policy investigations:* (a) After noting wide variation in proportion of "A" and "C" grades given by instructors and by divisions, the committee assigns a subcommittee to develop a statement of the meaning of each letter grade. Arranges for consideration, revision, and approval of the statement in order by the committee, the faculty, and the board of trustees. (b) Investigates teacher load, by departments, in other colleges, as a basis for considering a redefinition.
4. *Faculty studies:* (a) The committee sponsors a study by each division of the college, under leadership of the division chairmen, of the meaning and application of the aims of general education in its own classrooms. After this consideration, some changes may be recommended in the requirements for graduation or in the nature of specific courses offered by several of the divisions. (b) Recommends the financing and planning of a workshop during the summer in which instructors will attempt to clarify their purposes and outline of materials in one or more of the required courses.

Ingles suggests several criteria to be used by a curriculum committee and the administrator in deciding whether to install a proposed new course. He suggests that evidence should be gathered for each proposed course on:

1. *Need:* Does the course contribute measurably to transfer, occupational, or remedial education? Could an existing course be modified to satisfy the need?
2. *Relation to other courses:* Will the proposed course duplicate, supplement, or replace another course?
3. *Scholarship level:* Is it clearly a course appropriate for the junior

college, rather than to upper division or to high school? Is the unit
value in harmony with that of similar offerings?[1]

The administration, after receiving the proposal from the curriculum
committee, will consider the problems of the need for a lay advisory
committee, the need for added staff, the duplication unnecessarily of
offerings in nearby institutions, the present and future cost of the course
in relation to other desirable expenditures, and the long-range prospects
of student enrollment.

In view of its responsibilities and its functions, the curriculum
committee in the community junior college exerts a decisive influence on
the scope and the quality of the class offerings; it is equally effective in
safeguarding the conditions that encourage excellent teaching and in
interpreting the faculty to the administration and vice versa. It helps to
create the enthusiasm and morale among the instructors that arise from
the recognition by the entire college that its purposes are achieved only
when they are achieved in the classroom.

*Research.*    Constant reference has been made in the pages of this
chapter to the need for continuous research as a basis for curricular
decisions. Such fact gathering is never completed. The questioning faculty
is an improving faculty, if it discovers answers. For this reason, the
collection and interpretation of all kinds of information are essential
elements of a program of curriculum development. Many useful facts are
easily and conveniently available, if only someone has the time to gather
and tabulate them and the interest to search for their meaning. The list
that follows is not intended to be exhaustive. It merely suggests some of
the kinds of information that must be kept up to date and made available
to teachers, deans, counselors, curriculum committees, and junior college
administrators as essential tools in their daily tasks.

Many kinds of knowledge about the community of the public junior
college are needed. The college offering is affected by population growth
or decline, economic stability, breadth of industrial, commercial, or
agricultural employment, socioeconomic composition of the community,
other colleges in the area, median personal income, and assessed valuation
trends, to name only a few of the factors. The students require careful
analysis also. How many are coming through the lower schools? What are
the characteristics of those who enroll at the junior college? What trends
are discernible in age, health, marital status, aptitude, and educational
plans? How long do they persist in attendance, and how well do they do
their studies? What of the success of the graduate in his next endeavor,
whether work or study? Administratively, how do annual unit costs
compare with those of comparable junior colleges? What legislation

affects the college, in the state or nation? Are the student-faculty ratios and the teaching load within acceptable limits? What evidence is available about the quality of instruction, through observation, faculty opinion, student reaction, available tests of achievement, later study, and other sources? The community junior college that gathers such data as a basis for its educational planning will be a busy institution; by the same token, it will almost certainly be one of high instructional quality.

## FOOTNOTE

1.  Ingles, E. T. "Criteria for Adding New Courses to the Junior College Curriculum," *California Journal of Secondary Education,* 32: (April, 1957). pp. 218-221.

## BIBLIOGRAPHY

Furniss, W. Todd. "Racial Minorities and Curriculum Change," *Educational Record,* **50**, No. 4 (Fall 1969), pp. 360-370.

Hardner, Robert J., and Don L. Pratton. "Curriculum Reform Through Behavioral Objectives," *Junior College Journal,* **41**, No. 2 (October, 1970), pp. 12-16.

Harris, Norman C. *Technical Education in the Junior College: New Programs for New Jobs.* Washington, D.C.: American Association of Junior Colleges, 1964.

Henderson, John T. *Program Planning with Surveys in Occupational Education.* Washington, D.C.: American Association of Junior Colleges, 1970.

Ingles, E. T. "Criteria for Adding New Courses to the Junior College Curriculum," *California Journal of Secondary Education,* **32** (April, 1957), pp. 218-221.

Jennings, Frank G. "Junior Colleges in America: The Two Year Stretch," *Change,* (March-April 1970), pp. 15-25.

Johnson, B. Lamar. *Islands of Innovation Expanding.* Beverly Hills, California: Glencoe Press, 1969.

———*Systems Approaches to Curriculum and Instruction in the Open-Door College* (Occasional Report No. 9, Junior College Leadership Program). Los Angeles: University of California, 1967.

McCabe, Robert H. "A New Course: 'Man and Environment,'" *Junior College Journal,* **41**, No. 4 (December/January, 1970-1971), pp. 16-17.

Resnick, Solomon, and Barbara Kaplan. "College Programs for Black Adults," *Journal of Higher Education,* **42** (March, 1971), pp. 202-218.

Riendeau, Albert J. *The Role of the Advisory Committee in Occupational Education in the Junior College.* Washington, D.C.: American Association of Junior Colleges, 1967.

Roueche, John E., George A. Baker III, and Richard L. Brownell. *Accountability and the Community College.* Washington, D.C.: American Association of Junior Colleges, 1971.

# 13 | The Curriculum: Occupational Education

"Everyone is affected by the accelerating pace of scientific and industrial change. A whole new array of occupations has been created, rapidly outmoding many of yesterday's skills and techniques. In the years ahead, millions of us will be required to relearn our jobs as the skills required become more sophisticated.

Earlier fears of mass unemployment because of automation and other new technology have proved unwarranted. Millions of new jobs requiring higher levels of skills have been created. At the same time, however, many unskilled jobs once available to untrained high school graduates, school dropouts, the disadvantaged, and the handicapped have been wiped away."[1]

For more than 50 years, writers about the community college have advocated the estab-

**175**

lishment of courses to prepare students for immediate employment. This concept of one of the functions of the junior college has been recognized officially by several of the states in their laws authorizing the establishment of public junior colleges. Since its first issue in 1930, the *Junior College Journal* has carried articles and editorials about occupational studies. A great majority of the community colleges in America offer one or more courses designed to prepare students for immediate entry into employment.

Nevertheless, the idea of college education for occupational life has not yet achieved full acceptance by high-school graduates and their parents. The lay citizen, even in communities with extensive community college occupational offerings, is only partially aware of the nature of and the need for these courses. Workers in other segments of the educational system, both secondary and higher education, are likely to share the lack of information and the misconceptions of the layman. Students as they come to the community college to enroll are often unaware of the nature of occupational offerings. As a result, only 9% of vocational education enrollments at all levels (secondary, post-secondary, adult) are in post-secondary programs, and not all of these are in community college programs.[2]

Although the Office of Education does not report community college vocational education enrollments separately, an estimate may be reached by comparison of total post-secondary vocational enrollments in fiscal 1969 with October, 1968 total enrollments in junior colleges. Post-secondary vocational education enrollments were 706,085; total junior college enrollments were 1,924,970. Vocational enrollments in the colleges could not have been greater than 36% of total junior college enrollments. Because noncollege post-secondary vocational enrollments are included in the 760,085, it is permissible to estimate that fewer than one-third of all junior college students are enrolled in organized vocational curriculums.

The definition of occupational education in community colleges is made difficult by the lack of agreement, even among institutions that have established such courses, on the kinds of occupations for which community colleges should prepare students and on the scope and level of appropriate instruction. Chapter 13 attempts to clarify the field of community college occupational education. It presents a series of definitions of terms frequently used in discussing this function. Thereafter, evidence about the nature and prevalence of occupational courses is presented, followed by a discussion of some of the current issues in the development of occupational education.

## A. Terminology of Occupational Education

In the literature dealing with junior college preparation for employment, several terms with overlapping connotations are employed, sometimes interchangeably. A brief discussion of the background and meaning of each term will lead to a clearer understanding of the field of community junior college occupational education. Among the phrases essential to an understanding of this aspect of the curriculum are "terminal education," "vocational education," "paraprofessional education," "technical education," and "occupational education." In addition, some of these are at times used in combination, as "terminal-technical" or "vocational-technical."

*Terminal Education.*    In 1925, Koos contrasted the "isthmian" function of the junior college with its "terminal" function.[3] The term "isthmian," intended to indicate that the junior college serves as a bridge between high school and senior college, was never widely adopted. The word "terminal," indicating education planned for those students who did not intend to continue their attendance beyond the junior college, proved to be a more useful term. Several authors object to it because of a growing understanding of the fact that learning is lifelong, that it does not cease at the end of any period of school attendance. Another objection arose from an early tendency in some junior colleges to segregate students unnecessarily into classes of "transfer" and "terminal" students; this practice in effect created two distinct student bodies with certain unwholesome social and even educational consequences. According to one point of view, moreoever, the distinction between transfer and terminal functions was invalid and unnecessary, since occupational training might result from appropriate combinations of transfer courses. With the growing recognition of the need for technical education, this concept of the dual-purpose course is losing its earlier degree of acceptance.

In spite of the objections, there is a use for a term with the implications of "terminal education in the junior college." "Terminal" may be defined as applying to community junior college courses of study planned primarily for the student who intends that the completion of the program will mark the end of his full-time enrollment in organized classes in schools. By extension, of course, the adjective may apply to the student who enrolls in such courses. Certain corollaries of the definition should be understood. Terminal courses may be of any appropriate length, whether a semester, a year, or two years, as the majority of occupational courses. Again, a change in the objective of the student who may decide after all to continue his education does not invalidate the concept of terminal courses; a major purpose of the program of studies and the original intention of the student were both "terminal." Finally, it should be noted that terminal courses are not necessarily occupational in nature; a general course of study leading to no specific occupation may be terminal, depending on the purposes of the college in planning it and of the student in enrolling in it.

*Vocational Education.* "Vocational education" has come to be restricted, in much educational writing, to preparation of "less than college grade" for specific job fields in the areas of agriculture, trades and industry, distributive education, and homemaking. Such preparation has been federally subsidized since 1917 and has been developed mostly in the high schools. Some junior colleges have offered vocational education programs which qualified for federal aid under this series of acts; recently, however, there is a tendency to develop junior college courses of study that prepare for families of occupations and to give up the specific training programs required under earlier federal legislation.

The limits of the concept of vocational education may be established by means of a series of sentences taken from an official bulletin:

To the learner, vocational education is learning how to work . . . To the educator, vocational education is teaching others how to work. It is a systematic program for discovering the knowledge, skills, and attitudes people must have for successful participation in a specific area of work, for organizing these inter-related elements into graded courses and experiences, and for integrating these courses and experiences within the total educational program . . . Vocational education is always specific. It must prepare the individual to *understand,* and to be able to *do* the specific activities found to be necessary in accomplishing a given task . . . It must be set in a laboratory equipped with the actual tools and materials which are used in the occupation and operated in such a way as to parallel the activities on a real job.[4]

In the limited and usual sense, then, vocational education implies a series of courses preparing for a specific occupation in the fields of agriculture, trades and industry, distributive occupations, or homemaking. When offered in a community junior college, it forms only a part of the total program of studies of the student; its major emphasis is on practice rather than on theory. The concept is a more limited one than either "terminal" or "special" education.

In the "Vocational Education Act of 1963," the entire traditional concept of federally supported vocational education was revised. Support for specific occupational fields was withdrawn, and funds were made available at any appropriate level of education, so that all persons might have access to training or retraining in any occupation. Vocational education, under this Act, emphasizes the citizen who needs training, rather than the industry that needs workers. The Vocational Amendments of 1968 established a national policy of providing all persons with "ready access to vocational training or retraining which is of high quality, which is realistic in light of actual or anticipated opportunities for gainful employment, and which is suited to their needs, interests, and ability to benefit from such training." Two emphases predominate in the application of this policy—vocational education as a necessary step in education for disadvantaged and handicapped persons, and the need to supplement skill training with broader educational opportunity.

*Paraprofessional Education.*    The increasing application of technology in professional fields has introduced the concept of professional teams to free the fully educated worker—physician, engineer, teacher, lawyer, social worker, etc.,—from much of the drudgery formerly associated with each area of work. At the same time, new fields have been opened for persons who can operate technical instruments under the direction of the professional. Such helpers need more than high-school training but in many cases less than the bachelor's degree. They include teacher's assistants, engineering technicians, laboratory technicians, dental assistants, and other workers in manufacturing, in business, and in service occupations who must combine a measurable understanding of the field with a considerable skill in technique. It is also possible for paraprofessional training and employment to be the first steps on a career ladder leading for at least some workers to full professional status.

*Technical Education.*    This is a specialized category of community college two-year education; it prepares for jobs in which some manipulative skill is required but in which technical knowledge is emphasized. In general, "technical education" implies preparation for occupations within scientific and engineering fields where the worker will make use of instruments rather than tools and mental effort rather than muscular exertion. It requires more depth of understanding and allows more independence in judgment than most paraprofessional tasks. With the advent of the electronic age, the demand is increasing for technicians in all fields—business, national defense, construction, manufacturing, medicine, service, and design, to name but a few. The preparation of technicians is an appropriate undertaking for junior colleges, since these workers require more maturity and depth of scientific knowledge than the high-school graduate has achieved, although the scope of their operation and education is likely to be narrower than that of the graduate engineer or scientist under whose direction they will work.

A publication of the Office of Education lists six examples of day programs in "Vocational-Technical Education;" all but the third description apply to courses appropriate for community junior colleges:

1. Curriculums with broad technical content in specific industrial fields, designed to prepare persons for engineering technician occupations; usually two years in length, on the post-high-school level; commonly known as educational programs of the technical institute type.
2. Curriculums designed to prepare persons for technical specialist occupations, usually confined to one area within an industry; commonly six months to two years in length, on the post-high-school level; scope of content narrower than that of technical institute type curriculums.
3. Vocational-technical curriculums in technical high schools, designed to prepare youth for positions similar to those of engineering technicians but on a somewhat lower level.
4. Curriculums which combine technical content with sales content, cost content, and the like; frequently two years in length, on the post-high-school level.
5. Vocational-technical curriculums which lie outside the fields of engineering, such as biological laboratory technology, or medical assistant technology; usually two years in length, on the post-high-school level.
6. Short intensive programs designed to prepare persons for specific vocational-technical occupations of comparatively low level.[5]

***Occupational Education.*** Each of the terms just defined is inadequate as a single designation for all the courses of study offered in community junior colleges for the purpose of preparing students to enter an occupation at the end of the course and to succeed and advance in it. The term "occupational education" is sufficiently broad to include areas such as nursing education or secretarial training together with technical and trade training; at the same time, it has not been pre-empted by specialized segments of the entire field of training or employment. "Occupational education" is used in this chapter to denote all organized community college programs of study, of whatever length, that combine appropriate proportions of technical, manipulative, general, and elective courses to prepare the student for employment upon the successful completion of the course.

The practice of occupational education in community junior colleges may be demonstrated by the course of study suggested in a bulletin of the Automobile Manufacturers' Assocation.[6] The two-year sequence is intended to prepare personnel for entry level work in automotive servicing, with capability for advancement to management after on-the-job experience. Entrance requirements to the program include high-school graduation and competence in English and arithmetic. The curriculum outline on pages 181-182 shows the combination of general and specialized courses suggested by the Association.

## Suggested Curriculum for Automotive Servicing

| Courses | Credit Hours | Class Hours | Laboratory Hours |
|---|---|---|---|
| FIRST YEAR | | | |
| Semester I | | | |
| Communication Skills I | 3 | 3 | 0 |
| Mathematics I | 3 | 3 | 0 |
| Engines | 3 | 2 | 3 |
| Electricity | 4 | 2 | 6 |
| Service Orientation and Maintenance | 3 | 1 | 6 |
| TOTAL HOURS | 16 | 11 | 15 |
| Semester II | | | |
| Service Management I | 2 | 2 | 0 |
| Mathematics II | 3 | 3 | 0 |
| Suspension and Brakes I | 3 | 2 | 3 |
| Auto Accessories | 3 | 2 | 3 |
| Engine Diagnosis and Tune Up | 3 | 2 | 3 |
| Cranking and Charging Systems | 2 | 1 | 3 |
| TOTAL HOURS | 16 | 12 | 12 |

SUMMER PROGRAM (Institutional or cooperative with industry.)

During the summer session, the school will arrange programs with local dealerships to provide school-supervised work and study experience on operational vehicles. If institutional facilities are adequate, programs providing this type of practical experience may be scheduled at school.

Instruction or working experience should concentrate on: Tune-up, Electrical, Brakes, Chassis Service, Engines, Transmission and Drive Lines, Service Orientation and Maintenance. Maximum of 4 credit hours.

## Suggested Curriculum *(Continued)*

| Courses | Credit Hours | Class Hours | Laboratory Hours |
|---|---|---|---|
| **SECOND YEAR** | | | |
| Semester III | | | |
| Social Science I | 3 | 3 | 0 |
| Science I | 3 | 2 | 3 |
| Suspension and Brakes II | 2 | 1 | 3 |
| Transmissions and Drive Lines | 3 | 2 | 3 |
| Service Management II | 2 | 2 | 0 |
| Accounting and Business Organization | 3 | 3 | 0 |
| TOTAL HOURS | 16 | 13 | 9 |
| Semester IV | | | |
| Social Science II | 3 | 3 | 0 |
| Science II | 3 | 2 | 3 |
| Electrical Circuits | 2 | 1 | 3 |
| Communications Skills II | 3 | 3 | 0 |
| Elective | 3 | 1 | 6 |
| Air Conditioning | 2 | 1 | 3 |
| TOTAL HOURS | 16 | 11 | 15 |

# B. Kinds of Occupational Courses

*American Junior Colleges* (Seventh Edition) presents information on the curriculum of each of 751 accredited public and independent junior colleges. The information in Table I on occupational courses is derived from listing in Appendix Three of that work.[7]

It is apparent that *secretarial and clerical* courses, with 394 opportunities, are the most frequent occupational offerings in junior colleges. The total business field, with an additional 748 curriculums, is also the most frequently taught broad field. The total of 1142 curriculums compares with a similar tally of 728 four years earlier. Since the general category of business accounts for more than one-fourth of all employment in the United States, even smaller junior colleges can enroll enough students to justify the offering of business training and find suitable employment for them when they finish the course. For this reason, business courses are usually the first occupational offering of junior colleges.

*Engineering Technology.*    This heading was not listed as a separate category in the Fifth Edition of American Junior Colleges, although some 279 of the curriculums listed at that time might be broadly defined as technically based. The recognition of the need for technicians is demonstrated by the emergence between the Fifth and Sixth Editions of 403 curriculums specifically labeled as engineering technologies and the increase by the Seventh Edition to 574 technology curriculums. The electrical and electronic emphasis is most frequent, with 141 colleges offering work, followed by a total of 112 curriculums in engineering technology and 98 in mechanical engineering technology.

*Trades and Industry.*    These courses are offered in almost half of the total of 751 public and private colleges summarized. Electricity and electronics as vocational courses lead the list, as the parallel technology courses did in that listing. Machine shop and mechanics courses are also popular offerings, with 94 and 90 curriculums, respectively.

*Miscellaneous.*    Technical assistance in the health fields is an important curriculum area in community colleges. Curriculums for registered nurses (190), practical nurses (138), dental assistants (56), dental hygienists (16), therapists (16), dental technologists (14), and medical laboratory assistants (60) are supplemented by radiologists and x-ray technicians (17) and medical assistants (43), tallied under miscellaneous curriculums to yield a total of 550 opportunities to prepare for paraprofessional work in health fields.

In the *service area,* police science is represented with 100 colleges

**TABLE I.**

**Number of Accredited Junior Colleges Offering Named Occupational Courses, 1965-1966**[a]

| Course | | Number of Colleges |
|---|---|---|
| **TOTAL BUSINESS COURSES** | | **1,142** |
| Secretarial and Clerical | 394 | |
| Accounting | 159 | |
| Administration and Management | 149 | |
| Sales and Retailing | 149 | |
| General Business | 148 | |
| Data Processing | 143 | |
| **TOTAL ENGINEERING TECHNOLOGY** | | **574** |
| Electrical and Electronic Technology | 141 | |
| Engineering Technology | 112 | |
| Mechanical Engineering Technology | 98 | |
| Architectural and Civil Engineering Technology | 68 | |
| Chemical Engineering Technology | 48 | |
| Industrial Engineering Technology | 45 | |
| Air Conditioning Engineering Technology | 30 | |
| Metallurgical Engineering Technology | 17 | |
| Aeronautical Engineering Technology | 15 | |
| **TOTAL TRADES AND INDUSTRY** | | **457** |
| Electricity and Electronics | 121 | |
| Mechanical | 90 | |
| Metal and Machine | 94 | |
| Trades and Industrial Arts | 77 | |
| Construction | 52 | |
| Aviation | 23 | |

**TABLE I.** *(Continued)*

| Course | Number of Colleges |
| --- | --- |
| TOTAL MISCELLANEOUS | 1887 |
| Nursing (registered) | 190 |
| Drafting | 150 |
| Nursing (practical) | 138 |
| Police Science | 100 |
| Agriculture | 88 |
| Art | 85 |
| Home Economics | 70 |
| Architectural Drafting | 62 |
| Medical Laboratory Assisting | 60 |
| Dental Assisting | 56 |
| Hotel, Motel, and Restaurant Technology | 50 |
| Physical Education and Recreation | 46 |
| Music | 38 |
| Teaching | 35 |
| Forestry | 31 |
| Journalism | 30 |
| Printing | 24 |
| Speech and Drama | 24 |
| Clothing Technology | 17 |
| Dental Hygiene | 16 |
| Therapy | 16 |
| Dental Technology | 14 |
| Other Miscellaneous Curriculums[b] | 547 |

[a]Source: Appendix Three, "Curricula Offered by Junior Colleges," American Junior Colleges, (Seventh Edition).

[b]Some 547 miscellaneous courses were offered under 55 different occupational titles. Specialized courses in mortuary service, child study, cosmotology, gunsmithing, real estate, and watch repair were included among those available in one or more of the colleges listed.

offering training. Teaching as a terminal curriculum in community colleges appears 35 times, indicating the emergence of paraprofessional preparation for the schools as a field of study. Hotel, motel, and restaurant technologies reflect the growth in tourism with 50 colleges presenting courses. Agriculture, with the newer emphasis on the business opportunities in that field, has rebounded to 88 offerings listed in the Seventh Edition, compared to only 52 in the Sixth Edition of *American Junior Colleges*.

Taken all together, the 751 public and independent accredited junior colleges studied offered 4060 two-year occupational courses of study, a mean of about six per college. The listing justifies the conclusion that junior colleges have fully accepted the responsibility for occupational education. In addition, the listing points up the fact that each college defines its own responsibility for these courses in the light of the demands of its constituency and its own philosophy of junior college education. A few colleges offer occupational courses only of a technical nature, whereas others concentrate almost entirely on business or business and trade courses. The statistical picture presented in Table I may be somewhat more extensive than the reality, since some colleges may at times list in their descriptions courses for which very few students enroll or which are not offered at all in a given year.

Reference to three junior college catalogs will illustrate the diversity of practice in occupational education. The three colleges are located in different areas of the nation; all three enroll between 2000 and 3000 full-time freshman and sophomore students. Each of the three cities is a prosperous, industrial community. Yet the differences in their occupational courses are greater than the similarity of college size and situation would lead one to expect. One college offers 922 semester units of technical nontransfer courses in 40 two-year degree curriculums including business (149 units), law enforcement (32 units), engineering technologies (242 units), nursing (36 units), and machine trades (86 units). In addition, this same college offers 27 certificate programs for less than two years and an extensive program for full-time apprentices who are part-time students. The total part-time annual enrollment in this college is a little more than twice as large as its full-time freshman and sophomore enrollment.

The second college, situated in a similar city in another area of the nation, enrolls almost 4,000 part-time students. It offers technical courses for full-time students in 38 occupations, including five business specialties. Its two-year curriculums total 934 semester units, including electronics (72), business fields (125), nursing (62), and 124 units of other health-related courses. Evening courses for part-time students are offered in 13 occupational fields and amount to a total of 175 units.

The third college has half as many part-time students as full-time freshmen and sophomores. It offers a total of 574 semester units of technical study, but no trades courses. It has business (144 units), and engineering technologies (275 units), but no health-related courses.

The three colleges exemplify three stages of occupational education in the junior college. The first, with its all-inclusive coverage of full-time technical and vocational education, apprenticeship-related training, and extension courses for vocational advancement, represents the fullest possible development of this aspect of junior college curriculum. There is some evidence that nationally the trend is away from such complete coverage and that trade and apprenticeship courses may be decreasing in the junior colleges in favor of technical education. On the other hand, if junior colleges generally accept the role of "area vocational school" authorized in the Vocational Education Act of 1963, this community junior college may become the model for future development of other colleges.

The second college takes a middle position. It offers both pre-employment and extension work, but limits its courses to the technical and business areas. It has a balanced appeal to the full-time and the part-time student. It can defend each of its offerings as of junior-college level and is probably representative of the modal position of community junior colleges of this size. The third college seems much more conservative in its approach to occupational education and may well be just at the beginning of its development of this aspect of the curriculum. It makes only minor provision for the part-time employed student and limits its offerings to courses that have been tested in other colleges in other communities.

*Frequency of Occupational Courses.*     From the individual exhibits in the body of American Junior Colleges (Seventh Edition), another insight may be gained into the scope and frequency of occupational or career education in accredited junior colleges. Each college lists its transfer curriculums and its occupational curriculums separately. It is possible to tally the frequency of occupational course titles listed by the 751 colleges. This information is summarized in Table II. It is of interest to note that 149 of these 751 junior colleges (20%) offer no occupational courses; in the Sixth Edition, 181 out of 655 colleges (28%) offered no such courses. The occupational function is being adopted more generally. The median offering is four occupational courses, including the independent colleges and the community colleges that offered no occupational study at all; 17 colleges offered more than 25 such courses.

## C. Current Problems in Community College Occupational Education

***Rapid Change in Occupational Requirements.***   Manpower statistics always show proportions of the labor force as unemployed; the ratios in recent years have varied from 3.5% to about 6.0% of the total labor force.

**TABLE II.**

**Frequency of Occupational Offerings in 751 Accredited Junior Colleges, 1965-1966[a]**

| Number of Occupational Offerings | Number of Colleges | % of Colleges | Cumulative Percentage |
|---|---|---|---|
| 0 | 149 | 19.9 | 19.9 |
| 1 | 68 | 9.0 | 28.9 |
| 2 | 60 | 8.0 | 36.9 |
| 3 | 67 | 8.8 | 45.7 |
| 4 | 53 | 7.1 | 52.8 |
| 5 | 54 | 7.2 | 60.0 |
| 6 | 49 | 6.5 | 66.5 |
| 7 | 32 | 4.3 | 70.8 |
| 8 | 26 | 3.5 | 74.3 |
| 9 | 20 | 2.7 | 77.0 |
| 10 | 20 | 2.7 | 79.7 |
| 11-15 | 76 | 10.1 | 89.8 |
| 16-20 | 42 | 5.6 | 95.4 |
| 21-25 | 18 | 2.4 | 97.8 |
| 26 and more | 17 | 2.2 | 100.0 |
| TOTAL | 751 | 100.0 | --- |

[a]Source: Author's tabulation from exhibits in American Junior Colleges, (Seventh Edition).

Unemployment, however, is not distributed evenly over the categories of workers. For example,

"approximately 13 per cent of all persons aged 16 to 19 and 8.7 per cent of those aged 16 to 24 were unemployed in 1968. In nearly every age group and in almost every geographical area, unemployment rates among nonwhites were twice as high as those for whites. Seventeen out of the 20 largest metropolitan areas in the country reported a higher unemployment rate in their central cities than was reported as a national average. Much of the unemployment among nonwhites and younger persons was structural: the result of insufficient education and training . . . The untrained person may still find a job, but he will probably have difficulty finding and maintaining a rewarding occupational career."[8]

The problem for the community college has two aspects—one of forecasting occupational trends so as to eliminate obsolescent programs and to introduce new programs; the other to convince unemployable and displaced workers that the occupational programs it offers provide valid preparation for jobs that are really open to graduates of all colors and ages. As a bridge between the career needs of young people and the manpower needs of the economy, the college must become much more aware of and more readily responsive to constant shifts in both sets of needs.

*Expansion of the Occupational Curriculum.*    Data presented in Section B of this chapter indicate that in most community colleges the occupational offering is still very limited in scope. The idea that occupational education is a function of the community college is readily accepted, but the planning and introduction of courses have lagged. The employment crisis of the seventies is based in part on the increasingly cognitive nature of a great amount of employment. Human strength and docility are no longer prime qualities in the employment market. The unemployed are largely the uneducated, the unprepared; yet there is still a constant market for workers with skills suited to automated production. White-collar jobs outnumber blue-collar jobs in the labor force, and their share of the total force increases yearly. In spite of these trends, more than half of all junior colleges offer fewer than five curriculums emphasizing any occupational skills; among the courses offered, the business rather than the technical competences predominate.

The issue may be simply stated: either the community junior colleges will accept in practice the responsibility for middle-level technical education, or some other institution will be established to carry out this essential educational task.

*Articulation with Other Institutions.*  In developing its occupational programs and in its role in occupational education within any region, the community junior college must work closely with other educational institutions. It seems to be true that the public high school will play a diminishing role in specific vocational education as the age of first employment rises and the technical requirements for many jobs are increased. During the transitional period, however, the junior college staff must work closely with the high-school authorities, in the interests both of fiscal economy and of educational efficiency.

Several of the states that are developing or extending their system of public junior colleges have previously established separate trade, vocational, or technical schools. In most instances, these schools have concentrated on the direct preparation of their students for immediate employment in a given occupation, without concern for more than a bare minimum of education in nonvocational subject matter. Junior college occupational education includes a balance of special and general education and may be presumed to have greater value both for the student and for society. It may well be that in the long run the vocational schools and the junior colleges will be amalgamated in all states as they have been in North Carolina and Hawaii; until such unification of effort is possible, however, junior colleges face continuing problems in the coordination of their occupational offerings with the existing, although limited, opportunities already available in the community.

A third area of articulation concerns the relation of junior college occupational courses to advanced standing requirements in four-year colleges and universities. Students sometimes hesitate to enroll in terminal occupational courses because they fear that credit will be denied for such study if later they decide to seek a bachelor's degree. The question of appropriate credit in bachelor's degree programs for such courses has long been a source of concern to junior college counselors and to university registrars. In general, it may be stated (1) that no single rule can possibly apply to the acceptance of credit for all occupational courses from all junior colleges in fulfilling requirements at all four-year colleges and universities in every major field; (2) that the quality of a student's junior college achievement is a more reliable predictor of his success in upper-division study than is the specific pattern of lower-division courses he has completed; (3) that necessary prerequisites to specific advanced courses cannot be dispensed with, no matter how high the level of a student's marks in other junior college courses; and (4) that each junior college and each senior college will need to analyze the applicability of specific occupational courses to specific degree programs to determine whether the courses that were established for one (terminal) purpose may or may not be accepted in certain cases as meeting another (transfer) purpose.

***Balance of Elements in Occupational Programs.*** Because of the briefness of the junior college period and the multiplicity of its functions, curriculum makers are constantly faced with a choice among educational values. The enthusiastic occupational instructor often feels that he could engage the entire two years of the student's full-time study without preparing him adequately for employment. A contrary pressure is exerted by the generalists on the faculty, who realize how far from ready their students are to bear the responsibilities of life in present-day civilization. The suggested pattern of studies set forth in any organized program is a compromise between these two forces, complicated further by the possibility of legal requirements of courses that must be taught to all students or completed by all graduates.

Several rule-of-thumb suggestions have been made for the resolution of this conflict. Eells has suggested that an occupational program should include 40% specialized study and 40% general courses. He recommended that 20% of the total study for graduation be reserved for elective courses so that the student might pursue any field in which he had a personal need or a worthy interest. Several of the examples of curriculum patterns described by Harris[9] require from 72 to 76 semester units of study. Of these, about 20 are assigned to general education subjects—about 25%, with limited opportunity for free elective courses. A more traditional curriculum pattern of 62-64 semester hours would permit most students to complete their degree and occupational requirements in four semesters of full-time study. Of this, about half, or 30 semester hours, should be assigned to specific technical courses; about one-third, or 20 semester hours, to required general education; and the remaining one-sixth, or 10 semester hours, for elective courses. The important consideration is to assure a reasonable balance of breadth and specialization in each occupational program, so that it may constitute for each student a harmonious collegiate experience.

***Program Organization.*** The organization of instruction in occupational areas varies between junior colleges and also between several occupational fields in the same junior college. Little research is available to help determine which pattern of organization is more effective in training for any given employment. In trade training, a "global" organization is frequently found. Under this plan, one instructor is in charge of all the lecture and laboratory work in the occupational course for a comparatively long period of time; periods of three or four hours scheduled on three or five days a week are usual. This plan has the

## A Global Course Organization in Building Trades

| Number and Name of Course | | Units of Credit | |
|---|---|---|---|
| | | Semester I | Semester II |
| | The First-Year Program | | |
| English 51A-51B | Language Skills | 3 | 3 |
| American Problems 10A-10B | History and Government | 3 | 3 |
| Orientation 1 | Educational and Vocational Planning | 1 | |
| Industrial Drawing 30A | Fundamentals | | 3 |
| Building Construction 58A-58B | Vocational Course | 8 | 8 |
| Physical Education | | ½ | ½ |
| | SEMESTER TOTAL | 15½ | 17½ |
| | The Second-Year Program | | |
| Psychology 51 | Applied Psychology | 3 | |
| Speech 51 | Business Speech | | 3 |
| Health Education 1 | Physical and Mental Health | 2 | |
| Physical Education 31A | First Aid | | 1 |
| Electives | | 2 | 3 |
| Industrial Mathematics 53 | Fundamentals | 3 | |
| Architectural Drawing 30A | Working Drawings | | 3 |
| Industrial Science 63A-63B | Physical Sciences | 3 | 3 |
| Building Construction 64A-64B | Vocational Course | 4 | 4 |
| Physical Education | | ½ | ½ |
| | SEMESTER TOTAL | 17½ | 17½ |

## A Specialized Course Organization in Automotive Technology

| Number and Name of Course | | Units of Credit | |
|---|---|---|---|
| | | Semester I | Semester II |
| **The First-Year Program** | | | |
| English 1-2 | Composition | 3 | 3 |
| Political Science 5 | Survey of American Government | 3 | |
| Physics A | Introductory Physics | 3 | |
| Psychology 5 | Personality Development | | 2 |
| Shop Practice 1 | Basic Machine Tools | | 2 |
| Automotive Training 1 | The Automotive Industry | 2 | |
| Automotive Training 2 | Construction of the Automobile | 4 | |
| Automotive Training 3 | Elementary Electricity | 2 | |
| Automotive Training 4 | Internal Combustion Engines | | 4 |
| Automotive Training 5 | Starting and Lighting Systems | | 4 |
| SEMESTER TOTAL | | 17 | 15 |
| **The Second-Year Program** | | | |
| Speech 3 | Elementary Speech | 2 | |
| Business Mathematics 1 | Business Arithmetic | 2 | |
| Business Administration 1 | Business Organization | | 3 |
| Accounting A | Practical Accounting | | 4 |
| Retailing 1 | Fundamentals of Retailing | | 4 |
| Automotive Training 6 | Generating and Battery Systems | 4 | |
| Automotive Training 7 | Fuel Systems and Carburetion | 4 | |
| Automotive Training 8 | Ignition Systems | 3 | |
| Automotive Training 9 | Diagnostic Laboratory | | 4 |
| SEMESTER TOTAL | | 15 | 15 |

advantage of flexibility in that lecture and laboratory work may be combined in any proportions; laboratory periods are of economical length, so that only a minor fraction of the time need be used in changing clothes, issuing tools, and cleaning up. Field trips can be arranged within the time schedule for the class, without the need for excusing students from other teachers' classes. Disadvantages of the global pattern may include the difficulty of finding a single instructor who is able to teach all aspects of the course, the fact that the laboratory or shop is not used with greatest economy, since it will be vacant whenever the instructor is lecturing, and the inability to care for the student who does not desire the entire occupational course but only a single aspect of it.

The alternate plan, a series of separate courses in various aspects of the occupation, is more usual in business, home economics, and agriculture. This plan allows for specialization of teaching; it also permits a single class section to be used as a portion of the course of study for students in varying major fields. It separates laboratory time from lecture time and so may make possible a greater utilization of specialized equipment. It suffers a disadvantage in that conflicts in schedule with general education courses are more frequent; moreover, some students will not enroll in all the courses essential for complete occupational preparation; their related training may be taught by instructors with only a minimum acquaintance with the specialized occupational field (when technical mathematics, for example, is taught by a mathematics teacher who does not know electronics); and the single courses may be elected by students whose objectives are not occupational. In a community junior college of medium size, moreover, it may well be that a single instructor is required to teach the entire series of separate courses, so that no advantage of specialization is gained over the global course organization.

The detailed courses of study from two community junior colleges demonstrate the difference between the global and the specialized course organizations. The global organization is represented by a major-field program entitled Building Trades, with concentration in Pre-trade Carpentry. This program includes 68 units, of which 24 (35%) are in the major course and an additional six units (9%) are in drafting. General courses account for a total of 33 units (48%), if Industrial Science and Mathematics and Business Speech may be considered a part of the general rather than occupational studies. Electives are limited to five units (7%) of the total of 68. The vocational course requires 15 hours of classtime weekly in the first year, and 10 hours weekly in the second year.

A course for Automotive Technicians at another community college demonstrates the use of a variety of courses of lesser unit value to achieve a similar intensity of occupational training.

In this program, the major course accounts for 31 units (50%) of the total recommended program in addition to the two units in shop practice (3%). A series of vocationally related courses in the business field requires 13 units (21%) of the student's total credit and 16 units (26%) are allocated to general education. In this suggested program no time is provided for free election of courses. Both programs provide for intensive study of occupational topics and related knowledge, and both provide a good opportunity for general education. The elective opportunity, however, is limited in the one program and nonexistent in the other.

*Modular Scheduling.* Educational needs of displaced workers and lateblooming dropouts do not coincide with the academic calendar. Increasingly also, employed workers want refresher instruction in single aspects of their trade and are able to enroll for periods shorter than a semester. Recognition of these facts leads to reorganization of course materials into brief segments (modules) that can be completed in periods of two to three weeks, independently of other sections of the total offering.

The restructuring of occupational courses is facilitated by introduction of auto-tutorial materials and behavioral objectives. In a fully developed modular course, it would be possible for a student to start at any time of the year, to establish the level of his entering mastery of the subject by examination or by performance, and to proceed at his own rate to completion of the course. His contacts with the instructor would be nearly all individual conferences and tutoring at points of difficulty. Success in a basic unit would be prerequisite to succeeding modules; competence instead of time spent in the shops or laboratory would be the measure of completion. Mastery of expected behavior could be required of almost all students, although some would achieve it more slowly than others.

A less thorough adaptation of instruction to student needs consists in increasing the number of entry points within the term. Instead of requiring all students to start every course at the opening of a semester, independent four- or six- or eight-week modules can be scheduled within a course. This plan can be made to fit with other courses that are scheduled for full terms. It causes complications in record-keeping, but these are not insuperable. It is perhaps more adaptable to trade-technical studies and to science than to mathematics or foreign languages. At any rate, greater flexibility in scheduling will contribute to concentration on the specific needs of individual students rather than on the convenience of the system.

*Specialization of Training.*    The desirable degree of specialization of the offering is another problem in program development. It is not difficult to determine the content and the equipment of a course that trains carpenters, body and fender workers, or television repairmen; but the realities of technological change suggest that broader training may be advisable to prepare graduates adequately for their futures. For this reason, community junior colleges have attempted to develop courses which prepare for families of occupations, such as mechanical technology, electronic technology, or civil engineering technology. Not only does such training prepare the graduate to progress to a position of responsibility in his work; its scope and variety make it more suitable to the junior college than the more limited trade training that may properly be found in vocational schools or in high schools.

Cooperative work experience is a further opportunity in the development of occupational programs. In cooperative education, students preparing for occupations spend part of their time in classes on the college campus, both in general education and in occupational courses. In addition, a part of their junior college course is devoted to work in the occupation for which they are preparing. The junior college staff arranges for the student's placement, supervises his work, and grants limited credit for successful completion of the assignment. In some plans, the students work as much as half-time and receive learners' rates of pay; in others their work is limited to fewer than ten hours weekly, and they receive no pay. Under either plan, the important outcomes from the standpoint of the community junior college are the first-hand acquaintance the student gains with the requirements of employment and the added understanding he brings to his class work.

*Cooperation with Labor and Management.*    Occupational courses are soundly established only as a result of thorough and continuing study of the employment opportunities and the training needs of the industry. This information is available most readily from those who are currently working in the field, either as workers or managers. Advisory committees including representatives of both interests are essential to the development and maintenance of any occupational course. Such a committee can keep the community junior college abreast of trends in the occupation. It can help with placement of students and graduates, with choice and procurement of equipment, and with interpretation of the training program to workers and to employers. No occupational course should be established without the advice and encouragement of a broadly representative local advisory committee.

*Retention of Students.*   In a period of low employment opportunity, the junior college is more concerned with finding work for its graduates than it is with keeping them in school until completion of the program. In a time of high employment, however, the timing of student employment may be a perplexing problem. The community junior college, with the cooperation of its advisory committee, plans an occupational program which it considers to be well-rounded and unified. The student who completes the program will have received training enabling him to obtain and to progress on a job; if he leaves before completion, he leaves with only partial training. Employers and students, however, sometimes fail to take this long-term attitude. The employer is certain that the half-trained bookkeeper, technician, draftsman, or secretary is superior to any of the untrained persons otherwise available to him. The student feels, justifiably, that he came to the community junior college to prepare to get a job which is now offered to him; it is difficult to convince him that an additional year of schooling would increase either his earning power or his preparation for living. The advisory committee may take a stand in this area by discouraging employers from hiring students prior to their graduation, but for the most part, the decision to work or to study will be reached by the student in the light of the values that have become apparent to him.

*Selection of Students.*   One of the most pressing issues in occupational education continues to be that of helping students to choose the course for which they are best fitted. Some degree of error is unavoidable; some students must be permitted to attempt curriculums in which their success seems unlikely. A good deal of the disproportion between ambition and achievement, however, derives from inadequacies of the junior colleges. In part, there is a failure to provide a suitable diversity of nontransfer courses. One or two terminal business courses (and a third of the junior colleges offer no more) will not meet the needs of all nontransfer students. A second inadequacy lies in the failure to inform students and their parents, early in their high-school careers, of the availability and of the purposes of junior college occupational education. A good many students would choose their programs realistically, if only they had appropriate information. Lack of effective personal guidance is another contributor to failure and dropout. Students who are helped to see the relationship between their patterns of interest and abilities and the requirements of available occupations and of educational programs are enabled to choose wisely. Without such information, their choices must be blind and almost haphazard. It is becoming increasingly important to provide for some students a semester or more of preparatory studies so that they may have the educational background to succeed in the chosen technical course.

*The Recruitment and Training of Occupational Instructors.* Studies of certification standards for community college teachers stress a combination of academic training equal to a master's degree or beyond, plus a meaningful period of work experience in a field related to the major subject. For teachers in occupational fields, the preparation requirements are even more stringent than those for teachers of traditional subjects. These teachers, in business, in technologies, or in trade subjects, need thorough academic knowledge of their specialty and adequate training in the methods and materials of teaching. Beyond this, they need actual vocational experience of sufficient scope to enable them to prepare their students realistically for the conditions and responsibilities of employment. They need to have achieved sufficient standing in their occupational field to work with members of the advisory committee on a basis of equality and mutual respect. Since such experience connotes considerable maturity, salary schedules must recognize this kind of experience and preparation as well as academic degrees and experience in teaching. Further, since such mature persons can rarely devote a year or more to full-time teacher-training programs, it is often necessary to enable them to complete the requirements for certification while they are teaching.

It seems probable that a major deterrent to the development of occupational education in junior colleges has been the scarcity of qualified instructors in these subjects. Until plans can be elaborated for the effective recruitment and training of instructors, the offerings will continue to be scanty and only partially suited to the educational needs of junior college students.

### FOOTNOTES

1.  *Learning for Earning: New Opportunities for Paycheck Education.* Washington, D.C.: Government Printing Office (OE-80063), 1969. Unpaged.
2.  *State Vocational Education Statistics, Fiscal Year 1969* (Preliminary Report). Washington, D.C.: Government Printing Office (OE-80017), 1969. Tables IV and XII.
3.  Koos, Leonard V. *The Junior College Movement.* Boston: Ginn and Company, 1925.
4.  Vocational Education Staff, "Vocational Education in California,"

*Bulletin of the California State Department of Education,* **XIV,** No. 4 (October, 1945), pp. 1-3.

5.     Emerson, Lynn A. "Vocational-Technical Education for American Industry," *Office of Education Circular,* No. 530. Washington, D.C.: U.S. Government Printing Office, 1958, p. 9.

6.     *Community College Guide for Associate Degree Programs in Auto and Truck Service/Management.* Detroit: Automobile Manufacturers' Association, Inc., 1969.

7.     Gleazer, Edmund J., Jr. (ed.), *American Junior Colleges.* (Seventh edition). Washington, D.C.: American Council on Education, 1967.

8.     *Vocational and Technical Education* (Annual Report, Fiscal Year 1968). Washington, D.C.: U.S. Government Printing Office (OE 80008-68), 1968, p. 23.

9.     Harris, Norman C. *Technical Education in the Junior College: New Programs for New Jobs.* Washington, D.C.: American Association of Junior Colleges, 1964, pp. 63-76.

## BIBLIOGRAPHY

De Carlo, Charles R. "Changing Industrial Needs and Job Training," *Compact,* June, 1968, pp. 38-40.

Gleazer, Edmund J., Jr. *American Junior Colleges* (Seventh Edition), 1967. Washington, D.C.: American Council on Education, 1968.

Harris, Norman C. *Technical Education in the Junior College: New Programs for New Jobs.* Washington, D.C.: American Association for Junior Colleges, 1964.

Hilton, E. P. and Steven J. Gyuro. *A Systems Approach—1970: Vocational Education Handbook for State Plan Development and Preparation.* Lexington, Kentucky: Kentucky Research Coordinating Unit for Vocational Education, University of Kentucky, 1970.

Miller, Aaron J., and Angelo C. Gillie. *A Suggested Guide for Post-Secondary Vocational and Technical Education.* Columbus, Ohio: Center for Vocational and Technical Education, The Ohio State University, 1970.

Rhodes, James A. *Vocational Education and Guidance: A System for the Seventies.* Columbus, Ohio: Charles E. Merrill Publishing Company, 1970.

Riendeau, Albert J. *The Role of the Advisory Committee in Occupational Education in the Junior College.* Washington, D.C.: American Association of Junior Colleges, 1967.

Schaefer, Carl J. and Jacob J. Kaufman. *New Directions for Vocational*

*Education*. Lexington, Massachusetts: D. C. Heath and Company, 1971.

Venn, Grant. *Man, Education, and Work*. Washington, D.C.: American Council on Education, 1964.

*Vocational Education: The Bridge Between Man and His Work*. Washington, D.C.: U.S. Government Printing Office (OE 80052), 1968.

Young, Earl B., et al. *Vocational Education for Handicapped Persons*. Washington, D.C.: U.S. Government Printing Office (OE-35096), 1970.

# 14 The Curriculum: General Education

Each student's program of studies is made up of three elements: preparation for occupational specialization, elective courses, and general education courses. Occupational specialization courses appear in many forms, but they include all the subjects required of any individual student as a part of his total preparation, immediate or remote, for his life's work. In this sense, calculus for the pre-engineering freshman and zoology for the premedical freshman are just as truly occupational education as technical electronics or stenography for the technician or the secretary.

The elective section of a given student's college education may include any course listed in the college catalog. After the graduation requirements of the college and the specific requirements for occupational specialization have been met, a student may complete his education by free choice from any of the courses for which he mas met the prerequisites. For others, the same course may be a part of specialization; for him, it is an elective, chosen to satisfy an individual interest. The only distinction, in this case, arises from the student's purpose in enrolling in the course. "Shakespeare" serves a different function for the English major than it does for the future architect who happens to enjoy drama. Many courses, as in sociology, psychology, history, art, music, philosophy, trades, or sciences, have an inherent interest for students who have no intention ever to use them vocationally. By enriching the personality, such courses may in fact improve the student's working effectiveness, but that is not his reason for enrolling in them.

Some writers include this category of elective courses under the heading of general education. Such a confusion of purpose then leads to suggestions that "Anthropology (or astronomy, or ceramics) is a good general education course." More enthusiastic advocates see general education as inhering in all aspects of the curriculum. Yet other writers object that if the program is collegewide in its scope, the responsibility for it becomes so diffuse that no precise provision will be made. Chapter 14 examines the concept and definition of general education, presents some of the patterns of general education courses discovered in junior college curriculums, and describes courses in several fields which might contribute to the achievement of the goals of general education.

## A. Definition of General Education

General education is but one element of a complete education; nearly all students will need to add to it courses which prepare them for their occupations and courses which satisfy specialized interests of a nonvocational nature. General education refers to programs of education specifically designed to prepare young people for the responsibilities that they share in common as citizens of a free society and for wholesome and creative participation in a wide range of life activities. It is that part of education which prepares the student to assume:

> his roles as an individual, as a member of a family, and as a citizen. While it may contribute to his choice of occupation and to his success as a worker, vocational skills are not its main objective. It is called "general" because its purposes are conceived to be common to all men; it is that part of the total collegiate offering which is concerned with men's likenesses rather than with their divergent interests. It intends to assist the student to feel intellectually and psychologically at home

in a world which makes new economic, social, civic, physiological, spiritual, and intellectual demands upon him.[1]

Several phrases in the definition deserve elaboration. General education programs, it states, are "specifically designed." This concept is not shared by all students of general education; college lower-division programs often attempt to provide for general education by recommending a sampling of established introductory courses from several areas— English, science, social sciences, and humanities. The sampling plan has the advantage of fiscal economy, since a single course may be made to serve several purposes. In most subjects, however, the introductory course is planned principally for those students who will study further in the field; the purposes of the nonmajor students are likely to be subordinated or completely ignored by the instructor, himself a specialist in the field. The establishment of a separate pattern of general education courses is justifiable on the grounds of (1) economy of the student's time, (2) the impossibility of a student's enrolling in all the needed introductory courses, (3) the student's need for a coherent and unified interpretation of modern scholarship rather than for an introduction to five or six unrelated aspects of it, and (4) efficiency in organizing instruction to achieve general education purposes directly rather than as by-products of specialized courses.

The key phrase in the definition, that which distinguishes general education from vocational and elective education is "preparation for the responsibilities which they share in common." In previous chapters, attention has been called to the range of student differences in the public junior colleges and to the need for many varieties of educational opportunity to accommodate these differences. At the same time, common citizenship and common humanity beget common educational needs that may be overlooked under the pressure of our increasing specialization and the sheer volume of modern knowledge. The multiplication of courses in every department of our colleges makes necessary the conscious exertion of a countering centripetal force; too rigid a concentration in any field may deprive the student of the opportunity to acquire understanding which he needs in his roles as citizen, parent, and person.

The specific meanings of the phrase "wholesome and creative participation in a wide range of life activities" have been enumerated by Johnson as a series of goals of general education:

The general education program aims to help each student increase his competence in

1. Exercising the privileges and responsibilities of democratic citizenship.
2. Developing a set of sound spiritual and moral values by which he guides his life.
3. Expressing his thoughts clearly in speaking and writing and in reading and listening with understanding.
4. Using the basic mathematical and mechanical skills necessary in everyday life.
5. Using methods of critical thinking for the solution of problems and for the discrimination among values.
6. Understanding his cultural heritage so that he may gain a perspective of his time and place in the world.
7. Understanding his interaction with his biological and physical environment so that he may better adjust to and improve that environment.
8. Maintaining good mental and physical health for himself, his family, and his community.
9. Developing a balanced personal and social adjustment.
10. Sharing in the development of a satisfactory home and family life.
11. Achieving a satisfactory vocational adjustment.
12. Taking part in some form of satisfying creative activity and in appreciating the creative activities of others.[2]

Such objectives are not new in American higher education; the novelty consists in their clear and explicit recognition and in the realization that students do not achieve them accidentally as a result of exposure to a random selection from the hundreds of available courses. Certainly no college will attempt to establish 12 courses, each to contribute to one of these goals. It is equally certain, however, that introductory courses in single disciplines are not the most direct means to effect the changes contemplated in the final six goals.

It is unfortunate when a community junior college commits itself to goals which it makes no provision for achieving. If the definition and the ideal of general education are valid, they are valid for all students. The college then must ensure that each student, and certainly each graduate, makes some progress in "improving his competence" in these areas. This obligation can be discharged in part through the establishment of a limited number of specially designed courses required for graduation. Because students differ in their competence, some provision for exemption or for advanced opportunity is necessary to serve those who already surpass the minimum standards. Organizing an attractive series of general courses, however, will not complete the task; especially in the community junior college, there simply is not time for the student to achieve these goals completely and finally in individual courses. Every instructor should become aware of these goals and be committed to them, so that every course in every department contributes as it can to general education; conscious planning is essential. The effective program of general education includes both a collegewide emphasis on general education outcomes and provision of courses which are addressed primarily to particular objectives.

## B. Practices in General Education

To some extent, the philosophy of general education which a community junior college adopts in practice maybe deduced from a study of its graduation requirements. It is true that such requirements are sometimes decided by agencies outside of the college; they may be copied after university curriculums or they may be prescribed by state law or regulation. Furthermore, if the college administration believes in a policy of individual election of general education courses, graduation requirements are unlikely to reflect that attitude.

In an effort to sample the offerings in the several areas of the curriculum, the catalogs of 40 community colleges were analyzed. These colleges represented 5% of the public junior college membership of the American Association of Junior Colleges. Enrollments ranged from more than 16,000 full-time students to fewer than 600. Public junior colleges in every region of the Association were included in the sample. Two cautions are necessary in considering data of this nature. Not every course described in a catalog is offered every year; and the catalog gives no indication of the numbers of students who actually enroll in a course. If a course is required, though, it may be assumed that a large proportion of the entering students will complete it.

Of the colleges sampled, 20 had specific course requirements for general education, and 12 others had a broad distributional requirement, with stated numbers of credits to be chosen from a list of courses in each of two, three, or four broad fields. Eight of the colleges listed no subjects that were required of all graduates, but in six of these every suggested program described in the catalog included one of several courses in English composition—the only element common to all programs. Practice in general education, in these 40 colleges, seems divided. Half hope to accomplish the purposes of general education by requiring the student to complete at least one course in each of the major areas of learning, and the other half require specific courses in English and social sciences, often in physical education and in health and hygiene, and sometimes in humanities or in sciences.

In 1952, Johnson concluded that few junior colleges had well-defined policies governing their provisions for the general education needs of their students. In the California Study of General Education in the Junior College, he reported that "As one examines the graduation requirements of California junior colleges with the goals of general education in mind, he is impressed (1) by diversity of practice, (2) by the spotty and limited recognition given some of the general education objectives, and (3) by the apparent failure as yet to make any provision for some of the others.[3] In the sample of 40 colleges, there is evidence that attention has been paid in principle to the need for general education. While Johnson's observations seem to be still applicable nationally as well as to California, more colleges are now making at least minimal provision for general education than at the time of his study (1952).

Sixteen of the 40 junior college catalogs included a statement about general education as one of the purposes of junior college students. The longest statement listed the 12 goals presented by Johnson. Another catalog contained the following listing of objectives:

The primary aim of_____Junior College is to create an educational environment which opens up opportunities for each student to learn and to work in a community of scholars and to develop the following abilities and attitudes:

To appraise realistically his goals, abilities, achievements, and behavior.

To expand his knowledge, understanding, and appreciation of the world about him.

To prepare for adult responsibilities as a citizen and a member of family and community groups.

To practice social conduct based on ethnical and spiritual values.

To develop skills and basic intellectual qualities for further higher education, continuing education, and occupational proficiency.

To develop aesthetic appreciation of literature, music, the visual arts, and his cultural heritage.

To develop social responsibilities, leadership characteristics and to learn how to participate in a democratic society.

To learn to judge men and issues critically and to base decisions and conduct on such judgment.

To understand conditions for healthful and effective living and to develop social poise and mature conduct.

***Communication.***    With two exceptions, all the public junior colleges in the sample group require for graduation some study of English. A one-year course is the usual prescription, with 22 of the 40 colleges listing this as their requirement. Thirteen colleges require either one or two additional semesters of English, and three add a requirement of a course in speech, for a total of 15 semester hours.

The second year in each college emphasizes literature more than basic composition. The universality of the requirement indicates that in the area of communication, at least, all public junior colleges attempt to increase their students' competence in expressing their thoughts. In composition, especially, the major purpose of the freshman course has always been that of general education rather than of introduction to further study. Although English faculties often question the efficacy of their efforts, at least the opportunity for general education in this area is available.

The effective emphasis on "increasing competence" in communication is demonstrated also in the prevalence of remedial or developmental opportunities. Thirty-five of the sample colleges offer some work in clinics, laboratories, or specialized classes to enable students to correct deficient skills in reading. These courses usually carry a minimum credit toward the associate degree but not toward transfer to a four-year college. The so-called "sub-freshman" course in the mechanics of writing is offered in 27 of these public junior colleges, and is usually required on the basis of a pretest of writing ability. The catalog statements, unfortunately, do not indicate how many students need or avail themselves of these opportunities to achieve minimum skills in communication.

An example of the nature of offerings in communication skills is the description of English 101-102, a two-semester course carrying six units of credit, in one of the catalogs in the sample group.

EN 101-102. TECHNIQUES OF READING AND WRITING.

Experiences in using the essential tools of communication. Selected readings analyzed intensively for both meaning and evaluation. Weekly written assignments correlated to develop logical thought in correct and effective expression.

EN101:    Studies in exposition.

EN102:    Studies in argumentation, rhetoric and persuasion, scientific writing. Introduction to and practice in the methods of library research and writing a research paper.

EN       Content and requirements are the same as those of
101X:    English 101. Two extra class periods a week give students
         who failed to demonstrate mastery of basic fundamentals
         the opportunity to remedy their deficiencies.

*Social Science.*    Thirty-eight of the 40 colleges require some study in
the field of social sciences for graduation. Usually this requirement is
either in American history or in a combination of American history and
government. The credit value of the requirement ranges from no credit
for passing a test of knowledge of American government in one junior
college, through ten units from a list of social sciences at another, to a
maximum graduation requirement of 12 units in social sciences. Although the social science requirement certainly is established in hope
that it may increase students' competence in democratic citizenship,
critical thinking, and understanding of the cultural heritage, the courses
which satisfy the requirement are usually organized as chronological
treatments of United States history.

In this sample, only 15 examples were found of courses in social sciences
which seemed to be specifically organized for the purposes of general
education. One of them is described in the catalog as carrying six semester
units of credit for the year's study:

SS 101, 102. SOCIAL SCIENCE—INTEGRATED
COURSE.

The nature of society and the manner in which the individual and
the social group interact, with emphasis on the role of the individual
as a family member, as a consumer-producer, and as an effective
participant in community life. Analysis of race relations, international conflicts, and consequences of social change. Makes use of those
findings, insights, and approaches from sociology, psychology, political science, and economics, which contribute to a better understanding of human relations, especially the significance of the student's
own participation in every-day living.

*Physical Education.*    Physical education is required for graduation in
36 of the 40 colleges, sometimes because of a prescription in state law.
The requirement usually includes two hours of participation weekly,
either for one year or for four semesters. In four of the colleges the
required participation earned no credit toward graduation, whereas in
seven it afforded a total of four units of credit. The pattern of two hours
weekly for one-half unit of credit is the most frequent one. The scope of
the offerings in physical education also varies greatly.

Some catalog descriptions indicate that the course consists mostly of calisthenics, supplemented by team play in two or three sports; others list as many as 40 kinds of physical education opportunities. The more extensive programs include classes for men, for women, and for mixed groups, and they supplement the usual intercollegiate team sports with activities of value in after-college life such as golf, badminton, and bowling. Only two of the colleges make mention of opportunities for special physical education for the convalescent, for the handicapped, or for other students with special needs such as posture improvement or weight reduction. The extent of variability of the offering indicates that although some public junior colleges are seriously attempting to improve their students' competence in maintaining good health and balanced personal adjustment, others have not yet developed any courses specifically directed toward the attainment of these goals.

An idea of the scope of physical education programs in a single community college may be gained from the description of the opportunities in the required course:

In the physical education programs a variety of activities are taught for physiological and recreational values. Courses include individual, dual and team sports and other activities designed to improve fitness, movement, and creative expression. Activities are scheduled for the skilled, unskilled, and handicapped. *To meet College requirements for an associate degree, five terms of physical education are required.*

Majors in health, physical education, and recreation must begin course work in professional activities during the freshman year if they are to complete a baccalaureate program in four years. Lower division professional courses are recommended for all students planning to transfer to teacher preparation programs offered by state system institutions.

Intramural and intercollegiate athletics are an integral part of the physical education program. Both men and women students of all levels of ability are urged to participate.

The broad aim of the intramural program is to provide an opportunity for every student to participate in some type of competitive sports activity as frequently as his interests, ability, and time will permit. The intramural program provides a full schedule of individual and team sports leading to school championships.

Intercollegiate athletics provide competitive opportunities for highly skilled students in selected sports with teams from other colleges. _____ College is a member of the _____ Community College Athletic Conference and the National Junior College Athletic Association. Teams compete in cross country, track, basketball, gymnastics, wrestling, soccer, swimming, tennis, baseball, and volleyball.

Instruction in personal and community hygiene is less usual than instruction in physical education. Twenty of the forty junior colleges include a one-semester course in hygiene, usually for two units, in their graduation requirements. Six additional colleges require a course in biological science, which may include health education topics.

***Other Requirements.*** Orientation, psychology, human relations, or personal adjustment courses are required for graduation in nine of the 40 colleges; most of the other schools offer an optional orientation course, or offer it without credit. Additional requirements in 12 colleges include courses in humanities, and in 21 colleges, courses in science or mathematics.

In so far as graduation requirements indicate the effective commitment of public junior colleges to the concept of a common minimum of general education for all students, it is possible to conclude that the colleges agree only on the skills of communication as elements in that minimum. There is substantial agreement on courses that are intended to prepare students to assume the duties of citizenship and on physical education courses. Beyond that, more than half of these colleges have attempted through prescription to ensure that their graduates have been exposed to a well-rounded and carefully planned curriculum in general education.

## C. Courses Planned for General Education

Section B of this Chapter reported that nearly all the public junior colleges require for graduation one or more courses which they consider to be part of the background essential for all their students. In addition, several of the colleges have made tentative and scattered attempts to devise appropriate courses. The courses so designed are rarely required for graduation; in student programs, they often take second place to the more "practical" and conventional courses in occupational training or in traditional disciplines. A brief discussion of some of the general education courses described in the 40 catalogs studied will indicate the nature and the extent of the effort being made at present to provide directly for these goals.

***Preparation for Marriage.*** Twenty-nine of the forty colleges list a course in "Marriage and Family Life," "Marriage Problems," or "Family Relations;" none of the 29 requires the course for graduation. The courses are developed in recognition of the increasing difficulty of establishing and preserving wholesome and stable families in an affluent, mobile, self-indulgent society. In general, they combine subject matter from the fields of sociology, psychology, biology, and home economics in an attempt to help students prepare to make rational choices of mates and to achieve attitudes and insights that will contribute to satisfactory home and family life. They are offered in the departments of sociology, home making, or psychology. It is not possible to determine what proportion of the students in these colleges actually enroll in these courses, nor what effect the courses have on improving students' later behavior as home-makers. They are examples, however, of direct attempts to achieve through classroom instruction several of the goals of general education.

One of the junior colleges in the sample group offers two separate courses in the area of preparation for marriage, both in the sociology department:

SO 157 FAMILY LIVING                                          3 credits

This is the study of the functions of the family and the effect of relationships within the family on the development of individuals in the home and community. Emphasis is placed on constructive attitudes toward marriage and the family. Open to all students.

SO 159 THE MODERN FAMILY                                     3 credits

An examination of the modern American family. Special emphasis is put on the changing functions and roles of individuals within society and an analysis of the basic problems confronting the American family. Open to all students.

*Applied Psychology.* Twenty-seven colleges offer no-prerequisite courses in the field of psychology, other than the university-parallel "Introduction to Psychology." These courses are planned to help the student increase his competence in maintaining good mental health for himself, his family, and his community, and in developing a balanced personal and social adjustment. Presumably they also contribute to the ability of critical thinking, as well as to several others of the goals of general education. The titles adopted for courses of this nature include: Psychology of Adjustment, Personality Development, Applied Psychology, and Human Relations. None of the colleges requires a course in psychology for graduation, although several have a requirement in Orientation, taught in the Psychology Department.

The nature of the human relations course is outlined in one of the catalogs surveyed.

## 12. HUMAN RELATIONS                          3 hours credit

A study of psychological principles is applied to everyday living, with emphasis on self understanding and on the building of successful relationships with others. This course is designed for the student who desires a practical course in human relations and who does not need general psychology to meet requirements in another college.

*Sciences.*   For some reason, the survey course in physical sciences, designed for the nonscientist, is offered more frequently than a survey in biological sciences. Of the sample of 40, 36 colleges offer an introduction to physical sciences, with credit ranging from three to six units. Laboratory experience is required in about half of these surveys. In biological sciences, only 13 of these colleges offer a course that is ostensibly different from the standard one-year transfer course in general biology. Credit value in this course also varies from three units in one semester to six units in a year-course.

In one college, a coordinated year-sequence is described as

### 10A-10B THE WORLD AND MAN (3-3)

Survey course with topics chosen principally from astronomy, meteorology, and geology in 10A and from the chemical and physical aspects of man's environment in 10B, developed in such a way as to attempt to influence significantly the beliefs, philosophy, behavior, and attitudes of the student. Lecture-demonstration and films.

NOTE: 10A may not be taken for credit by a student with previous credit in a college level course in astronomy, geology, or physical geography; 10B may not be taken for credit by a student with previous credit in a college level course in chemistry or physics; neither may be taken for credit as a repeat of a physical science course taken in another college.

*Other General Courses.*   Courses specifically designed to contribute to other accepted goals of general education appear infrequently and are rarely a part of a coordinated collegewide plan for a comprehensive general education. There are 20 examples of introductory courses in the social sciences, with titles such as Man's Cultural Heritage, Introduction to Social Sciences, or Man and Society. Only nine of the colleges offer courses in Consumer Economics or Personal Economics. In the integrated humanities field, 21 interdisciplinary courses are offered, seven for a full year and the rest for a single semester.

It is possible that the preceding paragraphs present an overly pessimistic picture of the present status of general education in the junior colleges.

The analysis of offerings and the comments about them were based on the two assumptions that general education courses should be specifically designed to achieve general education goals and that education for common responsibilities should be required of all students. It is certain that some courses which bear traditional subject titles are organized and taught primarily for general education. It is equally true that counselors in some junior colleges encourage students to broaden their education by the election of courses that will increase their general competence. Nevertheless, the fact remains that fewer than half of the colleges enforce any requirements beyond English, history, and physical education, and fewer than half organize any pattern of courses specifically for general education. The evidence is conclusive that the public junior colleges have not yet wholeheartedly accepted general education as one of their primary purposes.

## D. A Suggested Program

Many conditions contribute to the failure of community colleges to develop comprehensive patterns of required general education courses. Not the least of these is the sheer complexity of the undertaking; the leadership, the money, the time, and the faculty members simply have not been available for planning on the necessary scale. The autonomy of the public junior colleges makes it necessary for each one to work either independently or imitatively in developing its curriculum, and few of these colleges have the resources to initiate thorough studies independently.

Transfer requirements of universities are another restricting force. The investment required to prepare students for future study in engineering, sciences, business administration, education, social sciences, and the other hundreds of university specializations leaves little opportunity for the development of courses which deviate from accepted practices. These same requirements, moreover, so fill up the time of the students that it is difficult to obtain adequate enrollments of qualified students in experimental courses, even when they are provided.

The limitation of time affects the general education of the students in occupational courses as well. The advisory committees and the instructors who plan vocational training are convinced that their subjects are important and that they require a major part of the students' time and effort. They are likely to conclude that the financially unremunerative goals of general education can be ignored, or at least deferred, in planning programs of study. The students also may accept this judgment in their eagerness to achieve vocational competence so that they may begin to earn.

A further difficulty inheres in the uncertainty regarding the nature of the educational process itself. Is it possible to teach directly so as to achieve the intangible and attitudinal goals of general education? Or is the educator limited to teaching facts and skills in the hope that, from these, time and experience will bring about appropriate wisdom, attitudes, and practices? These doubts are reinforced by the inertia of faculty members, who find security in teaching as they were taught and a sense of immortality in preparing acolytes to follow in their footsteps and perpetuate the cult of their discipline. The net result of these difficulties has been to paralyze initiative and to discourage experimentation in general education, so that no public junior college exhibits a coherent, comprehensive, well-planned, and carefully evaluated curriculum to lead all its students toward the 12 goals of general education. The following suggestions are offered as a framework on which such a complete curriculum might be constructed. Several preliminary comments must be kept in mind as the proposals are evaluated.

In the first place, the community junior college cannot devote the major portion of its program to general education. Some four-year colleges require their students to complete a general program equivalent to as much as three-fourths of their entire lower-division credits; because of its functions in pretransfer and in occupational education, the community junior college will find that it cannot require more than 20 or 21 units of specific general education courses. In an era when all requirements are called in question, it may be necessary to depend on counseling rather than prescription even to achieve that goal of student exposure. Again, at present it is difficult for the junior colleges to secure university acceptance of experimentally developed courses. Careful preliminary planning of the course, perhaps in consultation with university officers, will help in gaining favorable evaluation, as will assignment of the ablest instructors available to the courses. Even so, for some time it may still be necessary to provide alternate courses by which students preparing for certain transfer specialties may meet the requirements. An easy evasion of university domination is to require newly developed courses only of the nontransfer students, but the experience of several colleges indicates that such a limitation on enrollment creates psychological barriers to the development of a course that can be taught enthusiastically and studied eagerly.

The problem of university domination of the community junior college curriculum has been mentioned before; it is one of the pervasive influences that must be recognized in any consideration of the curriculum. At times, this domination is advanced as an excuse for inactivity by the junior colleges; at other times, it proves to be a truly frustrating and unnecessary deterrent to soundly conceived experimentation. The solution lies partly in acceptance by the community junior colleges of full responsibility for the preparation of their graduates, with the implied guarantee that the transferring student has achieved an education equivalent to although not identical with that of the four-year-college junior. The other part of the solution lies in the recognition by senior institutions that community junior college faculties have the ability, the resources, the desire, and the obligation to develop curriculums for all their students. When these conditions are achieved, the community junior colleges will begin to develop acceptable general education offerings such as those here proposed.

Course titles present an added difficulty in devising a suggested program. Traditional titles such as History of the United States or Freshman Composition are both misleading and restricting when applied to broader courses that draw materials from several disciplines. The alternative practice is to devise titles that concentrate attention on the purposes of the courses rather than on their content, such as Preparation for Marriage. These titles may be so explicit or so unusual that considerable effort must be devoted to explaining and defending both the titles and the courses. The difficulty arises from attempting to compress great precision of meaning and a concise summary of content into a three-or-four-word title. A name should be adopted that affords a convenient and simple reference to the course, without confining the expectations of students and others too rigidly to a single discipline. American Civilization might be a better title for one course than Social Science I or History of the United States. For another, Communication might be a more acceptable title than either the traditional Composition and Rhetoric or the somewhat pretentious Elementary Linguistics.

The final caution has to do with content. The elimination of material is just as important as the selection of content in developing a course for general education. General education became necessary because the bulk of knowledge grew until no human, no college freshman, could hope to encompass any major part of it. Barzun has summarized the point of view as follows:

"That same abundance of information has turned into a barrier between one man and the next. They are mutually incommunicado, because each believes that his subject and his language cannot and should not be understood by the other. . . . Of true knowledge at any time, a good part is merely convenient, necessary indeed to the worker, but not to the understanding of his subject: one can judge a building without knowing where to buy the bricks; one can understand a violin sonata without knowing how to score for the instrument. . . . With a cautious confidence and sufficient intellectual training, it is possible to master the literature of a subject and gain a proper understanding of it: specifically, an understanding of the accepted truths, the disputed problems, the rival schools, and the methods now in favor. This will not enable one to add to what is known, but it will give possession of *all that the discipline has to offer the world.*"[4]

This concept is by no means an advocacy of superficiality. No useful purpose is served by teaching generalities. The haste, compression, and triviality that have sometimes characterized courses for the "nonmajor" student are useless, even harmful. General education demands the most careful selection of topics to be considered, coupled with thoroughness, depth, scholarship, rigor, and intellectual discipline in the study of these topics. It is not necessary to teach everything known in order to teach thoroughly.

In order to achieve a course of this quality, a faculty will need to steel itself to achieve some fundamental rethinking of educational practice. The first analytical task is the definition of purposes. These will be stated not as material to be covered but as changes expected in the students. In order to increase their competence in the desired activity, what attitudes must be developed? What skills achieved? What knowledge mastered? Through what educational avenues may these outcomes be reached? The answer to these questions may evoke a dozen possible answers. One analyst will suggest that his introductory course as now organized does just what has been described. Other suggestions will include an approach through biography, a laboratory experience, concentration on a single problem of contemporary America, a sampling of interesting units from several disciplines, or a thorough study of a current problem as it appeared in an earlier society. The planning group may realize that the goals may be approached in any of several ways, and that it must select the course organization that seems most adaptable to available instructors, facilities, and students.

Detailed planning will follow upon choice of basic approach. Here again selection of material is crucial. The temptation is to cram too much into a single course, so that a great many topics are mentioned, not mastered. Instead, conscious effort should be exerted to provide for depth of understanding in a few areas rather than breadth and superficiality over the entire field. This is why a planning committee is necessary to bring to light contributions from various specialties; at the same time, a single instructor, training himself to succeed in all phases of the new course, is likely to be more effective than a corps of instructors, each presenting a single aspect of it.

Can a series of such courses be organized to require no more than one-third of a junior college student's time and to contribute significantly to the increase of each student's competence in the 12 goals of general education? It should be possible to construct a series of four courses, comprising 21 semester units and affording all students opportunity to improve their preparation "for the responsibilities they share in common as citizens in a free society, and for wholesome and creative participation in a wide range of life activities." The following suggestions are presented as a demonstration of the feasibility of this approach and in the hope that one or more public junior college faculties may undertake to refine the analysis and to develop an experimental program. Such experimentation might help to determine whether or not it is possible to organize instruction with emphasis on the purposes of the learners, rather than on the complete and logical organization of single disciplines.

Certain of the objectives quoted at the beginning of the chapter are closely related to each other and can be achieved at the same time and in a single course. It is possible to imagine four manageable courses which in combination would contribute directly to the student's attainment of every one of the 12 goals. Additional study in elective and in vocational courses would extend each student's competence in one or several of the goals, whereas the suggested basic offering in general education would attempt to make sure that no student ignored completely any one of the goals. The four courses proposed may be summarized thus:

| | | |
|---|---|---|
| Course A Communications | 6 units; | Primary goals 3,5,12, secondary, 2,9. |
| Course B American Civilization | 6 units; | Primary goals 1,5,6, secondary, 2,11. |
| Course C The Physical World | 6 units; | Primary goals 4,5,7,8, secondary, 11. |
| Course D Human Behavior | 3 units; | Primary goals 8,9,10, secondary, 11. |

*Course A, Communications,* would combine the purposes of helping each student increase his competence in expressing his thoughts, thinking critically, working creatively, and appreciating the creative activities of others; indirectly, the activities of the course should lead to a clarification of his values and to a more balanced personal and social adjustment. The *content* of the course would consist of consideration of excellent examples of communication in all mediums. Subject matter could be drawn from written materials in any field and from music, painting, sculpture, and dramatics. Such content can be adapted to any level of previous student achievement by selection of examples; the purpose is to help each student increase his competence. The experience of considering the communicative effort of other men will provide the students with rich incentives for writing and speaking. Some of the difficulty in freshman composition has come from the student's lack of desire to compose because he has nothing to say. In a course such as this, his reactions and his attempts to clarify his critical thinking will provide ample stimulation to write and to discuss. For the teacher, English as a deadening service course in mechanics, concentrating on uninspiring sentence errors and inspired misspellings, will be replaced by the exciting experience of watching young minds increase in appreciation, in critical thinking, and in desire to express their thoughts clearly.

*Course B, American Civilization,* would explain and prepare for participation in American civilization by concentrating on helping the student increase his competence in citizenship, in critical thinking, and in understanding his cultural heritage. The development of spiritual and moral values and of satisfactory vocational insights would be a concomitant but indirect outcome of the methods and the materials of study. A chronological study of history might not be the most effective approach to these goals. Rather, the analysis of a selected few aspects of present American society might prove both more stimulating to the students and more effective in contributing to the desired goals. It seems likely that such an approach in depth might both increase understanding and help to encourage thoughtful involvement in civic affairs.

At Honolulu Community College, an Introduction to Social Science was taught by a team that included a historian, a political scientist, and a sociologist. The basic theme was "Understanding the Culture of Hawaii." In addition to lectures and discussion groups, the course emphasized attendance at meetings of community agencies, city council, and State Legislature. Participation in Hawaiian customs and visits to Polynesian enclaves on the island of Oahu were arranged. Perhaps the most effective part of the course for a dozen students was their assignment as unpaid assistants to members of the State Legislature during the session. All of the students observed, discussed, and evaluated aspects of American civilization with which they had not previously had any contact at all.

*Course C, The Physical World,* or perhaps Sciences and Mathematics, will be difficult to plan and to teach. A decision to devote, for example, six weeks to chemistry, six to physics, and six each to botany, zoology, community hygiene, and mathematics would destroy the entire concept of the course. The materials must be selected, in this general education course, for their contribution toward "helping each student increase his competence" in using basic mathematical and mechanical skills, in critical thinking, in understanding his interaction with his environment, and in maintaining good health for himself and for others. From these studies, some indirect contribution to vocational choice and adjustment may also arise. The purpose of this course is not to train scientists—it is to achieve the goals stated. For these comparatively modest goals, it is possible that content might be drawn almost exclusively from one discipline; on the other hand, principles from several sciences might be brought together to help the student increase his understanding. The goals that are accepted for this, as for other courses, may be attained by means of quite different organizations of experiences. The important consideration is to plan for the achievement of goals and not for the coverage of all the content of a scientific discipline. A study of biography might provide a stimulating vehicle for learning in this field. The work of men such as Galileo, Francis Bacon, Lavoisier, Pasteur, Newton, the Curies, Albert Einstein, and Charles Darwin could yield many insights into the skills and understandings which are sought here.

*Course D, Human Behavior,* is restricted to one semester and to three units because of time limitation rather than because of the lesser importance of the topic. A junior college which began the experimental development of its general education along the lines suggested here might soon find it necessary to rearrange the allocation of goals to specific blocks of content and to increase or diminish the relative credit values. It will be possible to make some contribution, within one semester, to student competence in maintaining mental health, developing balanced adjustment, and sharing in developing satisfactory family life; if these abilities are improved, vocational adjustment will also improve. In a course directed toward the achievement of these goals, content would be drawn as needed from psychology, biology, sociology, home economics, philosophy, and perhaps from other disciplines. Once more it is essential to state that this sampling would not be done through a series of brief superficial presentations of each separate subject. In this course, presenting each topic is not the primary goal; the personal and intellectual growth of the student is the objective. Content may be chosen by asking at every point "Will this material assist students to gain the insights which will enable them to improve their practices in human relations?" It goes without saying that the instructors in such a course must add to a thorough knowledge of psychology a broad acquaintance with other fields, and in addition, they must be themselves fully mature and balanced personalities.

In colleges and community colleges throughout America, examples may be found of courses similar in organization and purpose to each of the courses suggested here. None of the public junior colleges in the sample of 40 offered all the courses leading to the attainment of all the goals of general education. Yet these goals are too important to be subordinated to other objectives. The community colleges must begin to adopt them and to institute patterns of instruction specifically designed in accord with them or continue to fail in one of their primary functions. Courageous experimentation in general education is one way in which community colleges may prepare for their constantly increasing responsibility in American higher education.

## FOOTNOTES

1.  Thornton, James W. Jr. *General Education: Establishing the Program* (pamphlet). Washington, D.C.: American Association for Higher Education, 1958, p. 2.
2.  Johnson, Lamar B. *General Education in Action.* Washington, D.C.: American Council on Education, 1952, pp. 21-22.
3.  *op. cit.*, p. 49.
4.  Quoted by permission from Jacques Barzun, *The House of Intellect* pp. 11-12. New York: Harper and Row, 1959. Copyright 1959 by Jacques Barzun. Italics in original.

## BIBLIOGRAPHY

Baskin, Samuel (ed.). *Higher Education: Some Newer Developments.* New York: McGraw-Hill Book Company, 1965.

Bell, Daniel. *The Reforming of General Education.* Garden City, N.Y.: Doubleday and Company, 1968.

Chickering, Arthur W. *Education and Identity.* San Francisco: Jossey-Bass, Inc., Publishers, 1969.

French, Sidney J. (ed.). *Accent on Teaching.* New York: Harper and Row, 1954.

Hatch, Winslow R. *The Experimental College* (New Dimensions in Higher Education, No. 3). Washington, D.C.: U.S. Government Printing Office, 1960.

Johnson, B. Lamar. *General Education in Action.* Washington, D.C.: American Council on Education, 1952.

_____ *Islands of Innovation Expanding.* Beverley Hills, California: Glencoe Press, 1969.

Ortega y Gasset, Jose. *Mission of the University.* New York: Norton Company (paperback), 1968.

Rice, James G. (ed.). *General Education: Current Ideas and Concerns.* Washington, D.C.: Association for Higher Education, 1964.

Sanford, Nevitt. *Where Colleges Fail.* San Francisco: Jossey-Bass, Inc., Publishers, 1968.

Stickler, W. Hugh (ed.). *Experimental Colleges.* Tallahassee: Florida State University, 1964.

Thomas, Russell. *The Search for a Common Learning: General Education, 1800-1960.* New York: McGraw-Hill Book Company, 1962.

# 15 The Curriculum: Education for Transfer

In devising the pattern of course offerings that will prepare a large percentage of its students for further college study, the community junior college must reconcile several conflicting forces. Students who hope to earn bachelors' degrees in every conceivable field of study have a right to expect that their junior college will provide the lower-division courses that are required as preparation for later specialization. Each college and university that accepts transfer students expects the junior college to offer freshman and sophomore courses which are fully parallel, in content and in standard, to its own offering. Graduates of any junior college will apply for admission to many senior colleges, each of which has its own highly individualized concept of the content of lower-division preparation. The junior college, on the other hand, must use its human and fiscal resources economically, limiting the number and variety of its offerings. It must reserve some part of its teaching personnel and financial assets to meet the needs of its students who do not plan to transfer. It realizes that many of its students with transfer ambitions will not transfer after all, and so it tries to develop courses that are not solely preparatory, but which have an inherent value as well.

In their reactions to all these forces, community junior colleges seem to have been influenced most by the lower-division requirements of nearby universities and by fiscal limitations. Previous chapters have demonstrated that junior colleges are financed, organized and administered according to a number of regional patterns. In their transfer curriculums, however, they show much greater uniformity. In the various lower-division disciplines, community colleges all over the nation provide a very similar minimum offering, organized and titled in conformity with the practice of the nearby public university and comprising in essence the same traditional subject matter. *Report on Higher Education* charges:[1]

> . . . The expansion of American colleges and universities is failing to help the majority of those individuals to learn for whom the expansion was designed.
> With a few notable exceptions, the most sweeping reform is at the selective institutions, while it is at the unselective that the need to develop new approaches is the greatest. Even if the effectiveness of teaching at these institutions could be greatly improved, we believe that about half of the entering students would continue to find the present academic format unattractive. And many students who have developed the necessary academic skills to succeed in the present format would prefer other approaches if they were available.

It is possible that the increasing demand for higher education may encourage community colleges to be more active in defining anew the nature of lower-division preparation for further study. Suggestions are increasing in frequency that transfer students from junior colleges should be accepted only after they have completed the full two-year junior college course. If such a practice comes to be adopted throughout the nation, qualitative standards for transfer will follow. At present, receiving colleges are likely to scrutinize the transcript of the entering junior college transfer in search of a one-to-one conformity of courses completed at the junior college with those required of their own freshmen and sophomores. Courses for which the university offers no parallel may not be accepted for full credit; on the other hand, if the transfer student has neglected to complete a specific course required in the freshman or sophomore pattern of the receiving institution, he is refused junior standing until the course is "made up." This additive or quantitative approach to education for further study denies the junior colleges the right to develop, in mature and responsible fashion, courses which might well constitute superior intellectual fare for all their students. It causes frequent criticism and ill-feeling among the universities, the junior colleges, and the transferring student. Furthermore, it hinders the development by the junior colleges of courses appropriate for their terminal students, since they must concentrate too much of their attention on copying the offerings of several departments of several colleges and universities.

The community colleges will very soon be faced with the responsibility of exerting leadership in the development of lower-division preparatory curriculums. University leaders continue to be critical of the quality and nature of these programs, within their own institutions as well as in junior colleges. Many community college leaders have expressed dissatisfaction at dictation of details of their curriculum by outside agencies—the universities. If present trends continue, it seems inevitable that the greatest part of freshman and sophomore study will be completed in community colleges. All these trends combine to encourage university and community college leaders in each region to agree on statements of the purposes of this segment of education and to define standards of equivalence and training. Clearly stated behavioral objectives would permit all students, native and transfer, to demonstrate their readiness for the next stage of education. With common understanding of purposes and standards, the junior colleges can accept the responsibility of developing curriculums that will be fully satisfactory to their several classes of students as well as to the receiving colleges and universities.

In the future, agreements must be negotiated to allow students to transfer with full junior standing, with status equivalent in every way to native students of the college, and to engage in any studies for which they have met the prerequisites, if they have earned the associate degree in an accredited junior college with satisfactory grade standing and if they have demonstrated, through courses or through examinations, aptitude for the field in which they intend to major. Such a pattern of admission would not only assure the senior college and university of the seriousness of purpose and the ability of its transfer students; it would also free the junior college to concentrate on a high quality of achievement in all its offerings, even though the exact course outlines of some university courses were not closely "paralleled" anywhere in the curriculum.

Such complete freedom of curricular experimentation is rare at present, although a few statewide systems have worked out agreements that permit the community college to certify completion of general require-

ments or equivalents, leaving only specific prerequisites in a major field to
be checked by the receiving college.

Chapter 15 presents brief descriptions of the usual offerings in each
major area of the lower-division curriculum in community colleges.
Conclusions on the extent of the offering are based on the same survey of
40 catalogs described in Chapter 14. In the present analysis, the courses
are those that serve as preparation for further study in a senior
institution; it may be assumed that the courses are in fact offered every
year in most of the colleges represented and that the students for whom
the courses are required are enrolled in them.

## A. Courses in English, Speech, and Journalism

The freshman composition course is one constant feature of almost every
college in America; in almost every college it is one of the requirements
for graduation. Countless hours have been spent in efforts to improve it,
to reorganize it, and to work out ways to make it more effective in
changing the communicative habits of students. Many emphases are
found, from the study of formal grammar to the use of materials from
philosophy or social sciences as a basis for more literate discussion and
writing. In colleges of all types, a provision is found for admission of the
entrant to the freshman English class only after he has passed a screening
examination or written a qualifying essay; those who fail to qualify
usually are required to complete noncredit courses until they can
demonstrate the minimum competence for entry into the required
freshman course. Other colleges enroll all students in a single first course
and require supplementary work in clinics or in remedial sections for
those students who need extra help in correcting faulty habits of
expression. The community colleges follow the four-year institutions
both in the uniformity of their requirement and in the variety of their
approaches to course organization.

Of the 40 community colleges sampled, four offer fewer than 30
semester units of transferable credit in English. The minimum listing
provides for freshmen a two-semester course in composition, often
including some speech training and an introduction to English literature.
This basic offering is exceeded in varying degrees, depending somewhat
on the size of the college. Twelve of the colleges offer between 31 and 39
transfer credits in English; these colleges usually add elective courses in
advanced or creative writing and some study of European or specialized
literature to the two-semester courses in composition and literature. The
largest colleges offer more than 50 semester units of transferable study in

English, expanding their offering by specialized composition courses for prospective engineers or teachers or by additional courses in creative writing or literature. Although exceptions are found, English courses are usually organized to afford three units of credit per semester and to meet three hours weekly.

Remedial courses in communication are not provided in all the community colleges. Six of the 40 studied list no work preparatory to freshman English and no clinics for the development of skill in reading or in writing. On the other hand, the colleges that do offer such courses exhibit a wide range of specialization. Twelve of them list only one course, without credit. Fifteen colleges offer English for Foreign Born, and 29 have special developmental courses in spelling, grammar, speech, or reading. Assignment to such courses is based on demonstrated lack of competence. In some colleges, students whose first papers·in the regular English course indicate that they need additional help are required to undertake remedial work as a supplement to their regular course. In others, tests of composition, mechanical skills, vocabulary, or reading ability are used as bases for assigning students either to regular or to subfreshman classes. Pooley concluded that:

> The problem of the less competent student seems best met by the creation of clinics. Several communications programs have developed excellent clinics in the fundamental skills to help the floundering student pull himself up to class level. Clinics are created for writing skills, speaking skills, and reading skills. Usually the student needing the help of the clinic is referred to it by his section teacher. In some cases he attends the clinic in lieu of class attendance; in other cases the clinic is additional. Teaching in the clinic is individualized. The typical clinic consists of a room with space for one or several instructors; it is equipped with books, materials, and apparatus of help in the particular skill. The student is tested, given a goal to work for, and provided with materials for his own self advancement. He practices the skills he needs, tests himself, and continues until he feels ready to be tested by the director of the clinic. When he has raised himself to reasonable competence in the skill for which he was referred he leaves the clinic, but may return for special help whenever he needs it.[2]

Except for the development of mechanical and electronic devices for teaching reading and the introduction of programmed materials for individual study in composition, there is little evidence in the 40 catalogs studied that fundamental changes have taken place in the clinic since Pooley's comments were written.

In many public junior colleges, some instruction in speech is a part of the basic required course in English. In addition, all the colleges in the analyzed sample offer separate courses in public speaking; the number of courses tends to increase with the enrollment of the college, although it conforms closely to the lower-division speech program of the state universities. The first course is likely to be for one semester, entitled Public Speaking. Other public junior colleges extend this course to a full year and provide additional experiences in debate, verse-speaking choirs, oral reading (for prospective teachers), and voice and diction. Speech correction is offered for credit in a very few instances. One large college lists 48 units of transferable work in speech; several of the courses are specifically planned to meet the needs of future elementary-school teachers. In two-thirds of the college catalogs analyzed, the total transferable offering in speech ranges between six and 15 units; again, the three-hour, three-unit credit pattern is universal.

Journalism also is frequently associated with the English department. The courses serve as an introduction to the place of the press in American life; at the same time they afford practice in newswriting and enable the college to issue a student newspaper at regular intervals. Ten of the colleges studied offer no work in journalism; the others range from a single three-unit course to as many as 37 units. A common practice is to offer a freshman two-semester course as Introduction to Journalism and to follow that by a second year in Newswriting or Editorial Techniques. Junior colleges expand their journalism departments by addition of Introduction to Media (five colleges), or by specialized courses in column writing, advertising, or news photography. Since similar courses are often included in the upper-division programs of the university department of journalism, these specializations are of doubtful preparatory credit value to the transferring major in journalism; they do offer an opportunity for students to gain valuable experience by working independently under the guidance of an instructor in publishing the junior college newspaper.

# B. Foreign Languages

Several objectives are offered to justify the inclusion of foreign languages in the curriculum. It is claimed that foreign language study helps one to understand and to use his native tongue better and that the study of a foreign tongue leads to appreciation of the culture of other peoples and so to international harmony and cooperation. Further, knowledge of a foreign language is urged on economic grounds; more extensive involvement in trade, in military defense, and in economic development of other countries requires more workers who can speak other tongues than

English. It has been argued that the effort itself of learning a foreign language has a salutary effect on the mind and the character of the student. Certainly some students will derive real enjoyment from the mastery of another tongue and from the ability to read and to converse in it, quite apart from economic or disciplinary rewards.

But the methods of instruction in foreign language have not always contributed directly to the attainment of such objectives. The parsing of sentences and memorization of paradigms seems to add little to cultural appreciation, and the labored, halting, senseless translations turned in by many students certainly are not calculated to improve their use of English. Even the economic value of the study of foreign languages may be largely illusory, unless the language is studied to the point of fluent and correct usage. Criticisms of this nature have led in recent years to marked changes in the materials and the methods of foreign language instruction. Classes are more frequently conducted in the language studied; films, meaningful reading materials, and instructional recordings are used to encourage students to listen, speak, read, and write the new language as a means of communication rather than to dissect it as an exercise in philology. Under such realistic approaches, there is encouraging evidence that usable skills can be attained by many students within the customary two-year period of study of foreign languages.

The community junior college is keeping pace with these developments in foreign language instruction. It receives from the secondary schools students at all levels of achievement in languages; some have had no instruction, others may have had four years of excellent high-school work in a single language. The junior college, in the same way as the four-year college, must assess each student's proficiency, compare that with the student's goal and with the requirements of his chosen four-year college and his major field, and then assign him to the next level of instruction. Because of this intermediate function, the patterns of foreign language instruction in public junior colleges in all parts of the country are remarkably similar. In any language that is taught, the junior college will usually offer four semesters of work; the first semester is a beginning course, and the fourth stresses reading and conversation.

The languages most usually taught, as revealed by the analysis of 40 catalogs, are French, Spanish, and German. French and Spanish were taught in all 40 colleges, and 33 colleges taught German. In addition, Russian appeared in 21; Italian, in 11; Hebrew, in five; and Latin, in three. Greek did not appear in the language offerings of any of these 40 colleges. One large college in the sample offered seven languages—Spanish, French, German, Russian, Hebrew, Italian, and Japanese.

The semester-credit value of the basic language courses varies from three to five units; for this reason, the four-semester offering may vary from 12 to 20 units. In a few programs, especially in the less popular languages, only two semesters of work are offered; most of the colleges offer additional courses beyond the four-semester pattern, in such areas as Conversational French, Scientific German, or Spanish Literature. Most public junior colleges offer foreign languages primarily for transfer purposes, and the organization of their courses is patterned very closely after that of the college or university to which most of their students go. There is a growing trend, however, toward emphasis on conversational courses in foreign languages, in tongues other than the traditional French, German, and Spanish.

## C. Social Sciences

Junior college courses in the social sciences share two major objectives with their counterpart courses in the four-year colleges. They are expected to contribute to the development of responsible and intelligent citizenship on the part of the student; at the same time, they must be planned so as to provide a foundation for further study to the small proportion of each class who will later specialize in any one of the social disciplines. The added responsibility to provide civic education for those students who do not plan to transfer may complicate the social science curriculum for the junior colleges, especially the smaller ones. The evidence indicates that the public junior colleges offer a considerable variety of social science courses and that the basic offering is nearly the same in all of them.

In developing the transfer curriculum in social sciences, the first effort is to provide two-semester courses that parallel the university offerings; subjects are introduced that meet lower-division requirements for a sufficient number of the students. As numbers of students and faculty increase, expansion within the social science areas takes two paths. The introductory courses in other social disciplines are added, and more specialized courses are introduced in the original subjects.

Every one of the 40 colleges studied offers two-semester courses in American history; all of them also offer at least a semester each of introductory psychology, political science, and sociology. Economics is available in 39 of the 40, usually in a two-semester sequence. Expansion of the curriculum within these five fields begins with the addition of European history or Western civilization in almost every college. A course entitled either mental hygiene or psychology of adjustment is the usual second offering in psychology. In political science, however, the second offering is not usually an additional opportunity for the student majoring in the field; rather it is a substitute course for students who need a course of limited scope to meet a state or a college requirement for graduation. In economics and sociology, nearly all of the colleges offer either one or two two-semester sequences. Those that offer second courses plan them primarily for specific occupational needs, such as for business students or teachers, and not as an additional year of advanced study.

Table I summarizes the offerings in all of the social sciences in the 40 colleges whose catalogs were analyzed. In general, a similar pattern of an introductory two-semester course, with the addition of additional specialization when conditions justify it, is indicated also in geography, philosophy, and anthropology. Education courses are taught extensively only in those states in which the public junior colleges are beginning to prepare teacher aides. In states where a bachelor's degree is a requirement for a teaching certificate, public junior colleges ordinarily offer no courses in education or only a single introductory course. Twenty colleges offer an integrated course in social sciences, carrying usually six semester hours of credit.

# D. Sciences and Mathematics

*Biological Sciences.*    Several professional fields require lower-division study in biological sciences. Some study in the area is required by many four-year colleges as part of the lower-division work of all liberal arts students, native or transfer, and some students in each year are likely to plan to specialize in one of these sciences, either as teachers or as researchers. The multiple nature of this student need obligates the public junior colleges to provide an extensive range of courses in the field. In the sample of 40 public junior college catalogs, courses are listed in the fields of zoology, botany, biology, anatomy and physiology, bacteriology, microbiology, and paleontology. In addition, there are 13 examples of generalized survey courses in biological or life sciences in colleges which offered biology also. The smallest of the sample colleges provides courses only in three fields of biological science; zoology appears in every catalog, and biology and anatomy-physiology are in all but three. In any biological science, expansion of the offering beyond the introductory course is provided to meet the needs of specific occupational groups, such as nurses, laboratory technicians, or agriculture majors; introductory courses of two different varieties are not found, as they were in social sciences. Rather, increasingly specialized courses or additional subject fields seem to be added in most of these colleges to care for specialized training needs.

**TABLE I.**
**Number of Public Junior Colleges Offering Instruction in Stated Social Sciences and Extent of Offering in a Sample of 40 Public Junior Colleges**

| Units Offered | Subject Fields | | | | | | | | | |
|---|---|---|---|---|---|---|---|---|---|---|
| | Hist. | Psych. | Pol. Sci. | Econ. | Sociol. | Geog. | Educ. | Philos. | Anthro. | Integrated Soc. Sci. |
| 31 or more | 14 | 2 | - | - | - | - | - | - | - | - |
| 25-30 | 12 | 2 | - | - | 2 | - | 1 | 1 | - | - |
| 19-24 | 10 | 8 | 5 | 3 | 3 | - | - | 3 | - | - |
| 13-18 | 2 | 9 | 12 | 3 | 5 | 8 | - | 8 | 2 | - |
| 7-12 | 2 | 9 | 18 | 19 | 18 | 9 | 7 | 8 | 8 | 3 |
| 1-6 | - | 10 | 5 | 14 | 12 | 13 | 18 | 12 | 16 | 17 |
| TOTAL COLLEGES | 40 | 40 | 40 | 39 | 40 | 30 | 26 | 32 | 26 | 20 |
| TOTAL UNITS | 1144 | 600 | 452 | 356 | 414 | 294 | 209 | 373 | 173 | 124 |
| MEAN UNITS[a] | 28.8 | 15.0 | 11.3 | 9.1 | 10.3 | 9.8 | 8.0 | 11.6 | 6.6 | 6.2 |

[a]"Mean Units" lists the arithmetic mean of units available in the subject in the public junior colleges of the sample which offer it.

A reader familiar with course-credit patterns in the life sciences will discern that the most frequent offerings in each area consist of only one or two semesters of work with laboratory. In Table II, the category "1-6 units" includes semester courses of four or five units as well as two-semester lecture courses, organized in the familiar pattern of three weekly meetings. In the "7-12 unit" group will be found the two-semester courses with laboratories, yielding credit value of four or five units each semester. The distribution of course titles and the extent of the offering indicates that these junior colleges offer ample opportunity for their students to prepare for further study in biological sciences.

*Physical Sciences.* In the public junior colleges, physical sciences are addressed principally to the education of engineers. A sequence of four unduplicating courses in chemistry is offered in every junior college in the sample group. In physics, a three-semester sequence is common; 23 of the 40 colleges offer that amount of work. In both sciences, catalog evidence indicates that the engineering requirements in the universities control the basic course offering, as well as the organization and sequence of topics. Junior colleges that offer work in chemistry and physics in addition to the minimum requirements for engineers do not ordinarily offer specialized advanced work. Instead, they offer other sequences of introductory study, often of shorter duration, which enable them to separate the engineering students from the general students and those preparing for other professions.

Thirty of these colleges offer geology, primarily as an additional elective course for the engineer. At times it also serves as a general physical science course for those transfer students who lack the mathematics to undertake a sequence of courses in chemistry or in physics, but who are required to complete some study in physical sciences. Except in petroleum-producing regions, not more than a single two-semester course combining physical and historical geology is usually offered. Introductory courses in astronomy and in meteorology are offered in a scattering of colleges. Even the colleges with planetariums offer limited transfer courses in astronomy. The distribution of courses is shown in Table III.

A survey course in the physical sciences is listed nearly three times as often as a survey of life sciences. This excess may exist merely in name, since the course titled General Biology or Introduction to Biology and offered in all 40 colleges may be in reality the same as a survey of life sciences. Thirty-six colleges studied, at any rate, list a Physical Sciences course; it is most frequently organized as a two-semester course.

The total of units offered in chemistry and physics in the public junior college is greater than that in any other subject area, except in the fine

**TABLE II.**
**Number of Public Junior Colleges Offering Instruction in Stated Biological Sciences and Extent of Offering in a Sample of 40 Public Junior Colleges**

| Units Offered | | Biological Sciences | | | | | | |
|---|---|---|---|---|---|---|---|---|
| | Zool. | Botany | Biol-ogy | Anat. Phys. | Bacte-riology | Micro-biology | Paleon-tology | Sur-vey |
| 10-24 | 2 | - | 11 | - | - | 1 | - | - |
| 13-18 | 2 | 6 | 11 | 6 | - | - | - | - |
| 7-12 | 23 | 11 | 8 | 10 | - | 7 | - | 2 |
| 1-6 | 9 | 14 | 10 | 21 | 8 | 26 | 4 | 11 |
| TOTAL COLLEGES | 36 | 31 | 40 | 37 | 8 | 34 | 4 | 13 |
| TOTAL UNITS | 301 | 244 | 469 | 269 | 36 | 192 | 12 | 59 |
| MEAN UNITS | 8.3 | 7.8 | 11.7 | 7.2 | 4.5 | 5.6 | 3.0 | 4.6 |

**TABLE III.**
**Number of Public Junior Colleges Offering Instruction in Stated Physical Sciences and Extent of Offering in a Sample of 40 Public Junior Colleges**

| Units Offered | Physical Sciences | | | | | |
|---|---|---|---|---|---|---|
| | Chem. | Physics | Geol. | Phys. Sci. | Astron. | Meteor-ology |
| 37 and over | 16 | 8 | - | - | - | - |
| 31-36 | 9 | 4 | - | - | - | - |
| 25-30 | 4 | 10 | 2 | - | - | - |
| 19-24 | 7 | 9 | 10 | - | - | - |
| 13-18 | 4 | 5 | 4 | 4 | 2 | - |
| 7-12 | - | 4 | 11 | 9 | 2 | - |
| 1-6 | - | - | 3 | 23 | 18 | 4 |
| TOTAL COLLEGES | 40 | 40 | 30 | 36 | 22 | 4 |
| TOTAL UNITS | 1323 | 1084 | 410 | 256 | 106 | 10 |
| MEAN UNITS | 33.0 | 27.1 | 13.6 | 7.1 | 4.8 | 2.5 |

arts. The nature of the courses offered indicates that the preparation of transfer students who have a professional need for these sciences—future engineers, physicians, and scientists— is being accomplished adequately. In addition, some provision of courses in physical science is becoming available to other students. For the most part, nonmajors in biological sciences must compete with the future specialists in extensive courses in zoology or biology or else avoid science altogether.

*Mathematics.*    Junior-college courses in mathematics also include all the courses in mathematics usually found in the lower-division curriculum of the scientific or the engineering student. The mean credit value of all courses in mathematics, in these 40 colleges, was 51.5 semester units. Thirty offered a course in college algebra, and all of them offered analytic geometry and calculus for credit ranging from ten to 18 units. In addition, several colleges offered a choice of patterns of analytic geometry and calculus either for honors courses or to permit more rapid completion and enrichment of the standard topics. These duplicating offerings were not included in the tally of the basic credit hours in calculus.

Thirty of the colleges offered the usual high school courses in intermediate algebra and plane trigonometry; of these, 23 also offered beginning algebra and geometry courses to permit students to complete the minimum requirements in mathematics for the baccalaureate degree. Thirty-five of the colleges surveyed offer a nontechnical course in mathematics for general education, with titles such as "Mathematics for General Education," "Structural Approach to Mathematics," "Contemporary," or "Modern Mathematics." This course is described in one catalog as follows: "Introduction to logic, the number system, set theory, functions and probability. This course is not remedial or fundamental in nature. A term paper is required. Recommended for pre-law students."

In discharging their responsibility to the "late-blooming" student and to the technical student who has neglected mathematics in his high school course, 34 of the colleges offer a refresher course in arithmetic under titles such as "Basic Mathematics" or "Fundamental Concepts in Mathematics." In some of the colleges, this course is a required prerequisite to other mathematics courses for students who fail to qualify on an entrance test in mathematics. It rarely carries credit toward the Associate in Arts degree and never for transfer purposes.

In sciences and mathematics, the evidence shows that the junior colleges provide a broad opportunity for the student to specialize in scientific study. In every college except the very smallest ones, transfer students can complete lower-division preparation for later study in engineering, in sciences, and in mathematics at the university, so that they need lose no time after transfer in making up subjects required of university freshmen or sophomores. Opportunities for the nonspecialist, especially in biological sciences, appear to be somewhat inadequate. There seems to have been little effort to discover whether other selections of material and of course organization are appropriate for these students. At any rate, there are few courses listed that are designed for them.

# E. Engineering

In addition to the science and mathematics courses required in the lower division of the engineering curriculum, public junior colleges also commonly offer a limited number of units in the department of engineering itself. Of the 40 colleges in the sample group analyzed for this Chapter, all but one offered some engineering subjects. The mean credit value of engineering subjects in these 39 colleges was 40.7 semester units, with a range from six to 105 units.

In all 39 colleges, engineering drawing is offered, with as many as four semesters of study made available. In addition, some of the colleges list also a high-school-level introductory course for those students who have had no previous drafting course. Surveying and a course in properties of materials are taught in more than half of the colleges, as part of the professional education of the civil engineer. The larger junior colleges, then, enrich their engineering offering by one or more introductory courses such as statics, mechanics, dynamics, and shop practices. The expansion of the curriculum beyond the universal offering in drafting is determined primarily, and properly, by study of the lower-division offering of the school of engineering to which most of the junior college graduates transfer.

## F. Fine Arts

*Music.*    Study of the catalogs of 40 public junior colleges demonstrates that junior colleges afford a wide variety of opportunities for group and individual study of vocal and instrumental music, supplemented by several courses in the theory of music. In one college, which enrolls approximately 2100 full-time students, the transferable units available in music total 131, with six music instructors. In this case, as in others with less extensive listings, it is evident that individual opportunity for practice under supervision was made available to students. It is probable also that students would not enroll for every one of the individual instruments listed in every semester. Listing the courses in the catalog indicates merely that students are encouraged to extend their musical ability while they are in junior college and that instructors stand ready to instruct, supervise, and examine any interested musical student. Table IV shows offerings in the fine arts.

This emphasis on music indicates also that a large proportion of the students in every public junior college are able to participate in some musical activity. There are courses suited to all qualities of musical talent; the credit earned is transferable, even though nontransfer students also enroll. Music appreciation and chorus classes are open to all students without prerequisites of vocal training or instruction. For the student whose interest in music is more serious, courses in sight reading, harmony, and counterpoint supplement group practice in glee clubs and a capella choir or in orchestra and band. In the colleges that have the personnel and facilities, this group instruction is supplemented by opportunity for individual vocal or instrumental study.

*Art and Photography.*    Thirty-eight of the public junior colleges in the sample offer some work in art. An introductory course in art appreciation is the most frequent offering, with design, color, and drawing

**TABLE IV.**
**Number of Public Junior Colleges Offering Instruction in Stated Fine Arts Subjects, and Extent of Offering in Sample of 40 Public Junior Colleges**

| Units Offered | Music | Art | Home Economics | Drama | Humanities | Architecture | Photography |
|---|---|---|---|---|---|---|---|
| | | | | Subjects | | | |
| 91 and over | 8 | 3 | - | - | - | - | - |
| 61-90 | 5 | 11 | 4 | 7 | - | - | - |
| 31-60 | 15 | 16 | 10 | - | - | 4 | 1 |
| 25-30 | 6 | 1 | 4 | - | - | - | - |
| 19-24 | - | 3 | - | 6 | 4 | 2 | - |
| 13-18 | 2 | - | 2 | 2 | - | - | 3 |
| 7-12 | - | 2 | - | 6 | 9 | 5 | 5 |
| 1-6 | 4 | 2 | 2 | 4 | 8 | 1 | 9 |
| TOTAL COLLEGES | 40 | 38 | 22 | 25 | 21 | 12 | 18 |
| TOTAL UNITS | 2168 | 2066 | 827 | 648 | 200 | 266 | 217 |
| MEAN UNITS | 54.2 | 54.1 | 37.6 | 25.9 | 9.5 | 22.1 | 12.0 |

as the usual basic offerings in applied work. Beyond these fundamental subjects, the junior colleges adapt their programs to the previous high-school study of their students, the artistic interest of the community, and the expectations of the universities. Some colleges content themselves with a minimum of choice in specialized art study; others seem to exert every effort to enable students to gain thorough background in many techniques. Such subjects as craft work, lapidary work, water color, oil painting, portrait painting, advertising art, and ceramics appear in one or more catalogs. In some junior colleges, only one semester of work is offered in one or two fields; yet there are junior colleges in which a student may pursue a four-semester course, meeting from six to 12 hours weekly, in painting or ceramics or advertising art. Such courses ordinarily are presented as part of the transfer offering of the junior college, even though few transfer students would be able to spare time, because of other requirements, for more than one or two of the specialized courses. In the colleges with the most extended listing of courses in art, it is likely that a good many nontransfer students enroll in some of the more advanced courses.

Photography is included in the art offering in several of the colleges, ordinarily as a two-semester course combining study of cameras and films with opportunity to expose, develop, and print pictures as a part of the laboratory work. It is not unusual for these classes to accept assignments to provide some photographs of campus activities for the college newspaper or annual. Although the courses in photography are presented as transferable rather than as occupational preparation, it is doubtful that any student can present as part of his preparation for the bachelor's degree all of the 39 units in photography listed in one public junior college catalog.

*Home Economics.*    Courses in this field are offered in 22 of the public junior colleges in the sample group of 40. The fundamental curriculum for transfer purposes includes one two-semester course in foods and nutrition and a second in clothing. Additional courses include home management, child development, family budgeting and purchasing, home planning and decoration, and specialized courses required in the pre-nursing or pre-teaching curriculums. In several junior colleges, these are offered as dual-purpose courses, appealing both to the young woman who plans to earn a degree in home economics and to the one who is looking toward early marriage. Other colleges find it desirable to separate the two sets of student objectives and to organize additional courses with appealing titles for the nonprofessional students. In these colleges, the home economics department may list such titles as Clothing for

Secretaries and Family Meal Planning among its course offerings. The opportunity exists for junior college women to prepare themselves for these important aspects of their lives; but the testimony of instructors indicates that only a minority of the students enroll in the courses.

***Drama.***    Another frequent offering of the public junior colleges is drama; 22 of the institutions in the sample group offer some experience in the field. As in the other arts, the offering includes study of the theory and the literature of dramatics, supplemented by application in stage craft and in acting, through a series of formal and informal theatrical presentations. Introduction to Theater is a two-semester course which may be taught in a usual classroom or in one with only a minimum stage. It concentrates on reading and analyzing plays and discussing techniques of acting and playwriting. If an auditorium is available, production of plays may be undertaken either as a noncredit activity or as a series of organized classes for credit. As the curriculum is expanded toward the 72-unit maximum offering found in these colleges, additional specialization is introduced in lighting, stage design, costuming, and makeup.

***Humanities.***    Courses under the departmental title, of "Humanities" are offered in 21 of the 40 public junior colleges studied. In general, the influences noted in the discussion of other subject areas operate here. If the universities in the state offer and require integrated courses in humanities, the junior colleges will offer similar courses. if the universities require credit in separate subject fields, the public junior colleges will be unlikely to develop strong and popular courses in humanities. For like reasons, even the junior colleges that do list a department of humanities sometimes include in it courses such as World Literature, Great Books, or Religious Concepts rather than experimental integrated courses that draw on materials from literature, drama, music, painting, sculpture, architecture, and the dance.

***Architecture.***    This is offered as a transferable subject in 12 of the 40 public junior colleges studied. Because of its severe limitations as a field of employment, not even all the larger universities have schools of architecture. It is unlikely that the smaller community junior colleges will enroll enough architectural aspirants to justify an extended preparatory specialization in the field. In most junior colleges, the pre-architectural student will be advised to choose the required mathematics, physics, drafting, and art courses from the available curriculum and then to transfer to a university school of architecture for the more specialized work. Four of the public junior colleges in the sample that offer architectural courses are in large cities close to university schools to which their students may transfer.

## G. Business Administration

Lower-division courses in the field of business administration are offered in every one of the 40 public junior colleges surveyed. Not all of the courses could be completed for transfer purposes by any one student, since 11 colleges listed more than 90 units of transfer business courses, and 33 have more than 24 units of courses. The large number of units in business indicates that specialized courses are offered for the needs of students with a variety of business administration objectives; undoubtedly the courses are taken by terminal and special students to prepare for work in the local community, as well as by those planning to earn degrees in business administration.

Principles of Economics, discussed under social sciences, is a course usually required of lower-division students in business. In addition, as many as four semesters of work in accounting may be offered as preparation for enrollment at some Schools of Business. A limited amount of work in typing and shorthand may be applied toward a business bachelor's degree, especially by students planning to be business teachers. Junior colleges sometimes consider the first year's work in each of these subjects as transferable and all work beyond one year as primarily occupational preparation. Other courses included in one or more of the catalog listings in business administration are Business Law and Introduction to Business, with Mathematics of Investment or Elementary Statistics offered in the mathematics departments of several colleges. The average number of transferable units in business offered in the 40-college sample was 34.3, sufficient to indicate that in business administration, also, the junior college student can complete the usual lower-division requirements for further study.

## H. Evaluation of the Curriculum for Transfer Students

Preparation of students for further study at the four-year college or university was the first responsibility of the junior college. It is still the function on which the junior colleges expend most of their effort and in which most of their students express interest. Evidence presented in previous sections of this Chapter indicates that public junior colleges offer the courses required to provide adequate lower-division preparation. In the larger colleges, the curriculum develops to a point at which preparation may be completed for almost every university area of specialization. It is possible that this multiplication of courses may in itself become a source of weakness and unnecessary expense.

Although his comments are addressed specifically to liberal arts college faculty, Earl J. McGrath has offered advice that is equally appropriate for community college curriculum committees as they develop their transfer programs:

> "The liberal arts curriculum has become a collection of subject-matter splinters. Only the most meager common body of instruction can be identified as the intellectual experience of all undergraduates. Many of the courses offered are highly specialized and beyond the level of college students. They typically attract few students, absorb a dispro-portionate portion of the faculty's time and energy, dissipate the institution's limited resources, and seldom contribute anything essential to undergraduate liberal education. These courses also tend unnecessarily to increase the faculties' teaching load and reduce the average salary which these teachers receive."[3]

Some indications of such overdevelopment of courses were noted in some of the fields of science, in business, in photography, and in music. Some of the excessive specialization, when it exists, arises from a desire to match similarly specialized university requirements in the same subject areas. In other instances, it is evident that the public junior colleges have elaborated transfer courses far beyond the lower-division needs of their students and beyond the limits of acceptability at the upper-division colleges. Although it must acknowledge responsibility for some of the shortcomings in junior college curriculums, the university is not the sole culprit. Exaggerated faculty enthusiasm causes a part of the uneconomical excess.

In an opposing vein, it seems probable that in some areas not enough courses have been developed. In their concentration upon preparing some of their students for professional specialization, the public junior colleges have tended to overlook the fact that other students need a layman's introduction to certain disciplines outside of their individual areas of concentration. The lack of conceptually rich and intellectually demanding nonprofessional courses in sciences, social sciences, and mathematics was mentioned as a case in point. In extenuation, community junior colleges may well point out that frequently they cannot afford to duplicate certain offerings. They feel that it is better to offer the specialized course, in that case, and to require too much of the nonspecialized student, than to serve the needs of the nonmajor student and so slight the education of the future professional.

If such a dilemma is in truth presented, the junior colleges have chosen the proper alternative. Yet it is possible that in some cases university domination is an excuse rather than an adequate cause for junior college conservatism. As a new and vigorous segment of American higher education, the community junior college should demonstrate ingenuity and energy in seeking solutions to curricular problems. With the extension of educational opportunity, new purposes of students have emerged that require new approaches to the organization of instruction. The community junior college too often has been complacently imitative, when it should have been diligently seeking better ways to educate its transfer students. Before many years, community junior colleges will enroll the major share of lower-division students; now is the time for them to prepare for the responsibilities that will accompany this role.

Finally, since the introduction of the concept of occupational education as a function of the community junior college, there has been a constant awareness that the provision of extensive transfer courses frequently interferes with the development of occupational education. The prestige of the transfer curriculum, in the minds of faculty as well as students, combines with the limitation of resources to constrict the breadth of offering. The community junior college that favors either aspect of its program at the expense of the other makes a serious error. The community that supports the college needs a well-developed college-transfer program of highest quality; it also needs, for a majority of those who enroll at the college, a vocational program of excellent quality. The two are equally respectable, equally important, and equally possible. The question is not so much one of priority as it is of the means for harmonious and concomitant development.

FOOTNOTES

1.    Newman, Frank (Chairman). *Report on Higher Education.* Washington, D.C.: U.S. Government Printing Office, 1971, p. 63.
2.    *In* French, Sidney J. *Accent on Teaching.* New York: Harper and Row, 1954, p. 119.
3.    McGrath, Earl J. *Memo to a College Faculty Member.* New York: Bureau of Publications, Teachers College, Columbia University, 1961, p. 53.

## BIBLIOGRAPHY

Dressel, Paul L. and Frances H. De Lisle. *Undergraduate Curriculum Trends.* Washington, D.C.: American Council on Education, 1969.

Knoell, Dorothy M. and Leland L. Medsker. *From Junior to Senior College: A National Study of the Transfer Student.* Washington, D.C.: American Council on Education, 1965.

Mayhew, Lewis B. *Contemporary College Students and the Curriculum.* Atlanta: Southern Regional Education Board, 1969.

McGrath, Earl J. *Memo to a College Faculty Member.* New York: Bureau of Publications, Teachers College, Columbia University, 1961.

McGrath, Earl J. (ed.). *Universal Higher Education.* New York: McGraw-Hill Book Company, 1966.

Medsker, Leland L. and Dale Tillery. *Breaking the Access Barriers: A Profile of Two-Year Colleges.* New York: McGraw-Hill Book Company, 1971.

Newman, Frank (chairman). *Report on Higher Education.* Washington, D.C.: U.S. Government Printing Office, 1971.

Trent, James W., and Leland L. Medsker. *Beyond High School.* San Francisco: Jossey-Bass, Inc., Publishers, 1968.

# 16

# The Curriculum: Continuing Education

In addition to the regularly organized daytime curriculum of transfer courses, general education, and occupational education, community colleges typically schedule extensive programs designed to satisfy the growing demand for continuing education. Citizens who are not full-time students desire to work toward a degree, to improve their occupational skills, to prepare for a new occupation, or simply to extend their understanding and knowledge. Community colleges accept the responsibility for providing opportunity for this continuing education.

The term "adult education," formerly used to describe this function of the community college, has become less appropriate as both the nature of the part-time student and the scope of the offerings change. At one time, it was possible to define adult education as consisting of courses offered to persons over 21 years of age who were employed full time, who attended classes only during evening hours, who were not interested in degree credit, and who probably needed the classes for Americanization or employment. At that time, these qualifications effectively distinguished the adult student from the regular day student. At present, none of the distinctions is fully accurate.

Nevertheless, community colleges are giving increased attention to providing evening courses identical to those given in the day, carrying the same requirements and credits, and leading to the same objectives. In the words of one catalog,

> . . . evening classes provide the adult community with freshman-sophomore level college-credit classes and non-credit activities. The courses in large part do not duplicate courses offered by other agencies in the community. They are designed to serve employed adults and others seeking enrichment of their lives and occupational values, who need or prefer evening hours for classes. Evening classes are an integral part of the college curriculum, and evening credits are not distinguished on transcripts from day credits.

Chapter 16 discusses the extent of the part-time enrollment in community colleges, considers the purposes of the students and of the colleges in making the courses available, and discusses several current issues in the development of programs of continuing education.

# A. The Extent of Part-Time Study in Community Colleges

Enrollment data in the *1971 Junior College Directory*[1] are based on figures reported in October, 1969. A part-time student is defined as one who is enrolled in at least one course for credit and who carries less than three-fourths (less than 12 semester hours) of a normal full-time load. There are, in addition, a large number of unclassified students, defined as students not counted as freshmen or sophomores, who may not have fulfilled requirements for matriculation or who are enrolled in college-level courses for which they receive no credit. It is apparent that the part-time category includes students who are fulfilling requirements toward a degree or certificate, students who take one or two courses for credit for any reason, and auditors.

The *1971 Junior College Directory* presents entries for 847 public and 244 independent junior colleges. Table I is derived from data presented in the *Directory*.

The exhibits indicate that part-time students are enrolled in public

**TABLE I.**
**Statistics of Part-Time Enrollments in Public and Independent Junior Colleges, October, 1969.**[a]

|  | Public | Independent | Total | Per Cent Public |
|---|---|---|---|---|
| Number of Junior Colleges | 847 | 244 | 1,091 | 77.6 |
| Number Listing Part Time Students | 759 | 187 | 946 | 80.2 |
| Percent Listing Part Time Students | 89.6 | 76.6 | 86.7 | -- |
| Enrollment, Part-Time | 1,039,089 | 25,098 | 1,064,187 | 97.5 |
| Enrollment, Full-Time | 1,064,508 | 105,974 | 1,170,482 | 91.0 |

[a] 1971 Junior College Directory, Tables I, II, III, and IV.

junior colleges more often than in independent ones, and in greater numbers. In fact, the part-time students almost equal the full-time students in the public colleges. In public junior colleges, part-time students account for 49.3% of total enrollments; in the independent colleges, 19% of all enrollments are part-time. In a few of the public colleges, part-time enrollments are more than twice as large as full-time enrollments; at Long Beach City College, for example, they are three times as large (19,703 as compared to 6185).

In 1948, Martorana reported a questionnaire survey based on offerings in "adult education;" of 337 respondents, 144 colleges reported having adult programs.[2] Of these, only 56% offered courses to adults that paralleled their transfer courses in the regular program. This finding contrasts markedly with the more limited sample of 40 community college catalogs for 1970-1971, in which most colleges describe their extended day programs as fully comparable to the daytime offerings, and avoid the use of the term "adult education."

In summary, except for the most recently established community colleges, all but a handful offer organized programs of instruction for several categories of part-time students, and the total of part-time students is almost equal to the regular full-time enrollment. There has been a distinct trend toward graded classes offered for credit, and away from the earlier concept of offering any class that was desired by a sufficient number of adults.

## B. Purposes of the Part-time Student

Bertram Gross has proposed the concept of the "Learning Force" as a parallel to "Labor Force." The "Learning Force" refers to "the total number of people developing their capacities through systematic education; that is, where learning is aided by teaching and there are formal, organized efforts to impart knowledge through instruction."[3] Until quite recently, most attention in higher education has been given to young people who devote their full-time to study, but it is probable that the major educational development of the last quarter of the Twentieth Century will be in the area of lifelong opportunity to reenter the learning force.

The need for more realistic access to part-time study by older persons has been explicitly and forcefully stated by the Task Force on Higher Education:

"Questions of who needs what kinds of education, and when, are impossible to answer precisely. People mature at different ages and arrive at the point of wanting to learn by different routes. Some 18-year-olds are simply not ready for any further education, and some for whom a conventional college education would be suitable are more ready at age 30. Others with job experience, either before or during or after undergraduate training, are ready for education that may be broader ranging or may be more specific and technical than the conventional.

The critical factor in answering "when" is precisely the one that students confined by the lockstep most often lack: motivation. The presence of high motivation is common to the doctor who realizes his training has become obsolete; the blue-collar worker who never went to college but whose aspirations and self-confidence rise; the welfare mother who has taken part in a Head Start program and now wants a professional career; or the returning serviceman who has found himself and seeks a place in a society he recognizes as complex.

It is not wholly a matter of subjective change, of course. Society and its technologies also change. Obsolescence of knowledge has long been recognized as a reason for continuing the learning process in technical fields—e.g., for doctors, engineers, and scientists. In other fields, altogether new skills may be needed. A police officer may suddenly realize that his career advancement calls for an understanding of urban sociology or law or criminal psychology."[4]

This need for continuing access has been met in part by community colleges. Several kinds of student motivation will lead to much more intensive efforts in the years ahead. The following are some of the purposes of part-time students in continuing their education.

*Basic Education.* Many Americans leave school before high-school graduation, only to learn later that they are handicapped through life by the lack of a diploma. If opportunity for further study is made available to them, many of these persons will enroll in order to complete their secondary education. Although some junior colleges require high-school graduation as a qualification for enrollment in all classes, an increasing number of community junior colleges are enabling adults to complete studies leading to a certificate of high-school equivalency. The same desire for ever higher educational attainment accounts also for a large proportion of the college-level work offered in extended day programs. As many as one-fifth of the ablest high-school graduates are financially unable to continue study in college. The presence of a junior college part-time program of continuing education enables such students to make some progress toward a college degree, even though the road may be difficult and painfully slow.

In addition, in any community there are numbers of mature persons whose interest in learning is still vivid, but who have no desire for additional college credits. Some of them may be largely self-educated; others will possess bachelors' or advanced degrees. Yet they are eager to pursue courses in subjects they were unable to study in college or to keep abreast of changing social and political conditions. For this class of students, the community college provides courses in great books, in philosophy and humanities, in current affairs, in geography, in interpretation of science, and in foreign languages. The "level" of the study is comparatively unimportant to these students; they can at last pursue knowledge for the sake of their own education, without concern for the evaluation of credit by the instructor or by another college. Teaching in the basic areas of education is, under these conditions, one of the most stimulating and rewarding experiences an instructor can have.

*Degree Objective.* Statistics of community junior college part-time enrollments indicate that there has been a substantial increase in the number of employed adults who intend to earn the associate degree through part-time study. As a result of this increase, more emphasis is being placed on organized patterns of evening courses which parallel the courses required of the full-time student. This degree objective is in part a manifestation of the long-term trend toward higher average educational attainment in America. In addition, the demand of industry for more highly educated employees contributes to increase, as does the desire of housewives to retrain themselves for office work or for teaching. The trend toward earlier marriage combines with compulsory military service to add another increment to degree-seeking part-time enrollments. Young men who marry during their military service still desire additional education upon release from active duty. Some of them can arrange to attend college full time; although others must seek full-time employment, they will avail themselves of the opportunity for part-time progress toward a degree if it is made available by the community junior college. This degree objective of part-time students is an appealing reason for the further development of community junior college continuing education programs.

*Occupational Training or Retraining.*    A consequence of expanding and developing technology has been the rapid obsolescence of vocational skills and the consequent need for refresher training or retraining for another occupation. The radio repairman is an example of this need. As television invaded the American home during the immediate postwar period, thousands of radio servicemen came to junior colleges and technical schools to learn the secrets of television repair. They had hardly become used to their new skills, when the introduction of color broadcasting sent them back to school for additional training. Almost immediately thereafter, the substitution of the transistor for the vacuum tube brought another set of technical problems and another demand for trade related classes.

Part-time occupational training also provides the skills needed for entry into an occupation. Men in blind-alley jobs and housewives whose children no longer need their full-time attention frequently seek this training. Introductory courses in machine shop, electronics, bookkeeping, real estate, or drafting are examples of courses offered for men; secretarial training and practical nursing courses may attract women who feel the need to qualify for employment.

The related training required of apprentices is another example of study in occupational areas suitable for the community junior college, especially in metropolitan areas. In addition to the trade-related courses that are required in the apprenticeship plan, apprentices are encouraged to complete general education requirements also, so that at the end of their four-year indenture they may earn both journeyman rating and the Associate in Arts degree.

A final class of continuing occupational training is that which prepares a worker for promotion on the job. Frequently, competent craftsmen are considered for promotion to supervisory positions in which they will need not only additional technical knowledge but greater understanding of personal relations and the techniques of leadership. When the demand in a community justifies courses of this nature, it is appropriate that they be offered at the community junior college.

*Homemaking Education.*    Although nearly all women will spend a major portion of their lives as homemakers, comparatively few college women or high-school girls elect courses designed to prepare them for homemaking. One reason for their neglect may well be a feeling that the need is remote, that there will be plenty of time to care for it later. In addition, readiness is an essential precondition for learning. Community junior college teachers of homemaking are becoming aware that the best time to teach many of the skills and understandings is after marriage and that in some courses, both the young wife and her husband can profit from instruction. Classes in homemaking, therefore, are among the usual offerings of community junior college evening programs. Consumer economics, low-cost cookery, family entertaining, and prenatal and infant care are some of the courses which may be offered to part-time students either in day or evening classes to suit the convenience of the class members. For parents of young children, combinations of nursery school and child psychology classes are offered in a few community junior colleges; such classes as advanced sewing, upholstery, and interior decorating are very popular also with young parents, especially if they are offered at a time when one parent can baby-sit while the other is in class.

*Avocational Courses.*    "Worthy use of leisure time" has been an accepted objective of public education at least since it was listed as one of the "Cardinal Principles" in 1918. Recent increases in the amount of leisure time combine with the monotonous and uninspiring nature of many occupations to encourage adults to seek avocational education through adult education programs. As Martorana discovered, 41% of the junior colleges with adult education offerings provided avocational and recreational courses. Critics of continuing education, in legislatures and in the popular press, comment scathingly on organized instruction in subjects such as "fly-tying" and "basket-weaving," as if these defined its entire scope. Nevertheless, increasing free time constitutes an important social problem. Some of this time can be filled with academic and vocational studies, but for some students, classes in avocational skills are equally valid and important. Among the recreational and avocational courses found in community junior college extended day programs are listed woodworking, mineral and lapidary work, oil painting, ceramics, weaving, craft work, and other manipulative skills. Astronomy, dramatics, music, and public speaking may be offered for the same reason. In addition, a good many of the adults who enroll in the more traditional courses choose them more for recreational values than because they seek college degrees or vocational competency.

*The Geriatric Purpose.*   A new educational purpose has been created by developments of the past half century. Increasingly urbanized split-level living in mechanized houses has combined with earlier retirement ages and longer life expectancies to create a new and numerous class of senior citizens. To many of them, the new-coined adjective, "roleless," applies with tragic exactitude. In each of our cities can be found a sizable group of retired men and widowed women who are still alert, able, reasonably healthy, but lonely and unoccupied. In the prime of life, men prize their hard-won free time; but when all of one's time is free, leisure becomes a dehumanizing burden rather than an opportunity. Society must face the increasing problem of its older members and search diligently for humane solutions. The junior college can contribute significantly to these solutions.

In the past, education has been considered essentially as a preparation for life. If this definition still delimits the scope of the schools, the aging citizen is no concern of theirs. On the other hand, if education can also be considered as a continuing part of life, it can make significant contributions both to the individual well-being of the older person and to the welfare of society. Engrossing interest in one or more courses of study and in the companionship of classmates can preserve mental vigor. It is possible also that such interest and activity can improve physical condition. Even the financial cost of continuing education for these citizens would be an economy in comparison with the custodial costs that might well be saved.

Community junior colleges are becoming aware of this emerging educational need, and some of them are experimenting with classes to meet it. Philosophy, history, current events, geography through travelogues, literature, and some hobby classes have all proved to be of interest and of value when offered primarily for classes of students over 60 years of age. Further experimentation is needed to determine the proper scope of junior college education for the aged. The need exists in every community.

## C. Purposes of the Community College in Continuing Education

The community college accepts the individualistic purposes of its part-time students as they request courses to satisfy their own needs. In addition, it realizes its obligation to society to use educational resources in seeking solutions of social problems. The evening curriculum is, therefore, extended to all hours of the day and to include activities that improve the life of the community. Among the social considerations that influence community colleges to substitute the function of community services for the more limited one of continuing education may be listed the unmet obligation of the college to the inner-city community; the rapid increase of knowledge; the demands of enlightened citizenship; and the fact of social lag.

***The Community College in the Inner City.***   The increase in numbers of metropolitan multicampus community college districts has focused attention on the relation of higher education to the solution of personal and social problems in the inner city. Urban poverty and ghetto dwelling involve much more than low annual income. They involve a chronic and self-perpetuating environment of unemployment, dependency, poor education, family instability, inadequate health care, and lack of any reasonable share in the visible goods of life. Education, if it is accessible, compassionate, and based on careful definition of the true learning needs of the urban poor can help to break this apocalyptic cycle.

If it is to help, the community college must go to the people of the ghetto. It must not go to the ghetto with monumental buildings and with upper middle class prejudgments, curriculums, and values. It must go with humility, with imagination and desire to learn how to teach people whose alienation comes from the past failures of the schools as much as from any other single factor.

Andrew L. Goodrich characterizes two aspects of community services to the inner city as "outreach" and "inreach."[5] The outreach involves concentrated effort to involve the inner-city community in developing educational plans, and to recruit reluctant and untrusting students to give schooling one more try. The inreach function comprises supportive activities aimed at the on-campus needs peculiar to minority and poor-white students: food and books, group work to build self-esteem, tutoring, and useful part-time work. In sum, inreach attempts to gain insight into conditions, attitudes, and practices that repel educable persons at any age from joining the learning force and to find ways to overcome these deterrents. Education for the urban poor is one of the primary tasks of

our time. The community college can become an instrument of our time
to accomplish the task; several districts are moving vigorously in that
direction.

***The Rapid Increase of Knowledge.***   Improved techniques of research
joined with electronic data-processing devices have brought about
geometric increases in the sheer bulk of available information in almost
every field of human endeavor. New information, too, causes the
obsolescence of certain procedures and creates a need to train operators in
new methods. No man may dare any longer to consider his education
completed. The physician, the engineer, the physicist, and the dentist,
among others, return to the university periodically in their specialties.
New knowledge on the professional level, however, must be accompanied
by new understanding at the level of the layman and by new skills on the
part of the technician. This lay and technical reeducation is a responsibility of the community junior college.

In a society based on technology and dependent for its continued well-
being on a constantly expanding technology, the rapid diffusion of
knowledge is essential. Advertisers and broadcasters certainly contribute,
from their partisan standpoints, to this diffusion; the community junior
college can work more dispassionately and thoroughly than the mass
media to help people to know and evaluate recent discoveries in all fields.
In part, the college discharges this obligation by offering organized college
credit courses for part-time students, paralleling in prerequisites and in
coverage courses offered to full-time students. Beyond this, many
approaches can contribute to the same ends. Individual lectures or lecture
series, weekend workshops for specialized interests, laboratory demonstra-
tions, forums, exhibitions, and conferences have been used by junior
colleges in bringing summaries of recent research to their communities.
Class sizes, in this sort of effort, may vary from seminars or laboratory
groups to large auditorium audiences assembled to hear especially
qualified speakers.

***The Demands of Enlightened Citizenship.***   Citizenship education
cannot be completed by the time of high-school graduation or at any
other fixed point in man's life. A citizen who had come to understand
thoroughly the civic problems and responsibilities of the 1950's might
find himself completely unprepared for the quandaries of the 1970's.
Some citizens, of course, through careful reading and civic participation,
have always kept their learning abreast of their times. That has never
been true of the majority of people; modern conditions make it ever more
difficult to achieve adequate political and civic insights without help. The
global nature of the national responsibility, the incomprehensible sums of

national budgets, the rapid growth of metropolitan complexes with suburban needs for services of all sorts, and the mobility of the population—all conspire to increase both the gravity of political decisions and the difficulty of making them wisely. The community junior college is equipped to contribute significantly to the quality of citizen participation in understanding and in solving local and national problems. Avoiding partisanship, it can still encourage study, fact finding, debate, and the acceptance by citizens of responsibility for informed action.

*The Reduction of "Social Lag."*    Social lag refers to the serious gap between scientific invention and technological advance, on the one hand, and changes in political and economic institutions, on the other. This lag often causes unnecessary human misunderstanding and discomfort. A simple example pairs the effect of technology in releasing women from economic production in the home so that they now make their economic contribution in the office and the factory, with the continuing social belief that "woman's place is in the home." As a result, women are employed but feel degraded, even though their drudgery is lessened; husbands, too, find it difficult to adjust the attitudes of their childhood to the realities of their maturity.

Community junior college evening programs can help to reduce this social lag and its effects. Serious adults welcome opportunities to explore developments in technology and to relate their effects on the quality of human life to the ideas that motivate so much of our activity. In many communities, the junior college will have on its faculty or readily available to it specialists in the social and technical disciplines. In addition, it will have lecture halls, classrooms, and laboratories. It avoids one of its most meaningful opportunities if it does not take the lead in bringing this sort of interpretation to its community.

# D. Issues in Community Junior College Continuing Education

*Elements of a Complete Program.*    Community junior college administrators are in substantial agreement that continuing education is distinguished from the regular daytime program as a matter of convenience rather than because of essential differences. The extended-day student is not clearly distinguished from the regular day student by age or educational purpose, not even by the number of units of credit he carries. The major differentiations are the facts that the part-time student considers his primary occupation to be something other than college attendance and that he may not be interested in college credit for his study. The continuing program, then, consists of learning opportunities organized primarily for this category of students, at any hour of the day, with or without degree credit. The fact that some "regular" students may also enroll in such courses does not affect the classification of the course; it is recognized that at times part-time students, as defined, will also enroll in " regular" courses.

The issues on which administrators are in disagreement have to do with the scope and diversity of the program. Should a community junior college offer courses leading to the certificate of high-school equivalency? Should it offer short courses, noncredit courses, hobby courses, or vocational courses? To what extent should the community junior college seek to meet all eduational needs of the adults of its community? Should it classify certain kinds of instruction as college work and worthy of its attention, relegating other studies to other agencies? Or should it decide that continuing education is accomplished best under a single administration, preferably that of the community junior college? Should the community junior college attempt, as some do, to offer any instruction for which there is student demand, so long as there is a reasonable body of knowledge, understanding, or skills, and an instructor available to conduct the course? Should it seek aggressively to extend its educational services to the community, or should it limit them to specified categories of college instruction? Those administrators who adopt the "community junior college" point of view lean toward the agressive, all-inclusive, extended-service concept of the adult education program. Their communities respond to this effort by enrolling in increasing numbers, as was suggested in the section of this Chapter dealing with part-time statistics.

*Academic Credit.* The proposed definition of the part-time student indicated that he is often uninterested in academic credit for his study. Some part-time students are working for credentials or degrees and must choose courses which carry credit, but many of the students who enroll in cultural, homemaking, vocational, or avocational courses are entirely uninterested in credit. They do not wish to be bothered with term papers or examinations; they feel competent to decide for themselves what values, and how much value, they wish to derive from the course. The question of credit is complicated in some courses by the presence of a small minority of students who need credit together with a majority who wish only to audit, for their own purposes.

The credit issue, then, revolves about two questions: Should a community junior college allow itself to offer courses that deviate from traditional and accreditable practices? To what extent does adulthood imply the ability of a person to choose values for himself rather than to accept those of tutors and scholars? Three sets of practices have developed in junior colleges in three attempts to reconcile the answers to these questions. Most junior colleges offer only credit courses in their continuing education program, paralleling subjects offered in the daytime schedule and supplementing these courses by credit-carrying pre-employment courses and occupational extension courses not offered during the day.

A second group of junior colleges insists that any course which is worthy of being offered is worthy of credit. These colleges attempt to provide a broad and comprehensive range of classes; they maintain credit and attendance records for all students and classify all students as either freshman or sophomores. Although this seems to be an extreme position, it does tend to add dignity and importance to the continuing education program and to those who enroll in it.

The third position is an intermediate one. Classes in any field which are equivalent to those offered in the regular program carry defined units of credit; students may enroll in these classes either for credit or as auditors. In addition, short courses and courses of limited scope or specialized interest are offered without credit toward any degree or diploma. It is probable that most of the community junior colleges that offer extensive evening programs of continuing education follow this eclectic pattern.

*Source of Support for Continuing Education.* Arrangements for the support of community junior college continuing education are complicated by the historical attitudes of legislators toward "adult education." At what point should free public education cease, and the student be required to carry all the costs of his education? How can such a stopping point be defined? Are years of age, years of attendance, diplomas achieved, stated purposes of the student, or courses taken better bases for distinguishing the tuition-free student from the paying adult? Even in private colleges, students pay only a part of the cost of their education; if fees are set so that part-time students do bear all the cost of their classes, will not many of them be unable to afford further education? It is not likely that those least able to pay for additional education are those who are most in need of it? Inability to state consistent answers to questions like these is one reason why a few junior colleges offer minimum continuing programs, or none at all.

One pattern of support treats evening classes almost exactly the same as other community junior college classes. Requirements are established for the legal certification of teachers for adults, if that is required of other faculty members. State support, local support, and tuition policies apply equally to all classes of attendance; approval of courses by state departments of education is handled in the same fashion. Some method is worked out for equating part-time attendance, for purposes of state support, to that of full-time students, and foundation program funds are allocated on an equal basis. In states with laws of this nature, continuing education is fully accepted as one facet of the state's obligation to provide free public schooling for its citizens.

In other states, public junior colleges share in state support for post-high-school credit students, but are not given support for those in their adult classes. The junior college buildings, even though financed largely from state sources, are used by part-time students without additional charge. Costs of instructional materials, administrative costs, and teachers' salaries must be borne locally. In some of these states, local junior college boards may elect to bear the cost of these items entirely from public funds; in others, the local district and the continuing students share the costs through a nominal tuition charge. In still others, an attempt is made to collect the entire cost of evening instruction from the students or even to make a profit on the program. This last objective may be accomplished by authorizing only classes over a certain minimum size, charging fees which will cover the costs, and paying instructors a sliding scale in relation to the course enrollment.

There is, of course, no single best plan of financing continuing education for all states. Yet the financial plan does express in coldly factual terms the state's accepted philosophy of education. If individual and public needs for "lifelong learning" as expressed in this Chapter are valid, each state should work to make further education easily available to as many as possible of its citizens. A major step in this effort would be to reduce, as far as is feasible, the tuition charges for such opportunities.

*Flexibility in Curriculum Development.*    The ideal of some community junior college evening program administrators has been "to offer anything and everything of educational value for which there is sufficient and sustained demand ." The attainment of this principle requires a high degree of flexibility in schedule making and course approval. Courses will be inaugurated at any time of the year; instructors will be employed at short notice to teach courses which they may not have taught before. In fact, it is possible that some courses for which there is "sufficient and sustained demand" may not have been taught before by anyone. The issue created by this responsiveness to demand is that of academic control of the offerings of the college.

In Chapter 12, the careful process was described by which a curriculum committee examines new course proposals before including them in the curriculum. Under the principle stated above, however, demand, rather than the established procedures of committee deliberation, determines the curriculum. It is conceivable that a course that had been proposed and rejected in the regular curriculum might be accepted and established in the evening program. In other cases, courses paralleling regular courses might be offered in the evening program for credit toward the Associate in Arts degree or for transfer; but the instructor available might be one who would not have been employed as a full-time teacher of the same course. Standards of a junior college might suffer in such circumstances.

The enthusiastic extended-day administrator would counter these objections by pointing out that it is the purpose of his division to serve the community in all of its part-time educational needs. Many emerging needs of adults, he would claim, must be met energetically without undue red tape; the academic members of the curriculum committee might cause important damage to the total program of the college if they decided that responsible adult groups could not have a course or courses which they had petitioned for. Taxpaying patrons of the community college, in this view, are competent to analyze their own needs, and their requests should be complied with.

*Standards.*    The definition and maintenance of standards of achievement are closely related to the issue of flexibility. The problem of standards is complicated by several factors. The diversity of courses, from chemistry and calculus to ceramics and current events, is one source of difficulty. The shortage of qualified instructors for work which is usually overtime and often underpaid is another. The inadequacy of library services during evening hours, together with the fatigue of the students themselves, militates against rigorous assignments and requirements. The scheduling of classes for single weekly meetings of several hours' duration rather than for a series of one-hour meetings makes it difficult for the instructor to command unflagging attention and limits the number of papers he is likely to assign. Student diversity in background and in purpose is an additional stumbling block, since a class may enroll 20 persons as auditors who want to define their own goals in the course, together with four or five degree-credit students who must accept the requirements of the instructor.

The difficulties in definition and maintenance of standards do not absolve the teacher of part-time students from serious concern with them. As more and more students seek to earn degrees through part-time study, the question of comparable standards becomes more acute. Careful planning of the offering, in-service training of the faculty, extension of laboratory and library opportunities, and a clear-cut differentiation of credit and noncredit enrollments can help to clarify the value of evening program courses. The vigorous growth of community junior college continuing education can be stemmed abruptly if it becomes apparent that the quality of the achievement is inferior and unsound.

*Articulation with Other Agencies.* The creation of new community junior colleges brings a need for the articulation of all their efforts with previously existing educational agencies. This need may be particularly acute in the field of continuing education. Many school districts have developed over a period of years extensive plans for adult education with administrative staff, arrangements for use of facilities, well-established offerings, sources of faculty, and a continuing clientele. The new community junior college may then be seen as a threat to the status of the previous program. Especially if it is independently organized and administered, the new college may be tempted to duplicate and extend the existing program. Alternatively, it may decide to offer in the evening only the courses it offers in the day program to regular students. Either of these decisions is likely to prove unfortunate; the one will beget enmities, unnecessary competition, and excess cost, and the other will deprive some adults of needed educational services which can be provided most appropriately only by the community junior college.

A better solution would be an attempt to harmonize the efforts of the existing and the new agencies, looking toward a time when unification of program and of administration will become possible. In these situations, neither the prestige of previous workers nor the ambitions of the newer faculty should be the controlling consideration. Organizational decisions should be sought that will result in making available to the people of the community the finest possible continuing education program, with due regard for economy to the school districts and for harmony among all workers.

The underlying conflict in each of the issues presented lies in the philosophies of those who hold the varying positions. An emphasis on the responsibility of the community college to meet any educational needs of any citizens beyond high-school age will lead to one kind of decision about continuing education, course credit, financial support, curriculum development, and interagency cooperation. Emphasis on the historical role of the college, on the other hand, and on its responsibility to preserve the integrity of the academic disciplines, will lead to other decisions. As yet, no clear-cut evidence indicates which tendency will prevail as public junior colleges gain experience in continuing education. There is little doubt, however, that the continuing education function of junior colleges will continue to increase in importance, both in numbers of institutions providing it and in numbers of students enrolled.

## FOOTNOTES

1. *1971 Junior College Directory.* Washington, D.C.: American Association of Junior Colleges, 1971.
2. Martorana, S.V., "Status of Adult Education in Junior Colleges," *Junior College Journal,* **18** (February, 1948), pp. 322-331.
3. Cohn, Wilbur. "Education and Learning,"*The Annals,* **373** (September, 1967), p. 83.
4. Newman, Frank (chairman). *Report on Higher Education.* Washington, D.C.: U.S. Government Printing Office, 1971, pp. 8-9.
5. Goodrich, Andrew L., *Community Services for the "New Student" at Inner City Community Colleges.* East Lansing, Michigan: Kellogg Community Services Leadership Program, Michigan State Univeristy, 1970.

## BIBLIOGRAPHY

Carnegie Commission on Higher Education. *Less Time, More Options: Education Beyond the High School.* New York: McGraw-Hill Book Company, 1971.

Goodrich, Andrew L. *Community Services for the "New Student" at Inner City Community Colleges.* East Lansing, Michigan: Kellogg Community Services Leadership Program, Michigan State Univeristy, 1970.

Harlacker, Ervin L. *The Community Dimension of the Community College.* Englewood Cliffs, New Jersey: Prentice-Hall, Inc., 1969.

_____*Effective Junior College Programs of Community Services: Rationale, Guidelines, Practices.* Junior College Leadership Program, Occasional Report No. 10. Los Angeles: School of Education, University of California, 1967.

Johnson, B. Lamar. *Starting a Community Junior College.* Washington, D.C.: American Association of Junior Colleges, 1964.

Myran, Gunder A. *Community Services in the Community College.* Washington, D.C.: American Association of Junior Colleges, 1969.

_____*Community Services Perceptions of the National Council on Community Services.* East Lansing, Michigan: Kellogg Community Services Leadership Program, Michigan State University, 1971.

Reynolds, James W. *The Comprehensive Junior College Curriculum.* Berkeley, California: McCutchan Publishing Corporation, 1969.

*Urban Community College Project: Los Angeles Peer Counseling Program.* Report No. 2. Washington, D.C.: Office of Economic Opportunity and American Association of Junior Colleges, 1971.

*Urban Community College Project: Peralta's Inner City Project.* Report No. 1. Washington, D.C.: Office of Economic Opportunity and American Association of Junior Colleges, 1970.

Weindenthal, Bud. *The Community College Commitment to the Inner City.* Washington, D.C.: American Association of Junior Colleges, 1967.

# 17

# Student Personnel Services

A key word in the description of the community college student body is "diversity." Students vary in backgrounds, in personal qualities, in abilities, and in ambitions. At the same time, the college offers a broadly diversified program of instructional opportunities. Effective matching of students to programs requires extensive and competent guidance. In addition, realization of the educational values of student-directed activities requires the coordination and advice of faculty members. The entire field of out-of-class services to students constitutes the responsibility of student personnel services.

Although these responsibilities have been recognized throughout the history of junior colleges, student services are still judged to be only partly effective. Many reasons for this evaluation are listed—insufficient supply of fully trained and competent workers, assignment to them of inappropriate clerical tasks, excessive numbers of students per counselor, appointment to guidance positions of good teachers who are untrained in personnel theory and practice, and unrealistic expectations of the effectiveness of guidance. Evaluations of personnel practices, either within single institutions or more broadly sampled, consistently report dissatisfaction with the scope of the program in relation to the need.

Chapter 17 presents the elements of a comprehensive student personnel program. Although the author knows of no single program that includes all the practices described, each may be found in successful operation in one or another community junior college. A complete student personnel program will include the guidance service with its multitude of functions; special student services; student activities; placement and follow-up services; records, research, and evaluation; and an administrative agency to carry out the services.

## A. The Guidance Service

*Guidance Workers.* In his study of student personnel services in 73 two-year colleges, Medsker found that student counseling was usually done by instructors and sometimes by the general administrators or deans of the college.[1]

In only 16 of the 73 colleges studied was most of the counseling performed by counselors who had been trained in student personnel work. The instructors who do counseling are ordinarily neither trained nor qualified to do more than assist students in selecting their term schedule of classes. Problems of choice of vocational objective, improvement of study skills, and growth in personal adjustment are beyond the instructors' usual competence or interest. Since their full-time responsibility is in teaching, the instructor-advisers may feel that their guidance duties are an imposition. In practice, they may become for most of the students assigned to them merely schedule checkers rather than advisers or counselors.

The administrator-counselor, except in the smallest colleges, may also find it difficult to provide adequate service for his students. His experience and training may have equipped him to serve ably as a counselor, but the pressure of other duties and his frequent absences from the campus will tend to interrupt the progress of counseling and distract the administrator's attention from the student, even in the midst of an important interview. The instructors and the administrators have definite functions in guidance. The former will stand ready to assist any of their students in problems associated with success in their courses and will advise students referred to them by other workers about educational and occupational matters in which they are competent. The administrator can help by being convinced of the importance of personnel services as another aspect of instruction and by providing workers and facilities to carry on the services. In addition, trained guidance workers are required as the center of the organization for guidance. The scope of their responsibility may be presented by means of a description of a guidance program in operation.

*The Purpose of Guidance.*    The purpose of guidance is to assist the student in reaching sound decisions in matters of vocational choice, educational planning, and personal concern. Sound decisions are based on adequate information made available to the student and so interpreted that he is willing to accept it and to act in harmony with it. One category of such information includes knowledge of educational opportunities. An effective guidance service will provide for informing prospective students and their parents about the purposes and achievements of the local junior college. Such orientation must take many forms and must be accomplished over a period of time, rather than in one concentrated effort during the spring before high-school graduation. Understanding of a comparatively new institution such as the community junior college, especially of its broader and less traditional kinds of educational opportunity, requires constant and untiring interpretation. For this reason, there is an intimate relation between the public relations of the college and its guidance service. Effective liaison between the two operations will prove helpful to both.

*Information Giving.*    The information-giving process upon which guidance is based starts with the interpretation of the college to the community through the press, through the speakers' bureau, and through the various publications of the college. Each of these efforts must be planned and carried out with a realization of its collateral importance in the guidance of students and their parents. Press releases, then, will concentrate not only on athletics and on the university success of graduates; they will include stories about vocational advisory committees, about placement of graduates of occupational curriculums, and about all aspects of the community junior college program. Pamphlets describing the work of the college or the nature of a single curriculum will be given widespread circulation, all so that the patrons of the junior college may know of its existence and become ever more conscious of the varieties of educational opportunity it offers. The student newspaper, the annual, and the catalog will attempt to present in a manner appropriate to each the full scope of college activities, so as to clarify misconceptions and to contribute to adequate understanding of the purposes and the programs of the community junior college.

Such efforts are directed at the entire supporting community and only incidentally toward those who will become students. It is necessary to intensify and to focus the information-giving process for the prospective full-time student as the time for his enrollment approaches. At this stage, the wholehearted cooperation of the high-school administrative and teaching staffs becomes necessary. If they are convinced that the college officers are interested primarily in the welfare of their students and not just in "recruiting," this cooperation will be offered willingly. Early in the senior year, college counselors may be asked to explain to each section of senior English or perhaps to an assembly of all seniors, the growing necessity for higher education in American society and the opportunities afforded by the community junior college. Questions comparing the junior college with other available forms of higher education can be answered candidly; perhaps a brief letter of information may be passed out for discussion at home. If such presentation of community college purposes, offerings, and quality is to affect student decisions, it must occur comparatively early in the senior year—preferably before Christmas vacation. In February or March, the community junior college can perform a service to the students, to the high schools, and to itself by arranging for the administration of a college aptitude test battery and perhaps of an achievement examination to all graduating seniors in those high schools from which most of its students come. The costs of such administration may be shared in any agreed proportion; even if the college bears the entire cost of administering and scoring the examinations, the expense is a good investment. The high-school counselors can use the results in informing students of their likelihood of success in achieving various educational objectives and of being admitted to various available colleges. Since choices of college are unstable until the students have completed enrollment, availability of scores of all students during the summer will be very convenient for junior college counselors. Some students are sure to appear for registration interviews after insisting that they planned to attend another college. Participation in the testing of high-school seniors within its enrollment area has four additional values for the community college. It tends to ensure standardized administration of the tests in accordance with the instructions of the publishers; it provides comparable scores on the same examinations for all students from contributing high schools; it simplifies the problem of arranging a time and a place that will be convenient both for students and test administrators; and it focuses the attention of seniors once more on the need for decision about whether to attend college and which one to choose.

An organized visit by high-school seniors to the college campus is another valuable step in providing the information students need as a basis for decisions about college attendance. On this occasion, college administrators can tell the seniors about high points in the history of the college, about its excellent or unique features, and about other interesting and important facts. Division chairmen can present details of the work of their divisions and conduct tours of the facilities; each senior will attend only one or two of these divisional presentations. Student officers will describe the nature of the student government and opportunities for participation in athletics and activities. At the conclusion of this campus visit, each senior should have sufficient information to make a considered choice between attendance at the community junior college and the other possibilities open to him, such as work or another college.

He may still be undecided about choice of vocational goal and the educational requirements for it. Individual counseling in the high school has surely contributed to his decisions; it now becomes necessary for the college counselors to assist in the process of selection of appropriate curriculums and individual courses. Armed with high-school achievement records, junior college catalogs, and scores from standardized tests, the counselors arrange a time when they can be available, preferably at the high schools, for comparatively brief interviews with any student who thinks that he is likely to attend the community college. At this time, a tentative first-semester program is worked out for discussion with parents and other trusted advisers but subject to later confirmation at the summer registration appointment. The major values of this tentative individual discussion are that it affords the student an opportunity to clear up any questions he may have in mind and that it stimulates him to think in concrete terms of his possible course for the fall.

In some colleges, this pre-graduation interview will serve as the only individual counseling prior to enrollment in classes on registration day; other colleges may forego it in favor of application for admission and registration interview by appointment during the summer. Colleges that have been able to provide for both interviews, however, feel that they have reduced the number of schedule changes during the first days of instruction and have also reduced the rate of withdrawal from college. In any case, the college will need to provide other opportunities for testing and enrollment for older students and for those from more distant high schools.

*Orientation.*    Information-giving as a part of the counseling service continues after the initial enrollment. Nearly all junior colleges devote some time at the opening of each year to orientation of new students. Through a single "freshman day" or through a course designed in part for this purpose, the freshman are introduced to the facilities of the campus, such as the library, cafeteria, auditorium, gymnasium, and specialized classrooms. They are encouraged to participate in the student life of the college and to make use of its services such as the testing office, the reading laboratory, and the health service. In orientation courses they ordinarily consider the improvement of their study skills, complete several examinations useful in guidance, and develop individual four-semester schedules of courses that will fulfill their several junior college objectives of occupational preparation, graduation, general education, and preparation for transfer.

Some of the community junior colleges require courses in personal adjustment or in psychology as a part of their group guidance efforts. One pattern of such courses is a required introductory psychology course which contributes to general education by its emphasis on the under-standing of the causes and processes of human behavior. At the same time, the activity of the course serves as a preparation for more efficient personal counseling. Tests administered and discussed in the unit on individual differences serve as a basis for individual conferences on the relation between stated goals and measured personal qualities; this conference, in turn, leads to the development of detailed plans for the students' remaining semesters in the junior college. In the same way, the unit on personal adjustment may encourage a troubled student to approach his counselor for individual help while giving him the factual information he needs if he is to profit from such help.

*Individual Counseling.*    Students in every college exhibit a variety of needs for help in reaching decisions and in correcting conditions that interfere with their success in classwork. The trained counselor is charged with the responsibility of providing this help.

Vocational choice is fundamental to many other decisions of the student. As many as half of the high-school graduates who come to the community junior college will have made a firm and realistic vocational choice; they can plan an educational course and pursue it. The other half are not so fortunate. They have not yet managed to develop a firm self-concept or to relate it to occupational opportunities. The counselor will help these students to interpret and accept information about themselves derived from records of previous accomplishment and from tests. He will guide them to sources of information about occupations, such as the library, instructors in all departments of the community junior college, and employers in the community, in the hope that they can form firm occupational choices as a foundation for their educational planning.

After making a vocational choice, many students still lack information on educational requirements and opportunities. One of the major tasks of the community junior college counselor is assisting students to develop realistic long-term educational plans. Such plans will include specific semester schedules for the period to be spent at the community junior college, and the next choice of institution, if any, together with an estimate of additional time to be required and financial resources to be consumed in completing the plan. Students are confused by university catalogs and if left to themselves will often fail to include all the courses required as preparation for their specialty. The duration, grade requirements, and cost of programs such as engineering or medicine are often a shock to the eager freshman. Some also are unaware of physical requirements for certain types of work, such as size or color vision or dexterity. The sooner these matters are made clear to them, the better chance they will have to select and to complete an educational plan suited to their own aptitudes, interests, and potentialities.

Problems of personal adjustment are another concern of the counselor. A good deal of college failure is attributable not to low ability or to lack of funds so much as to personal difficulties. Such conflicts may involve self-concept, classmates, instructors, family members, or life in general. They may be temporary and relatively superficial or deep seated and potentially dangerous. The counselor's task in relation to personal problems is first and foremost to recognize the nature of the difficulty. In some cases, he himself can help the student work out his solution; in others, he will need to convince the student, or perhaps his family, of the need for expert help. Every community junior college counselor needs, therefore, to maintain acquaintance with a wide range of community agencies to which students may be referred. Welfare organizations, employment offices, family service bureaus, psychiatrists, veterans' service offices, and religious counseling agencies are among the resources upon which a counseling service may call within the course of a month. An important qualification of a counselor is the humility which helps him to know his limitations and leads him to seek specialized help for his students when it is needed.

The community junior college will maintain also a limited health service in connection with its student personnel office. The service is much less extensive than that found in residential colleges. Its purpose in the community junior college will never be medical treatment, except in cases needing emergency first aid. The staff consists ordinarily of a full-time public health nurse, competent to advise students about minor difficulties, to present some topics to classes upon request of the instructor, to perform needed first aid, and to know when to insist that the student see his personal physician. A program of medical examinations of all students is very helpful to the counseling office, if it can be arranged; even a cursory examination by a physician may enable the staff to improve the educational opportunity of many students, either by arranging for correction of defects or by calling them to the attention of instructors.

The broad purpose of the guidance aspect of student personnel services is to help each student to know, to accept, and to respect his own abilities, so that he may match them with realistic educational and occupational goals and proceed with maximum effectiveness toward those goals. In achieving this purpose, the community college provides consultation before college enrollment and during registration periods; it uses convocations and individual counseling; it assigns instructors to some parts of the task, trained counselors, psychometrists, or physicians to other parts of the task, and administrative officers to still others. The entire coordinated guidance effort is founded on the realization that the misdirected student wastes both his time and that of his instructors; the development of an appropriate and attainable educational goal is prerequisite to any worthwhile student achievement.

## B. Special Student Services

The increasing recognition of the fact that many nonachievers and school dropouts represent a waste of good or even high ability has led to concerted efforts to induce these persons to make one more attempt at school success. As the efforts succeed, it quickly becomes apparent that it is a mistake to simply introduce these reluctant learners into the traditional curriculum; it is almost equally futile to set up remedial or sub-college courses that repeat the irrelevancies that first drove them from school. A few of the unprepared, especially those who are older and return to school after maturing their ambitions, can succeed in such programs, but most will experience one more defeat and depart once more.

The educational response to their need must be personal and individual. It is concentrated on providing the new student some experiences of success, no matter how elemental the task, and some growth in self-esteem. This approach to education is not congenial to many instructors, and they have not been prepared for it. It does not permit organized preplanned presentations or the assignment of tidy packages of credits and grades. For this reason, specialists must be employed to help these students bridge the gap between the street and the classroom. One-to-one counseling and work in small groups are required. High levels of academic scholarship are not nearly so important at this point as ability of the teacher to sense the student's fears and recognize his strengths. For these reasons, the initial college contacts of unprepared students are most appropriately assigned to persons with counseling training, within the student personnel division.

Special services for unprepared students include the initial recruitment, an outreach by counselors or even by successful students from the peer group to encourage the young person to give school another try. Because college is an unfamiliar situation, but similar to one that previously has meant frustration and defeat, the new high-risk student needs to establish at the beginning a relationship with a trustworthy and accepting guide, one who can tutor him, reassure him, and encourage him. Since poverty is one of the major reasons for discouragement with school, support funds are a help in recruiting and retaining these students. If such funds are available, they should be administered by the special services counselor.

Small groups under the leadership of the special counselor are useful in providing a sense of security and belonging for each participant. If it is possible to include in each group members of several ethnic backgrounds, the polarization of attitudes can be lessened. Members of the group will find it possible to assist each other in their studies, to the benefit of the helper and the helped. The group as a whole can serve to encourage a lagging member to keep on trying rather than to drop out once more.

The concept of special services is a relatively recent development. It may be rejected as spoonfeeding by some on the grounds that the student who needs so much help will never become a scholar. The justification of the program lies in the fact that it opens doors of opportunity that had previously been slammed shut; it gives hope of access to the enjoyment of life by citizens who had earlier been without hope. Special student services aim to develop self-sufficient persons rather than specialists in academic disciplines. This is a crucial social need of our time.

## C. Student Activities

The student personnel service of the community junior college encourages the establishment of a broad variety of student activities as a part of the total educational effort of the college. Participation in self-government, in interest clubs and social activities, and in organized athletics contributes importantly to the achievement of the purposes of the college. Skills in citinzenship are practiced, qualities of leadership are developed, broader interests are cultivated, worthwhile achievements are recognized, and wholesome social skills are encouraged when students participate in planning and carrying out the elements of a broad program of student activities. The educational growth of students is not the sole reward of these efforts, however. Many of the tasks accomplished by students through their organizations must be done by someone in the college, by employees if not by students; other tasks contribute notably to the student morale and to the local fame of the college.

The balance of these two aspects of student activities, their educational value and their service, constitutes the true art of student activity supervision. Student government, clubs, and athletics miss their true point if they focus only on artificial learning situations. In contrast, if their service to the college and to the community is overemphasized, the result may be exploitation of the students and such negative learnings as political chicanery or cynical sportsmanship. Student activities must have meaning and importance for the students and for the college, but the students, the faculty, and the community must never forget to keep them in their proper relation to all the other aspects of the college's offerings.

*Student Government.*     The organized student council or the associated students is the agency through which students exercise control over their activities and learn the skills of self-government. Since the final authority and responsibility for the operation of a community junior college rest with the board of trustees, it is usually advisable to develop a charter for student government. Such a document sets forth the duties, responsibilities, and areas of concern of the student officers together with provisions for administrative veto power over some classes of action. The power of revocation of the charter should be explicitly reserved to the board of trustees of the college. The need to invoke such power should never arise, but its mention serves to make clear the nature of delegated authority. For the same reason, a dignified ceremony can be developed for transmitting the charter to the new student officers at each annual inauguration. In this way, the students of each new generation are tactfully reminded both of their responsibility to the community and of the large measure of authority which is theirs to use wisely in their own interests.

*Activities.*     Student government properly concerns itself with the fostering and control of student interests outside of the classroom. Service to the college in such matters as orientation of new students, hospitality to college visitors, and some measure of control of student behavior outside of class is one suitable area of operations. Social activities, adapted to the interests and the desires of the students, ordinarily command the attention of student officers. In some colleges, business enterprises are conducted by the students. The student store, the cafeteria or coffee shop, and admission to intercollegiate athletic contests are frequently controlled by the student government and serve as sources of income for the support of other less profitable activities. Student clubs of all sorts—academic interest groups, denominational clubs, freshman and sophomore class associations, and hobby groups such as chess clubs and ski clubs—are chartered by the student government. This measure of control provides for the coordination of effort by all students; it enables the student government to approve the budgets and to appropriate funds for each of its constituent activities.

Several persistent problems plague junior college administrators and student officers in student government and related activities. It is very difficult to develop continuity of student leadership when all the tasks of orientation, apprenticeship, election, and office holding must be completed within a span of two college years. Lack of time also hinders the development of any significant body of useful campus tradition. Almost before a class has become fully acculturated, it must pass on its folklore to the next class; traditions, for good or ill, have little opportunity to mature and to become ingrained parts of the personality of the students. The high rate of withdrawal from the junior college contributes to the difficulties of the activity program; even elected officers at times drop out before completing their terms. Some of the clubs, for all practical purposes, must begin anew every year, since only a handful of former members may return for the second year's activity.

Under such conditions the personality and the enthusiasm of the faculty advisers of the student government and of the several subordinate organizations are of major importance. Since they provide the only long-term continuity for activities, the advisers may begin either to dictate the details of the annual program or else to despair of any substantial achievement for their student group. In either case, the faculty adviser must remind himself that the purpose of student activities is to help students learn through their own participation. The adviser is just as truly a teacher in this setting as he is in his classrooms, and the fact that teaching here may be more difficult does not mean that the learning is less worthwhile. The difficulties do point up the need for careful selection, both of the activities to be sponsored and of the advisers for them. Once selected, the advisers should continue with the same activity over a period of years, so that they may grow annually more competent in exercising the unobtrusive leadership that helps students develop into citizens.

Important educational values inhere in student activities; the college that neglected or refused to encourage such out-of-class experiences would provide only a partial education. Although it is easy to demonstrate that all students need and can profit from working in self-government and the social life of the college, it is impossible to attract nearly all students to participate. Formidable barriers obstruct the path. First of these is certainly the lack of student time. Since students in community colleges live off campus and at distances as great as 30 miles, they will return in the evening only for events that seem highly important. The student who has completed his classes at noon will be unlikely to remain on campus for a late afternoon meeting. A fifth of the students are married, and more than half are employed; club meetings, all-college picnics, or the acceptance of responsibility in student government may seem comparatively unimportant to them. For students in a residential college, even frivolous organized activities may provide a welcome diversion from the loneliness of a dormitory room, but students in a community college are likely to find any optional campus event an unwelcome distraction from their busy routines of classes, employment, study, family life, and commuting.

A further deterrent often lies in the hidden or apparent costs of participation. To the student who is seeking higher education in spite of comparative poverty, the cost of a party dress, of tickets to several activities, of added gasoline or bus fares, and the loss of several hours of work may seem to prohibit unnecessary activity. These students are also likely to hold back because of a fear of rejection by other students who may have more time or money or more social experience. For such reasons, only half of public junior college students take part in student life, even under the best of circumstances.

On the other hand, some students participate so actively that their classwork suffers. Faculty advisers, in their desire to assure the success of a project by providing strong student leadership, may contribute to this exploitation. Overactivity by one student, of course, not only interferes with his own education but also deprives other able students of the opportunity for practice in leadership and for recognition. Some balance of honors is achieved through a quota limitation of activities. In most junior colleges, an officer of any organization must maintain an acceptable academic standard in order to continue in office. Beyond this, some student constitutions assign varying point values to several categories of responsibility and set a limit on the total points a student may assume at one time. Under a system of this sort, the presidency of the student body might be assigned a weight of five points. Other elective offices, athletic-team membership, and editorship of the newspaper might have weights of four points each. In the same manner, chairmanship or membership on committees and in clubs would be assigned point values. No student, then, is permitted to assume obligations exceeding an established total of points, worked out on the basis of experience in the college.

*Athletics.*    Intercollegiate athletics are a special category of student activities. Because of their inherent attraction for many junior college students as participants and as spectators and because of their appeal to the public at large, they offer unlimited opportunities to achieve the objectives of student activities. A well-balanced program of sports affords many students opportunity to develop physically and to learn the values of teamwork, the joys of wholesome competition, and American attitudes of sportsmanship. Through outstanding participation in sports, some two-year college students are enabled to continue their education into the four-year college or to qualify for a career in professional athletics.

When they are administered in accordance with the educational purposes of the community junior college, intercollegiate athletics can also make important contributions to the learning and to the morale of the nonplaying students. Wholesome rivalry, sportsmanlike support of one's own team, scorn for unworthy tactics, the elation of victory or the dejection of defeat are vivid and worthy experiences for the young. Athletic teams serve also as one part of the public posture of the college, attracting attention both from possible students in neighboring schools and from the sports-minded constituents in the community. These positive values amply justify the establishment of athletic conferences through which community junior colleges of comparable size within traveling distance may compete in all the usual competitive sports. In order to provide opportunity for the valuable learning experiences to as many students as possible, each junior college and each athletic league should feel obligated to provide team competition in every sport it can afford. To football, basketball, track, and baseball should be added also, as it is possible, handball, swimming, water polo, boxing, wrestling, tennis, and golf. Skiing, sailing, and ice skating are popular where conditions permit them. For women, too, the lessons of sportsmanship are important and should be encouraged by appropriate intramural competition in suitable sports.

But athletics are sources not only of positive values. Their drama—and their financial importance—too often blind the public, the coach, and even the administrator to their true purposes. Then overemphasis on gate receipts leads to exploitation of students, the purchase of able gladiators, the perversion of sportsmanship, and the philosophy of the hired athlete. Colleges and universities in America have struggled for years with indifferent success to establish gentlemen's agreements (buttressed by mutual spying) to control the abuses of competitive recruiting and extravagant aid to athletes. In spite of such efforts, values have been distorted to such an extent that at one time the football coach at a state university was paid more than any other public employee, including the governor; at the same university, professors' salaries averaged below the national average for colleges and universities. There are real values in athletics, and with proper safeguards for the welfare of the student and the educational objectives of the college, they should be encouraged. Constant vigilance by college administrators is needed, however, to avoid the excesses that have characterized university athletic programs.

## D. Placement and Follow-Up

An active placement office is an important adjunct to the student personnel service in a community junior college. Since most of the students work while attending college, they will appreciate help in finding suitable employment. It is not too much to say that a placement office may, for some young people, be the one agency that makes existing higher education truly available to them; it can enable them to find work to earn the money they need to stay in college. In larger communities, the placement office can be of real service also to the former students and to graduates in helping them to find full-time employment in the fields for which they studied in the junior college.

While serving the student and the graduate, the placement office can realize important by-products also for the entire program of the college. The constant contact of the placement officer with all kinds of employers in the entire community serves to keep him aware of emerging needs for trained employees.

In an unobtrusive way, the placement officer interprets the college and its purposes to the community while contributing a constant flow of important information to the continuing community survey carried on by the college. Clues to new and promising fields for occupational education, as well as to those declining in importance, may frequently come to the attention of the placement officer before they are noticed by any other staff member.

The "follow-up" of graduates and former students is an important part of the self-evaluation of the community junior college. It is functionally related to placement and is often under the direction of the same officer.

Of the two aspects of follow-up, junior colleges have been more concerned with former students who have gone on to upper-division study in colleges and universities. Few studies are reported of the success of vocationally trained graduates in finding employment in the area of their training and of their comparative success after placement. Both aspects are essential to a complete follow-up program.

The most usual method of estimating the success of the college in its transfer function is that of comparing grade-point averages achieved before and after transfer. Any college with a sizable number of transferring students will find such information about its own graduates comparatively easy to gather and of very real value in the continuing evaluation of parts of its curriculum. The registrars of nearly all receiving colleges are generous in supplying the needed facts; state institutions make routine reports of the first semester achievements of all new students to the school or college last attended. Other senior colleges will respond to a simple questionnaire listing students who had applied for admission and asking such questions as (1) Did he qualify for admission? (2) Did he enter? (3) What advanced standing was allowed? (4) Is he now enrolled in good standing? disqualified? on probation? withdrew before completing a semester? (5) Units attempted in his first semester? (6) Grade points achieved in his first semester? (7) Grade-point average?

Such quantitative data can be gathered also with somewhat greater difficulty from employers of occupational graduates. Since personnel officers in business and industry do not keep comparable "grade-averages" on all their employees, tact and knowledge of business procedures are needed in attempting this follow-up. Many times a personal interview must be substituted for a mailed questionnaire. Yet employers appreciate the interest of the college in preparing workers; the concept of quality control is one with which they are familiar; and they will cooperate enthusiastically if the reason for the interest of the college and the intended uses of the information are explained. Questions appropriate for this kind of interview might include (1) How was contact made—employer request to placement office, student initiative, other? (2) Starting wage, compared to usual beginning wage? (3) Advancement during employment? (4) Employer ratings of skills, personality, and training? (5) Reasons for separation, if applicable? (6) Employer suggestions for improved training programs?

Both of these follow-up studies use information only from the "consumer"—the receiving college or the employer. The reactions of former students about the quality of their preparation are equally meaningful, although more difficult to gather. Reactions are gathered most readily from the more satisfied graduate—the student who is still enrolled in the college to which he transferred or the one who is still employed in the field of his junior college major by his first employer. Such graduates are more easily located for questioning; they are also more likely to respond to a questionnaire than the graduate or dropout who has not been successful in his later work. In spite of such trends toward bias, it will be worthwhile to get as much evaluative information as possible from former students.

The mailed questionnaire is the simplest means of gathering such information. Even a double postal card can elicit helpful answers, if care is taken to ask only the most important questions. Since responses of students in any case will be qualitative and based on judgment rather than on quantitative facts, questionnaire follow-up should be supplemented whenever possible by a sampling of interviews. It will be possible, for instance, to arrange to talk to some transfer students on the campuses of universities after they have completed one or more semesters. Their opinions on the quality of their preparation and their difficulties in adjusting to the new college and their advice to later generations of students may not be soundly conceived in every instance. Yet they will deserve the attention of community college officials if only so that they may decide whether or not action is needed. Employed graduates may possibly be interviewed on the same visit as their employer. Skills omitted from the training program, unnecessary requirements in the college curriculum, and general observations about their preparation might provide the basic structure for the interview, again with concentration on the help which these former students can afford to later generations of students.

In the words of Mohs,

"Placement may be considered one of the culminating activities of personnel services in the college; it is so tied in with and related to other aspects of education, curricular as well as other student personnel services, that job placement *per se* can be regarded as only one, and by no means the most important, function of this office."[2]


# E. Records, Research, and Evaluation

The keeping of accurate records is one of the primary responsibilities of the student personnel service. Every student expects his college to maintain a complete and up-to-date record of his scholarly achievement and to be able to provide intelligible copies on short notice at his request. For this reason, every college provides an officer with the duties of registrar or recorder; and every college maintains a good system of academic records, mostly with individual student folders stored in a central location easily accessible to faculty members. Three considerations deserve comment in relation to student records: What materials become a part of the records; what constructive use is made of these materials; and how conveniently accessible are they for the reference of authorized personnel?

Two types of information are found in the student folder, the academic record and additional documents from several sources. The academic record is primarily a continuing account of the studies attempted by the student and of his success in them. It is designed in such a way as to facilitate the recording of new information at the end of each term of attendance; in an increasing number of colleges it is planned to permit rapid mechanical reproduction. In general, these records contain

1. Identifying Information
     full name
     sex
     birth date
     birth place
     name of parents or guardian
     permanent address
2. Background Information
     summary of previous school and college record
     date of high-school graduation
     major field of study
3. Progress in College
     date of entry to college
     dates of withdrawal and reentry
     date of graduation and degree
     semester by semester record of courses, units, and grades
     cumulative summary of progress toward graduation
     notations of honors or of academic disciplinary action
     notations of institutions to which transcripts have been sent
4. Information about the College
     name
     term plan (semester or quarter)
     grading policies
     signature of issuing officer
5. Optional Features
     photograph of student
     aptitude or placement test records with norms

Although this summary record, as the official evidence of the student's attendance and progress, must be guarded from every possible hazard, it contains in convenient form a wealth of information which should be readily accessible to any authorized person. It is an excellent practice, therefore, to duplicate a fresh copy of the permanent record for every student at the end of every semester, so that every counseling folder may contain an up-to-date record at the earliest possible moment. With suitable equipment and procedures, even colleges with large enrollments can make available to the counseling staff a complete report on the fall achievement of every student before classes begin in the spring. In this way, both honors earned and prerequisite courses failed may be recognized during the first days of the new semester and appropriate action taken.

The student folder, then, will include a single most recent copy of the student's permanent record. In addition, it should include such available information as will help counselors and instructors to work intelligently and professionally with the student. One school of thought would limit the contents of the folder to a bare minimum of official and quasi-public documents; at the opposite extreme are those who include every scrap of paper dealing with the student, so that the folder becomes bulky and disorganized. Some writers would restrict the use of the counseling folder to those who have extensive training in personnel work; others feel that anyone who is qualified to teach the young should be entitled to access to all pertinent information about them. The author leans toward a moderate economy of contents of the folder and the encouragement of all instructional faculty members to become acquainted with its contents. A typical student folder might include such materials as:

Application by the student for admission to the college.

A personal data sheet filled out by the student.

A four-semester educational plan, completed in conference with the counselor and adjusted at each registration period.

An up-to-date copy of the student's permanent record.

A sheet summarizing accurately the scores on any standardized tests of aptitude, achievement, interest, and personality.

Summaries of important interviews, and decisions reached in them.

Notations about other information available from the counselor, if it is of a nature to require careful interpretation to instructors by means of interview.

The personnel office, ideally, should make such folders conveniently available to any instructor who asks for them. If clerical workers can collect from the files the folders of an entire class and if a suitably quiet spot is available for the instructor to look through them, the use of the folders will increase. If this service is supplemented by a continuing plan of training the faculty in the proper use of test and other personnel information, both the quality of instruction and the quality of faculty advice to students will improve.

The availability in the student personnel office of such a wealth of information about students should encourage its use in institutional research. Many writers have pointed out the folly of giving tests that were not to be used in individual counseling. Yet if facts about students are used only as a basis for counseling interviews, fully half their value is lost. Personnel workers, the faculty, the curriculum committee, and the administration of the junior college ask many questions about the characteristics of their student body. The answers are available in the personnel files, if only some worker has the responsibility and the time to assemble them. Such studies provide concrete evidence on many problems; they bring to light the successful aspects of the college and the parts that need improvement. They aid in the process of decision by substituting facts for argumentation. No college should ignore this source of insight for curriculum development and for program evaluation.

A single public junior college, in the course of one academic year, prepared a study of characteristics of entering students, including college aptitude, economic and social status, ambitions, high-school achievement, and a dozen other traits that might affect curriculum and instruction. A report on sophomore achievement, as measured by the Sequential Tests of Educational Progress, was interpreted in its relation to aptitude scores at entrance; the study pointed up aspects of the curriculum that needed further study. A follow-up study of students graduating over a four-year period was completed, presenting the actual comments of graduates for faculty study, as well as summaries of their evaluation of the college.

## F. The Administration of Student Personnel Services

The administrative organization of student personnel services should grow out of the functions to be performed. A workable plan based on the analysis presented in the present Chapter would include a Dean of Students with appropriately trained staff members in charge of the several functions of student personnel. Such an organization is similar in most details to that described by McDaniel in *Essential Student Personnel Practices.*[3] Figure 17-1 concentrates on functions rather than on officers.

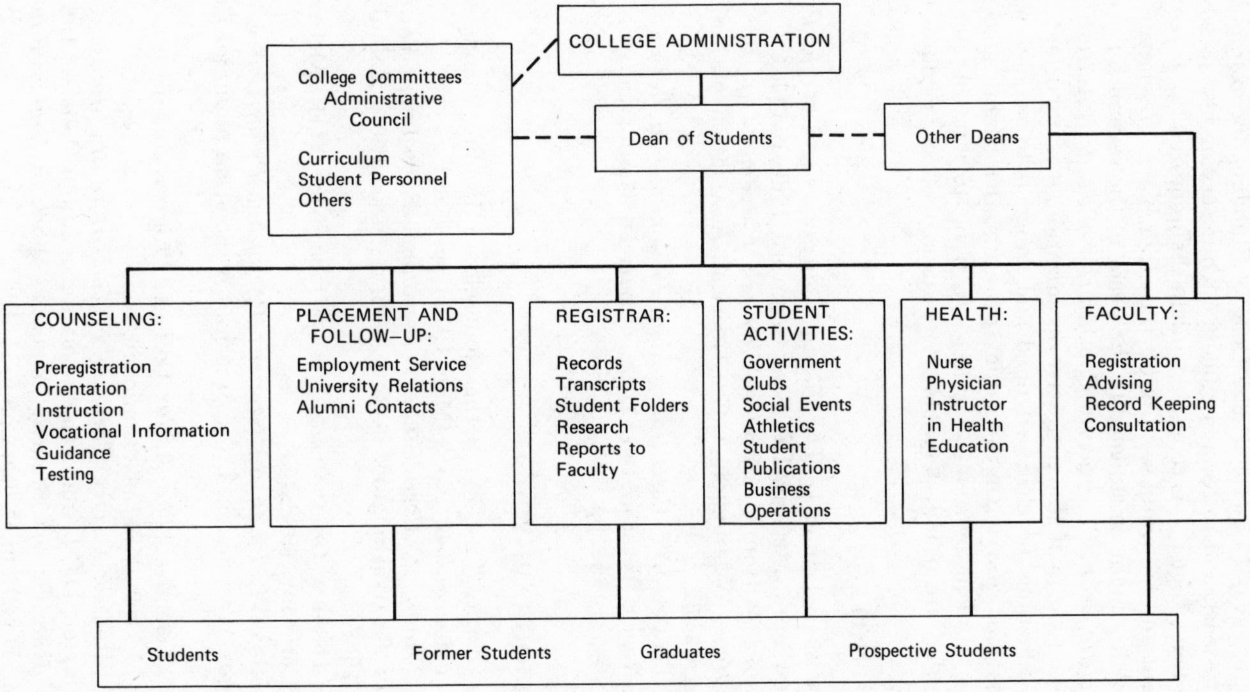

**COLLEGE ADMINISTRATION**

College Committees
Administrative Council

Curriculum
Student Personnel
Others

**Other Deans**

**Dean of Students**

**COUNSELING:**

Preregistration
Orientation
Instruction
Vocational Information
Guidance
Testing

**PLACEMENT AND FOLLOW–UP:**

Employment Service
University Relations
Alumni Contacts

**REGISTRAR:**

Records
Transcripts
Student Folders
Research
Reports to Faculty

**STUDENT ACTIVITIES:**

Government
Clubs
Social Events
Athletics
Student Publications
Business Operations

**HEALTH:**

Nurse
Physician
Instructor in Health Education

**FACULTY:**

Registration
Advising
Record Keeping
Consultation

Students

Former Students

Graduates

Prospective Students

**Figure 17-1  The organization of student personnel services.**

It is quite likely that in small colleges one person will be required to administer several functions. The Dean of Students, for example, might expect to teach and to counsel students, while serving also as adviser to the student council. A counselor might be required to care for the placement and follow-up service. On the other hand, in a larger college, special titles might be assigned to the heads of the several services, such as *Associate Dean, Recorder,* or *Coordinator of Student Activities.*

Under any form of administrative organization, it is important that the various functions be clearly defined and assigned to persons with the qualifications and with the time to accomplish them successfully. Intensive student personnel services are basic to student and faculty morale; they are an indispensable precondition of effective education.

## FOOTNOTES

1.    Medsker, Leland L. *The Junior College: Progress and Prospect.* New York: McGraw-Hill Book Company, 1960, p. 147.
2.    Mohs, Milton C. *Service Through Placement in the Junior College.* Washington, D.C.: American Association of Junior Colleges, 1962, p. 3.
3.    McDaniel, J.W. *Essential Student Personnel Practices for Junior Colleges.* Washington, D.C.: American Association of Junior Colleges, 1962, pp. 52-53.

## BIBLIOGRAPHY

Collins, Charles C. "Giving the Counselor a Helping Hand," *Junior College Journal.* **40**, No. 8 (May, 1970), pp. 17-20.

———— *Junior College Student Personnel Programs: What They Should Be.* Washington, D.C.: American Association of Junior Colleges, 1967.

Dawson, Helaine. *On the Outskirts of Hope.* New York: McGraw-Hill Book Company, 1968.

McDaniel, J.W. *Essential Student Personnel Practices in Junior Colleges.* Washington, D.C.: American Association of Junior Colleges, 1962.

Medsker, Leland L. *The Junior College: Progress and Prospect.* New York: McGraw-Hill Book Company, 1960.

Mohs, Milton C. *Service Through Placement in the Junior College.* Washington, D.C.: American Association of Junior Colleges, 1962.

Mueller, Kate Hefner. *Student Personnel Work in Higher Education.* Boston: Houghton Mifflin Company, 1961.

O'Connor, Thomas J. *Follow-Up Studies in Junior Colleges: A Tool for Institutional Improvement.* Washington, D.C.: American Association of Junior Colleges, 1965.

Raines, Max R. "The Student Personnel Situation," *Junior College Journal.* **36**, No. 5 (February, 1966), pp. 6-8

Sharland, Irma Blohm. "Health Services Programs for the Student," *Junior College Journal.* **41**, No. 8 (May, 1971), pp. 15-17.

# IV

## ISSUES AND OPPORTUNITIES

# 18 | The Future of the Community Junior College

Preceding chapters have presented the descriptive and statistical data from which an idealistic definition of the community junior college may be derived. Existing junior colleges differ widely in their characteristics; none will be found that conforms to all terms of the definition. In the future development of community junior colleges, as in the past, differences in local history, in local needs and fiscal ability, and in philosophy of education will combine to bring about adaptations and compromises within a common ideal. It is nonetheless worthwhile to state the ideal explicitly, so that the extent and the character of each departure from it may be recognized and evaluated.

287

## A. The Community Junior College Defined

The community junior college is a free public two-year educational institution that attempts to meet the post-high-school educational needs of its local community. In achieving this objective, its faculty studies the local community in order to determine these needs and works vigorously to develop appropriate kinds of instructional organization and techniques. The emphasis in the community junior college is on providing legitimate educational services, rather than on conforming to preconceived notions of what is or is not collegiate subject matter, or of who is or is not college material.

Because its purposes are broader in some respects than those traditionally associated with the liberal arts college and the university, its educational program will differ also in significant ways. It will offer for baccalaureate degree credit the courses appropriate to the first two years of the preprofessional school, the university, or the liberal arts college. In addition, it will develop many curriculums that are not appropriate to these institutions, curriculums designed to prepare students in a period of two years or less to participate intelligently in the work of the community. For all of its students, it will offer the basic elements of general education. It will present courses of many kinds for those citizens whose major occupation is something other than student. It will vigorously recruit for its educational programs youth who have not been successful in lower schools and attempt to provide for them both developmental courses and the full range of occupational and transfer courses. It will provide for its community, to the extent of its facilities and the community's need, educational, cultural, and recreational activities in music, art, drama, and public affairs. Finally, it will provide a program of guidance to assist its students to choose wisely from among its multiple offerings and to attain maximum benefit from their studies.

Several of the terms of the idealistic definition must be explained in greater detail, because they differ widely from present practice. The concept of tuition-free education has virtually disappeared. A majority of the states now provide for tuition payments by students to cover some part of the cost of their junior college instruction. The collection of tuition is justified practically on the basis of fiscal necessity and philosophically on the two premises that free public education ought to end at the completion of high school and that education is not truly valued unless the recipient is required to pay something for it. Nevertheless, the ideal community junior college is defined as tuition free.

Practically, American society can afford to provide for its citizens the level of education that is required for employment in the economy and for participation in civic responsibility. In answer to the philosophical argument, it may be pointed out that public education in America has been continuously extended as new conditions made more schooling both possible and desirable. There is no more inherent reason to set the terminal point at high-school graduation than at eighth grade or junior college or master's degree level. In the present stage of our economy, there are many cogent arguments for planning tuition-free education for qualified students at least through the junior college years. The motivational argument for tuition charges, on the other hand, has a certain degree of validity, even though one of the effects of tuition charges is to exclude some able students from further education. Every year of school attendance is costly to the student or his parents in living expenses and in loss of earnings, and tuition charges simply add to their total burden. Present social policy should encourage the development of talent, rather than place barriers in its path. The nation can better afford the costs of free tuition than it can the loss sustained from undeveloped human resources.

The term "public" in the definition is a second factor that requires elaboration. There are almost 250 independent junior colleges that provide a high quality of education to more than 130,000 students. Their function is useful and necessary; their existence should be recognized and encouraged in every feasible manner. Some of these private junior colleges, moreover, perform many of the services of the community junior college. Yet the private junior colleges can never accomplish the entire educational task here outlined, nor should they attempt it. The majority of community junior colleges are now and probably will continue to be publicly operated and financed, whereas the community junior colleges under private auspices will continue to be valued and rare exceptions.

Even the term "two-year" cannot be proposed as an entirely unqualified attribute of community junior colleges. There are in America a number of public four-year degree-granting colleges, established by municipalities and operated truly as community-serving institutions. Yet common usage in educational literature has tended to restrict the meaning of "community college" to the kind of institution described in this volume. Another objection to the limitation of "two-year" arises from the realization that community junior colleges will organize curriculums designed to last only one semester or one year; in a very few cases three-year programs have been offered. In addition, certain single courses may attract persons who have earned college degrees or those who have not graduated from high school. The term "two-year" is included in the definition in order to differentiate the community junior college from other kinds of colleges and because of the realization that most of the effort of the typical community college will be expended on those full-time students who are pursuing organized curriculums extending over two years of study and leading to the Associate degree.

The qualifications to the definition may leave the impression that the community junior college is an entirely amorphous institution, so fluid and adaptable as to lack character and defy consistent definition. Not so. For three-quarters of a century, these colleges have been progressing steadily toward a definition. They have explored various patterns of organization and experimented with types of control, concepts of function, and provisions for support. Their accumulated experience has brought a clarification of their role, a comprehension of the scope of their educational responsibility, and a well-defined direction for future development. At the same time, study of their present status discloses a series of problems and issues that must be resolved as community junior colleges, fully aware of the scope of their educational tasks, progress toward the period of consolidation and improvement of the scope and quality of their services.

## B. Problems of the Open Door

The open-door admission policy has been both the proudest claim and the knottiest dilemma of the community junior college. At a time when enrollments are rising annually by hundreds of thousands of students and when junior colleges are assuming an ever increasing share of freshmen and sophomore enrollments, is it possible to accept every student who requests admission? Is it possible to develop worthwhile college curriculums for all of them? Is it reasonable to accept students who are predestined to failure? Is it wise to conserve funds by denying admittance to applicants who fail to meet minimum intellectual or educational criteria? Does the American economy, or the "American dream," require that every high-school graduate be provided opportunity for further education?

If political theory does indeed seem to justify a liberal and welcoming admission policy, what consequences ensue? Should the open door for some applicants be simply a revolving door, or an entrance to a vestibule from which all doors are closed? How much remedial work in the skills of learning should be provided by the junior college in order to make real the opportunity promised by the open door? What limitations on study load, choice of courses, outside work, or student activities must be imposed on students who are admitted on probation?

Having admitted a student of doubtful potential, how long should the college encourage him to continue in dubious battle toward success in his studies? How can the open door provide access to real opportunity and not merely to one more experience of scholastic frustration and defeat? How can the distinction be made between the able idle, the slow but determined struggler, and the overly optimistic incompetent? By what means can students who are on the way to defeat in pursuit of one objective be helped to recognize and accept goals that are more realistic for them?

Alternatively, should all of these questions be evaded by abandoning any attempt to serve all post-high-school educational needs, and by establishing preconditions for admission that would eliminate many of the difficulties posed by the "open door"? If only students are admitted whose test scores and high-school grades predict acceptable chances for success, many problems do not arise. The scope of the curriculum is restricted, the task of the teacher is simplified, the costs of higher education are lower, and a high standard of scholarship is assured. On the other hand, a policy of restrictive admission would tend to diminish the total educational level of the population; it would certainly eliminate an appreciable number of applicants who would profit measurably from additional education. The benefits of a more restrictive admission policy seem to accrue more to the faculty and to the citizen as taxpayer, and to these only in the short run, than they do to the student and to the citizen as productive worker and as human being.

A more positive approach to the very real dilemmas of open admission will involve innovative and imaginative attempts to adapt the schedule and the curriculum to the needs of the less academic student. Acceptance of responsibility for developing the student's self-concept and motivation as well as his study and communication skills will help him survive the first term. Individual and small group instruction will restore a personal touch to instruction that has been lost as colleges grow larger. More frequent entry points as well as small self-contained instructional modules will diminish the penalties of initial course failure.

An open-door admission policy unquestionably poses difficult problems of educational strategy that have not been faced heretofore in higher education. Difficulties, however, by no means imply that problems are impossible to solve. On the contrary, the social and economic problems that arise as a result of failure to solve these educational problems will be of a much greater order of difficulty and of long-range consequences.

## C. Evaluation and Accountability

Education should make a difference to students and to the community at large. Too often in the past that difference has been indiscernible. Changes in personal qualities between the freshman year and graduation have been attributable to maturation or to contact with the peer group as much as to explicit and measurable purposes of the professors. The outcomes of training are demonstrable, especially in quantitative fields: chemists, engineers, accountants, or fullbacks were taught to do their jobs competently and efficiently. In the fields of ethical and intellectual development, on the other hand, outcomes have evaded evaluation because they were intangible, metaphysical, and qualitative rather than quantitative.

The community college of the future, along with the entire educational establishment, will not be permitted a pious evasion of the question; it will be required to justify its procedures and its expenditures by reference to output. Statistics and support will not be based on numbers of students enrolled in the fall, but on numbers of successful completions. Self-examination will be required of students, faculty, administration, and boards of control, so that each may justify his reason for participation in the educational enterprise and his rationale of operation.

> Basic questions to be raised include:
> "What is the purpose of higher education? Is there more than one? If so, what are they?
> "What are the benefits of higher education? To the individual? To society?
> Can we name the outputs of higher education? If we can name them, can we measure them? How?
> Where are we going? Where do we want to go? Where do we need to go?"[1]

Though still in a primitive stage, the techniques for accountability are available: the behavioral objective, the pre- and post-test, convenient computerized follow-up of student progress, program budgeting, and cost analysis. Community colleges can apply themselves to the tasks of demonstrating their effectiveness, or they can stand by and watch commercial enterprises take over the most easily quantified parts of their function. The defense that some important outcomes are unmeasurable will lead to the challenge, "Then how do you know that they are important, or that they exist, or that if they exist they exist because of your instruction?" In face of widespread questioning of the effectiveness of all educational institutions, community colleges as well as universities must examine purposes, priorities, procedures, alternatives, and capabilities. They must prepare to report their stewardship to their publics in explicit terms.

# D. Problems of Articulation

The transfer of credit from the community junior college to the four-year institution has been troublesome throughout the existence of junior colleges. The receiving college is concerned that the transfer student shall be fully and comparably prepared to succeed in competition with its "native" students. The junior college is equally concerned that transfer practices shall not seem to imply that its courses or its students are inferior to those in the four-year colleges. Enough evidence on performance of transfer students has been gathered to enable both sides of the discussion to agree on the basic principles of transfer policies, but still the debate goes on.

Developments are occurring in several of the states that will intensify the need for effective coordination of lower-division education. When a university or liberal arts college finds a greater number of transfers in its junior class than of native students, its whole concept of the four-year baccalaureate curriculum must change. To some extent, its ability to control the elements of lower-division requirements is diminished. These developments impose a new, perhaps not entirely welcome, burden on the junior college, to accept the obligation of defining and providing a lower-division education of high quality, as a basis for the specialized study at upper-division level.

A corollary of the effort to develop excellent lower-division programs is the necessity to improve the techniques of identifying and counseling the nontransfer student, and to develop appropriate curriculums for him so that he is not forced, in default of another opportunity, either to continue probation level work in transfer courses or drop out. It has been noted that two-thirds of junior college students classify themselves as transfer students, although year after year only one-third actually transfer. A large part of this discrepancy may be attributed to the fact that two-year courses simply are not available for many students. In Chapter 13, evidence was presented that half of all junior colleges offer fewer than five occupational courses; the nontransfer student who does not want any of the occupational courses offered in his junior college is forced to take a transfer course or drop out.

The techniques of recommending transfer students require additional study.[2] There is evidence that transfers with marginal grade records in junior college are often unable to succeed in larger universities, even though similar students succeed in other institutions. Long-term persuasive counseling might help students to become aware of the differences between colleges, and aware of their own characteristics, so that they may make their choices much more realistically.

A second area of articulation concerns relations with high schools. Constant communication between high schools and community junior college faculties will help to ensure that course sequences provide for planned progress in learning and avoid gaps or repetition in presentation. The transition from high school to college may be smoothed for the student through four types of high school-junior college cooperation.

1. The junior college and other colleges can be interpreted completely and accurately to the high-school student so that he may choose intelligently rather than on the basis of hearsay or purely extrinsic criteria.
2. The transfer of appropriate parts of the permanent records of students will assist junior college counselors in continuing effective guidance procedures.
3. The two institutions can plan jointly for orientation activities for the high-school graduates, to help them become familiar with the opportunities and requirements of the local junior college.
4. Faculty groups from parallel departments of the two institutions can meet regularly to become acquainted with mutual problems and to work toward sequential organization of instruction.

## E. Problems of Support

As community junior colleges assume an increasing share of rapidly growing college enrollments, their problems of adequate financial support grow more acute. They are in competition with elementary and secondary schools for local property tax money and with state universities and colleges for income from the state treasury. In each case, they are somewhat handicapped. At the local level, the numbers of students in the two-year community college are much smaller than in the 12 years of public schools, and so their claims for support are subordinated. In the competition for state revenues, on the other hand, they lack the prestige and the statewide appeal of the four-year institutions, and so find it difficult to secure adequate, not to say equal, appropriations.

Yet the burden of ad valorem property taxes on local real estate is approaching a maximum. If taxes rise too high, the homeowner cannot pay them from his annual income, and industry and commerce may intensify the revenue problem by moving away from high tax areas. Present state tax practices, although probably more elastic than local property taxes, are also subject to a law of diminishing returns. The Federal Government has enacted measures providing aid for construction of colleges, including junior colleges, and for financial aid to college students, but Congress has been unwilling until now to undertake a program of general support for the current expenses of education.

On the other hand, the gross national product, in real values, is higher than it has ever been and rising annually. The nation's children must not be denied education in favor of more frivolous or more temporary investments. The nation can afford to pay for a good education for its citizens, and it cannot afford to deny them a high level of excellent education. The problem then is to discover how best to allocate the necessary share of the national wealth to this essential purpose.

One source of increased income for colleges is higher tuition rates for students. In independent colleges and universities, this resource has been utilized increasingly since World War II, although it is likely that in many colleges costs have risen more rapidly than tuition. In state colleges and universities too, student fees have increased over the past two decades. Even in the community junior colleges, only two states specifically prohibit tuition charges to resident students; in other states, tuition charges may run as high as one-third of the per capita annual operating cost.

If the community junior college is really intended to keep open the doors of educational opportunity for able youth from all social and economic levels, tuition must be free or set at a nominal rate. There seems to be no question that most elements of the higher education establishment will continue to charge tuition and that the dollar amounts of tuition will continue to climb. All the more reason, then, that at least one segment of the system should avoid tuition, in order to permit and to encourage the nonscholarship student of good, but not superior capacity to develop his talents as far as he can. This policy would work to the eventual advantage not only of the student but of the nation as a whole.


# F. Problems of Control

The original ideal of the community junior college pictured a small institution, with a close personal relationship between faculty and students and with strong ties of service and support between the institution and the community. Present realities are quite different. Faculties number in the hundreds, and students in the thousands.

Communities grow until the once small and personalized junior college must establish another campus, or two or three. Administrative considerations lead to the merger of several junior college districts so that broader tax bases and some operational economies may be realized. As larger state contributions are needed for adequate support of higher education, state boards for coordination or control of community colleges are established. What effects do these developments portend on the essence of the community college?

Control by a board of local citizens chosen by the voters of a community was the earliest pattern of governance for community junior colleges. Recent developments in district organization raise the question of the ultimate size of a community. Can either Chicago, with seven branches of one junior college, or Los Angeles, with eight junior colleges, be considered in any meaningful sense a single community? There are at least 50 similar multicampus developments in operation or in prospect. The major problems in their establishment are to retain sufficient autonomy on each local campus and to provide for sufficient sampling of local community opinion, so that the basic values of college-community cooperation are not lost in the search for bigness, administrative convenience, or fiscal economy.

A similar set of problems—perhaps, in less populous states, the same problems—arise from the establishment of state boards of control for junior colleges. There is a strong appeal in the proposal for a single state junior college board. It can exert more influence on the Legislature in its competition with the university for funds; it can assure quality of education, equal treatment of faculty, and coordinated statewide development of a system of junior colleges. If the board responsible for junior colleges is also responsible for all higher education, it would seem that it would lead inevitably to a thoroughly coordinated, economical, and articulated pattern of higher education for the state.

Yet the losses under a statewide system should be considered as well as the gains. Recent governmental tendencies toward centralization of support and control have not guaranteed greater economy, efficiency, or improvement in quality of service. The remoteness of control from its center of impact may protect the controlling official from criticism; but it does not assure that control will be more acceptable, more intelligent, or more humane to the subjects. There is an educational advantage in the close relationship of a community to its junior college. It is true that universities become eminent without this relationship; but the junior college is not and should not aspire to be a university. It abandons its own unique nature when it imitates a different institution. The problems of control of the junior college should be settled with reference to the essential nature of that institution, and not on the basis of a possibly false analogy to other institutions.

Another emerging problem of control concerns the roles of faculty and students in the internal operation of each college. Beginning as upward extensions of the public schools, community colleges adopted the administrator-faculty relationships of the lower schools. The independent establishment of college districts, their self-concept as truly a part of higher education, the increasing levels of training of community college faculty members, and the growing concern of students—all combine to revise those relationships. Community college faculties feel that they have the competence and the responsibility to participate in policy formulation in the same way as faculty senates of colleges and universities, and students insist that they, too, have insights of value in the development of college policies. Shared responsibility in policy determination seems inevitable. The major problem lies in ensuring that faculty and students will exert their influence toward the realization of the full set of junior college tasks, rather than seeking to shape the institution in the image of the university. Land-grant colleges have become great state universities, to the point where they are embarrassed by the original purpose. Normal schools have become great state universities, without improving their competence or pride in the preparation of teachers for the public schools. Can community colleges resist this emulative drive and push on toward their own excellence? Or will it be necessary in another quarter century to establish anew an institution to perform the tasks that by then the junior college will have abandoned?

## G. Problems of Standards

Community junior colleges can become excellent educational institutions. In the past, too many of them have not achieved excellence. At present, conditions are favorable to their quest—growing higher education, improved preparation of administrators and of faculty, and greater cooperation and articulation among educational institutions. A remaining barrier is the confusion that still persists in the definition of excellence. Once junior college workers and their several publics accept internally as well as verbally that excellence may be a quality of an educational program at any level of abstraction, the road will be open to their pursuit of excellence in the entire junior college curriculum.

One of the first steps along that road will be the establishment of a dozen or more frankly experimental community junior colleges, dedicated to providing better educational opportunities for all elements of their student bodies. There are good reasons why community colleges have not been experimental—the domination of the universities, the association with the public schools, the cost of experimentation, and the local rather than universal outlook of boards and administrators. It would seem, however, that the time has now come when several communities might determine that they want the very best for their students, and work out in cooperation with an educational foundation plans for extended and fundamental controlled experiments in all areas of the curriculum. The successful techniques might then serve as models for less adventurous junior colleges.

The experimental junior college must carry its experimentation beyond independent studies in the humanities for the ablest 5% of the students. Excellence should be the goal of all faculty members and expected of all students. Excellence in education involves a high level of expectation on the part of the college community—citizens, board of trustees, administration, teachers, and students. It requires imagination in finding new ways to excite the interest and engage the active participation of all kinds of students in their own learning and development. It requires a willingness to pay for libraries, laboratories, varieties of learning spaces, and faculty time to plan for excellence. It cannot be achieved without flexibility in the use of time and space and personnel. In summation, institutional arrangements must encourage the faculty to be enthusiastic and creative about teaching and enable the students to become actively involved as they are caught up in this enthusiasm and creativity.

Improvement of junior college standards will require increased attention to the preparation and selection of faculty members. At present, the great majority of junior college teachers hold masters' degrees; more than half of them have had teaching experience in secondary schools. Few of them have prepared specifically and during their undergraduate years for college or junior college teaching. A good deal is known of the characteristics of junior college teachers in service, but there is no firm knowledge of what patterns of personal qualities are most closely related to stimulating and inspiring community college teaching. The problem of standards will not be solved until a great deal of research is done on this subject.

Better counseling is also associated with the improvement of standards, for the student who chooses an unsuitable curriculum is not a successful student, no matter how good his grade point average. Yet the quality of junior college counseling programs is reported to be far below the ideal that is set for this function. Until competent staffs are employed in sufficient numbers to be effective in junior college educational and occupational counseling, the best of junior college facilities will be hampered in their efforts.

The community junior college has successfully traversed the trials of infancy and adolescence. In its maturity, it must accept the obligation to strive for excellence at every level of its broad scope of educational tasks. High standards are possible in community junior colleges, but they are inseparable from diversification of the curriculum, exceptional teaching, and competent guidance. High standards are not demonstrated by the numbers of students who fail courses, but rather by the number who succeed in preparing themselves to cope creatively with the multifarious opportunities of life.

## FOOTNOTES

1.   Lawrence, Ben, George Weathersby, and Virginia W. Patterson (eds.), *The Outputs of Higher Education: Their Identification, Measurement, and Evaluation.* Boulder, Colorado: Western Interstate Commission for Higher Education, 1970, p. 1.
2.   Knoell, Dorothy M., and Leland L. Medsker, *From Junior to Senior College: A National Study of the Transfer Student.* Washington, D.C.: American Council on Education, 1965, pp. 89-91.

# INDEX

Legislation, 90-95
 authorizing community
  colleges, 101
 financial, 95-98
Lewis Institute, 48
Long Beach City College, 246

Marriage courses, 210
Mathematics courses, 234
Martorana, S. V., 246
McDaniel, J. W., 280
McDowell, Francis, 51
McGrath, Earl J., 153, 241
Medsker, Leland L., 73, 148, 263, 293
Minority students, 57
Modular scheduling, 194
Mohs, Milton C., 277
Montgomery Junior College, 102
Moore, William, Jr., 64
Morgan, Gordon D., 151
Multi-college districts, 86
Music courses, 236

Newman, John Henry, 4

Occupational education, 52, 175-200
 articulation, 190
 balance of offerings, 186
 courses, 163
 defined, 70, 180
 and disadvantaged, 71
 expansion of, 189
 instructors, 198
 part-time, 249
 program development, 191
 problems, 188-198
 specialization, 196
 table of frequencies, 184-185, 188
 terminology, 177-182
Open door admission policy, 35
Open door college, 290
Orange County Community
  College, 102
Orientation to college, 267

Palm Beach Junior College, 102
Paraprofessional education, 179
Part-time study, 245
 table, 246

Patterson, Virginia W., 292
Physical education courses, 208
Physical science courses, 232
 table, 234
Physical World course, 218
Placement services, 275
Population trends, 7, 25
Power, atomic, 21
Preparation of instructors, suggested
  program, 136-139
President, 127-130
President's Commission on Higher
  Education, 5
Private junior colleges, 81-84
Psychology, applied, 211
Public junior colleges, 84-88
Public relations, 127
Purposes of higher education, 4
 geriatric, 251
 in continuing education, 247-251
 individual, 34
 social, 33

Rank, academic, 141
Records, student, 277
Report on Higher Education, 223, 247
Research, institutional, 126, 172, 277
Research, scientific, 23
Ricciardi, Nicholas, 55

Salaries, 140
San Jose City College, 149
Sanford, Nevitt, 5, 63
Schedule, for establishing community
  college, 105-112
Schedule of classes, 122
Science courses, 212
Site, development, 125
 selection, 107
Skills, higher levels, 28
Snyder, William H., 37, 51, 53
Social change and higher education, 28
Social science courses, 208, 229
 table, 231
Speech courses, 227
Standards of instruction, 41-42, 297
Stanford University, 49, 51

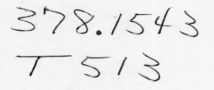